ADDITIONAL PRAISE FOR
THREADING A KAYAK DOWN THE MISSISSIPPI

"Dennis takes us on a fascinating thirteen-year sojourn in his quixotic effort to kayak the entire length of the Mississippi River. Starting as a complete kayaking novice, he grew into a legitimate 'River Man.' Dennis shares with us his river experiences through the full range of human emotions: serenity and solitude, purposeful engagement, and sheer adrenaline-fueled panic when dodging barges, rapids, and huge Asian Carp missiles. While the river is the main character, Dennis introduces us to many colorful people, historic towns, and delightful culinary experiences along the way. The book is a treat—for the mind and the soul." —**Jeff Wright, author of** *Breaking Bold: Capers from a Well-Spent Youth*

"I grew up on a channel of the Mississippi River and, along with many fellow Grey Cloud Islanders, acquired the appellation 'river rat.' But after reading Dennis's book, I realized how little I knew about the river. I thoroughly enjoyed and was impressed by his account of kayaking the entire length of 'Old Man River,' especially given that his age placed him quite appropriately on it. His book gives the reader an involving mix of history and geography of the river, sprinkled with a highly entertaining account of the river people Dennis met on his thirteen-year adventure." —**Steve Larson, author, screenwriter, movie director**

"Not since *Life on the Mississippi* by Mark Twain has there been such an elegant story about the mighty Mississippi. It's not about the river, it's about the people this river attracts. *Threading a Kayak down the Mississippi* captures with grace the essence of Dennis's journey and the people he met along the way. Great read." —**Jeffrey A. Redmon, author of** *Cash: The Fuel for Your Economic Engine*

"*Threading a Kayak down the Mississippi* follows in the footsteps (or wake) of Mark Twain along the Mississippi. It's a travelogue from Lake Itasca to New Orleans, with beautiful scenery, colorful (and generous) local characters, and numerous social currents and eddies. Dennis offers folksy comments, insightful observations, and literary allusions. This is both a well-guided tour and an appealing narrative of life on the Mississippi—both his and the river's residents." —**Michael B. Miller, retired lawyer**

THREADING A KAYAK DOWN THE MISSISSIPPI

A Journey through the River's Cultures and Characters

DENNIS VAN NORMAN

LYONS
PRESS

Essex, Connecticut

An imprint of Globe Pequot, the trade division of
The Rowman & Littlefield Publishing Group, Inc.
4501 Forbes Boulevard, Suite 200, Lanham, Maryland 20706
www.rowman.com

Distributed by NATIONAL BOOK NETWORK

British Library Cataloguing in Publication Information Available

Library of Congress Cataloging-in-Publication Data

Names: Van Norman, Dennis, author.
Title: Threading a kayak down the Mississippi : a journey through the
    river's cultures and characters / Dennis Van Norman.
Description: Essex, Connecticut : Lyons Press, [2023] | Includes
    bibliographical references.
Identifiers: LCCN 2023000373 (print) | LCCN 2023000374 (ebook) | ISBN
    9781493073559 (cloth) | ISBN 9781493073566 (epub)
Subjects: LCSH: Kayaking—Mississippi River. | Kayak touring—Mississippi
    River. | Mississippi River—Description and travel. | Van Norman,
    Dennis—Travel—Mississippi River. | Kayakers—United States—Biography.
Classification: LCC GV776.M7 V36 2023 (print) | LCC GV776.M7 (ebook) |
    DDC 797.122/40977—dc23/eng/20230207
LC record available at https://lccn.loc.gov/2023000373
LC ebook record available at https://lccn.loc.gov/2023000374

♾™ The paper used in this publication meets the minimum requirements of
American National Standard for Information Sciences—Permanence of Paper
for Printed Library Materials, ANSI/NISO Z39.48-1992.

This book is dedicated to our future . . .
Clara, Earl, Izzy, Joe, June, Natalie, and Penny

★ ★ ★

And in memory of

Captain Mike Coyle
Captain and our tour guide of the *Twyla Lure*
Died November 12, 2020

CONTENTS

FOREWORD

Some years ago, I met Dennis Van Norman. Seemed like a nice guy. He introduced himself as a "river rat." I knew I liked the cut of him, and with those two words, I knew he was a special kind of person.

One doesn't usually introduce oneself to a stranger that way, unless one senses that one is introducing oneself to another river rat. Perhaps he knew of my love of Mark Twain, or my board positions on the Mississippi River Connection, or maybe he had seen me hosting events sponsored by the St. Paul Riverfront Corporation.

He could not have known about the thousand volumes of river exploration books in my library, and he wouldn't have guessed that I had explored the Nile in Egypt, the Ganges in India, the Vilcabamba in Peru, and the Amazon basin. He didn't know that I had paddled large chunks of the Missouri River and the Yukon.

I like doing things in "chunks." Sometimes, unless you are a professional explorer, you have to work these explorations into busy schedules. Dennis Van Norman specializes in "chunks." He's my kind of explorer. And there is no quit in him.

Dennis asked me what he should read as he prepared for his Mississippi River journey. I told him to read Mark Twain's *Life on the Mississippi*. The river has changed dramatically since he wrote it, but the river's general shape hasn't changed much. Despite having been straightened in some places, it is a winding stream, like a hank of thread thrown across a smooth floor. Despite the manmade cutoffs and bypasses, it is still so crooked that you may have to paddle ten miles to travel a distance that would take just fifteen minutes across dry land. This is what Twain said:

Therefore, any calm person, who is not blind or idiotic, can see that in the Old Oolitic Silurian Period, just a million years ago next November, the Lower Mississippi River was upwards of one million three hundred thousand miles long, and stuck out over the Gulf of Mexico like a fishing-rod.

Dennis would learn this firsthand. In chunks.

I'm still astounded what would make a man like Dennis Van Norman take on this journey. My shelf is full of books by young men and women who have made the paddle from the headwaters of the Mississippi to the South Pass at the Gulf of Mexico. But Dennis is no spring chicken, and until shortly before he made his plan, his experience in a kayak was, to be kind, limited.

Nonetheless he planned and persevered, leaning on the help of people he met along the way. Some were kind strangers and others became true friends. Through his journey, Dennis experienced one of the most remarkable things about the river. River rats stick together and will do darn near anything for you.

Threading a Kayak down the Mississippi isn't a travelogue or an adventure novel. It is the story of an average guy, with average skills, and unaverage determination. Dennis faces some harrowing encounters while at the mercy of an ever-changing river, like monster barges and four-thousand-horsepower towboats that put up eight-foot wakes that can easily capsize a small kayak.

Yet in the margins, between those terrifying moments, he floats alone, watching a heron lifting from the surface of the water, basking in the sun or in the shade of the trees on the bank, and always, always wondering with trepidation and anticipation what lies just around the next bend.

This is a story of how Dennis Van Norman decided to live his life, and it is a story for us—a lesson—that we all do better when we can't wait to see what comes next into our view.

—Don Shelby
Veteran journalist, Peabody and Emmy award winner

PROLOGUE

Jump in! The Water's Fine

It was not a graceful moment, the first time I climbed into a kayak. It was a Saturday afternoon in autumn 2005. My son, grandson, and I pushed off for an afternoon of Huck Finning down the Mississippi River. We started in Minneapolis and pulled out a few hours later in my hometown of St. Paul, Minnesota.

I learned a lot that afternoon. I learned I was not Huck Finn, as I was fifty years his senior. I also learned that this was not Mark Twain's river—this was the modern Mississippi.

Within those first two miles, I paddled in and out of just three of the massive locks that mark the beginning of twenty-nine controlled river navigation pools, each under the authority of a morass of bureaus and agencies, stretching from Minneapolis to St. Louis.

In all its power and glory, the river exposed my impatience that day. It enticed me to be curious about what was up ahead, what was waiting beyond the next lock, and what could be discovered around the next bend. Maybe there was a little Huck in me after all.

Of course, at the time, I was oblivious to the significance of that outing. I had no idea it would be a watershed moment marking what would eventually become a top-to-bottom trip down the Mississippi River, crammed in a boat built for one.

Yes, I have taken a kayak down the center of the country, tracing a zig-zag pattern that slaloms a few degrees left and right of the ninetieth longitudinal meridian. Over thirteen years, I have paddled around thousands of "next bends," chasing buoys over 2,500 river miles covering both the Mississippi and Atchafalaya rivers, from northern Minnesota to the southern tip of Louisiana. While it's not exactly known how many people paddle the length of the Mississippi River each year, there aren't many of us. Somewhere around fifty is the number bandied about in the paddling world. By comparison, according to Google, about eight hundred people attempt to climb Mt. Everest every year, with a success rate of about 40 percent and a death rate that hovers around 1 percent.

I am not sure what the mortality measure is for Mississippi River paddlers. It may be easier to count the bodies on an icy slope five and a half miles above sea level than it is to track them over a nation-spanning, meandering, muddy river.

It can take anywhere from sixty to one hundred days to paddle from source to sea (S2S) for the typical paddler, if there were such a thing. (I can assure you, there is not.) There was a team of four paddlers that reset the Guinness World Record in 2021 by paddling a canoe down the entire length of the Mississippi in seventeen days and a few hours. Just a few years ago, a group of men paddled up the Mississippi. In my river journey, I encountered only three other paddlers who were on the same S2S paddling pilgrimage. Every year each one of these river paddlers is making their own story. This is mine.

My adventure has included a cast of characters from both the past and present. In addition to Huck and Tom, the Mississippi River currents carry the spirits of earlier travelers with names like Hernando De Soto, Zebulon Pike, Henry Schoolcraft, Jean Lafitte, James Eads, Henry Shreve, Meriwether Lewis, and William Clark.

Can today's river traveler sense the spiritual presence of these past adventurers? I guess it depends on the individual's level of romanticism. Too late to meet the early Spanish, French, and English explorers and expansionists, native tribes, pirates, slave traders, and riverboat gamblers, I had the good fortune of meeting with their descendants. They are the carpenters, artists, boat builders, early French furniture restorers, mountain climbers, authors, film makers, music makers, Cajuns, and Canadians who live and work along the river.

Early on in my river explorations I spoke with a Minnesota Department of Natural Resources (DNR) ranger, inquiring about a tricky section of the river given the swift current and challenging portages. He asked me, "Do you know what you're getting into?" I responded slowly, "No," adding, "but that's why I'm doing it."

This kayaking trip grew in unexpected directions over time, from a simple afternoon outing to years of planning, researching, paddling, and marking off the miles. I did not know what I was getting into. And I was fine with that.

I did it my way. My way was section by section. I never debated the pros and cons of through paddle versus section by section. I was already ten years into my bit-by-bit approach before I decided to do the whole thing. Section by section is different; it's not one long test of endurance, and the logistics process can be a major challenge! There is gas, money, time, restaurants, and lodging to consider. It's a lot more expensive to do it my way. When the multiple round trips to New Orleans, Natchez, Memphis, St. Louis, and all the waypoints in Wisconsin and Minnesota are tallied, the miles driven add up to about twenty-eight thousand.

On a road atlas, the Mississippi River is depicted as a thin blue line that divides our country east from west, carving the boundary line between ten states. It's also a thread that connects our country from the northern post of Minnesota to the southern shores of Louisiana. Traveling the length of this river, both the divider and the connector, I discovered it may be one river, but it offers a never-ending flow of Scheherazade-like tales.

One memory that is a perfect keynote for the pages ahead took place at the Playboy El Cappuccino Lounge in St. Louis, a local standing-room-only hotspot hidden in a not-so-gentrified neighborhood. My river companions and I had to wait forty-five minutes for our catfish fillets and hush puppies to go, but I wished it had been longer. We were under the spell of the bluesy headliner as her band rocked their hits, topping it off with the singer channeling Tina Turner with a raspy rendition of "Proud Mary." I recall the singer's sentiment as she soulfully expressed the giving nature of river folks. Yes, John Fogarty's classic, covered by Tina Turner and subsequently belted out by a rivertown local, served as fitting words for the miles ahead. I would be the benificiary of these river folks' generosity from Itasca to Louisiana.

The Mississippi River is a wise teacher. On my journey, I not only learned about the river itself but also the people living along its shores. I met scores of individuals—and characters—living or traveling this same path. I tasted their food, heard their music, and experienced their customs. I discovered a rich history, and an even richer present.

The scenes changed. There was the serenity of a northern Minnesota sunrise as a fawn and doe took a drink from the mirror-smooth Mississippi River. There were also moments of sheer terror, like when a towboat bore down on my unseen kayak in a choppy, tree-strewn, crowded St. Louis harbor.

This ordinary trip morphed into a first-class adventure early on. I was privileged to meet each precious, life-affirming moment head on, sandwiched between my anticipation and my memories.

Kayaking has taught me a lot about myself. Prior to this journey, I was rarely alone. On the river, I spent most days and nights alone. I was forced to learn who I was.

There are shelves of books written about being alone—alone at the bottom of the world, alone in the ocean, alone in the desert, alone in the woods—with authors ranging from Richard Evelyn Byrd to Henry David Thoreau. My moments of solitude covered a wide spectrum, too, from the state described in Warren Zevon's song "Splendid Isolation" to feeling very alone and very afraid.

As I learned to depend on myself, I also became acutely aware of the need for dependency on others. Some help from others, like river-guiding services, was planned and paid for, but there were also countless unexpected gestures of giving from both friends and strangers.

So is this a book about the Mississippi River? Or is it a book about travel, personal reflection, and adventure?

It's all of the above.

I started paddling in my early sixties and finished this adventure in my mid-seventies. The farther I went, the more I learned. As I realized my moments with the river were a story worth telling, I began adding keystrokes to my paddle strokes.

This is a journey of discovery on the country's most celebrated waterway, casting light on the Mississippi's treasures and warning of its dangers. It explores the wonderment, joy, and fear that will invariably grab hold of you when you're sitting alone in a fourteen-foot plastic boat on America's greatest river.

AUTHOR'S NOTE

My Mississippi River journey was not linear. Over a stretch of thirteen years, I made numerous paddling trips; some were day trips, others would last weeks, few were sequential. I did not pursue a top-down, Itasca-to-Mile-Zero track. One trip could be in Louisiana, and the next could jump back up to Wisconsin.

This book has been written to follow my hopscotch travel pattern, following a chronological order from 2005 to 2018, rather than a geographical, north to south journey. I hope you can go with the flow.

Upper Mississippi River - UMR 1347.0 to UMR 0.0

MINNESOTA

Coffee Pot Landing
UMR 1329

Itasca UMR 1347
"The Bear" UMR 1172

River Boat Depot Bar
UMR 933

Boom Island UMR 855

WISCONSIN

Big River Inn
Genoa, WI UMR 680

IOWA

Guttenberg, IA UMR 615
Muscatine, IA UMR 455

"Any Port in a Storm", Burlington, IA UMR 404
Iowa State Penitentiary UMR 382

Nauvoo, IL UMR 377

Flying Asian Carp UMR 357

ILLINOIS

Planter's Barn Theater,
Hannibal, MO UMR 309
Missouri and Mississippi
Confluence UMR 195
Lewis & Clark UMR 0.0 to UMR 195
Big Muddy's Kanu House,
St. Louis, MO UMR 180
Stuck in Cliff Cave Park UMR 167

Meet Rivergator
Expedition, Chester, IL
UMR 110

Grand Tower, IL
UMR 80

MISSOURI

Lower Mississippi River - LMR 953.3 to LMR 0.0

ILLINOIS

MISSOURI

KENTUCKY

Ohio and Mississippi
Confluence LMR 953.3 ●

● Goat Skull, Cairo, IL LMR 953.3

TENNESSEE

Ants, Ants, Ants LMR 754 ●

● Mud Island, Memphis, TN, Au Revoir to
Rivergator LMR 738

ARKANSAS

● Doe's Eat Place, Greenville, MS LMR 538

"Dangerous Eddy" LMR 490 ●
Bluz Cruise Start Line LMR 457 ●

MISSISSIPPI

● The Old Country Store, Lorman, MS

LOUISIANA

Under the Hill, Silver Street Gallery,
Natchez, MS LMR 364

Algiers Point,
Four Pisces LMR 95 ●
Yellowfin Tuna, Venice, LA LMR 10 ●

Part I

YEARS: 2005 TO 2009

Otsego, Minnesota, to Genoa, Wisconsin

River Miles: 190

Kayak: Open-cockpit recreation
Dagger Blackwater 11.5 ($350)

1

DIPPING A TOE IN THE WATER

Fall 2005

I t's funny how our passions find us.

Joe was eager to share his news. "I bought a kayak and Earl and I just checked out the Mississippi. We paddled through the locks at the Stone Arch Bridge. It's the best money I've ever spent!"

This was quite a surprise to me because for the first thirty years of my son's life, he lived the "you're not gonna be happy unless you're going Mach 2 with your hair on fire" lifestyle of Maverick in *Top Gun*. He endured painful scrapes and bruises from tangling his snowmobile with a barbed wire fence and he survived with just broken bones from a highway motorcycle crash at the age of sixteen. After he scrapped his motorcycle, I asked what speed was the fastest he had ever gone. "I'm not sure," he reflected. "After 120, I didn't want to take the chance to look at the speedometer."

Now my son, this adrenalin junkie, was fired up about floating peacefully down a river in a plastic boat.

"You should come with us," he said. "We're going again tomorrow." I was not going to pass on the invitation to spend time on the river with my son and two-year-old grandson.

SEPTEMBER 17, 2005
[UPPER MISSISSIPPI RIVER MILES (UMR¹) 855.0]

The next morning, we picked up my REI rental kayak, dropped a car at Hidden Falls Park in St. Paul, and traveled ten miles upriver to our launching site, Boom Island near downtown Minneapolis. After a thirty-second orientation, I was pushed off the concrete boat launch into the Mighty Mississippi. I was surprised how close to the water one is in a kayak—and how tippy they are. The feeling of an imminent capsize dissipated over the next few minutes, and soon I was kayaking! Joe and Earl quickly joined me, and we were headed together downriver. As we passed the Nicollet Island Inn, a corporate hangout of mine, I was fascinated by the new perspective, seeing the inn from twenty-four inches above the water. As I found myself taking in this new liquid experience, I realized I was approaching my first lock and dam.

For the record, I did have a moderate marine résumé. Years ago, I had dabbled with sailing. I had sailed with a couple trying out their new boat in Mobile Bay where we picked up an injured pelican, I spent a week on Lake Michigan out of Traverse City, I served as "rail meat"—scrambling from side to side to balance the boat—in a few regattas on the St. Croix River, and I helmed a catamaran on the Great Barrier Reef out of Cairns, Australia. With these varied experiences, there was still one thing I had always wanted to do but never had—boat through a lock.

Now with thirty minutes of kayaking experience under my skirt (a kayaking term I was not yet familiar with), I was one hundred yards from the Upper St. Anthony Falls lock and dam, the first lock on the Mississippi. My two-year-old grandson was my guide, as he was my senior in experience, having traveled this route just days before.

I learned that the locks have red, yellow, and green traffic lights, a signal cord to pull to announce one's arrival, and a lock master to drop you a mooring line.

---

1. For navigational purposes, the US Army Corps of Engineers (USACE) has divided the Mississippi River into two distinct sections: the Upper Mississippi River and the Lower Mississippi River. The Upper Mississippi begins at the headwaters at Lake Itasca in Minnesota, which is measured as Upper Mississippi River mile 1347.0, and it flows to Cairo, Illinois, at Upper Mississippi River mile 0. The Lower Mississippi River begins at Cairo, Illinois, and starts at mile 953.0 and flows to its mouth in Louisiana, in the Gulf of Mexico, at Lower Mississippi River mile 0. The convention adopted in this book for designating a location on the river is: Upper Mississippi River miles are depicted as UMR with the USACE mile number, for example UMR 404.0. Lower Mississippi River Miles are depicted with the prefix LMR and then the mile number, for example, LMR 379.2.

The first five minutes—framed in steel and stone (Photo by Joe Van Norman)

Our two kayaks were the only ones locking through. The lock and dam complex seemed so big, and our plastic boats so small. We paddled in, grabbed the mooring line, took some pictures, watched the doors close behind us, and waited as the big water elevator took us down. The descent was the equivalent of almost five stories, the deepest descent of all the locks on the Mississippi. Once we reached the lower level, we watched as the massive doors slowly opened and allowed us to paddle out. [This first lock has since been closed by the US Army Corps of Engineers (USACE) for a variety of reasons including creating a prophylactic barrier for the upriver advancement of Asian carp.]

Next, we traveled under the Stone Arch Bridge, a National Engineering Landmark. A quarter mile downriver was the Lower St. Anthony Falls lock and dam. I didn't need Earl's help for this one. I had been kayaking less than two miles and I felt ready to successfully navigate through my second lock.

However, managing my kayak was a different story. I was still trying to figure out the most basic moves; things like how to turn the boat, paddle, and look behind me without tipping felt pretty important. And I hadn't even thought about how to get out of my plastic casket! Like anyone's first

Rush hour in the first lock

Joe and Earl Van Norman checking out the first lock in Minneapolis, Minnesota

time skiing, golfing, or drinking, I didn't have a clue what I was doing, but I couldn't have had more fun. As we yelled across the water and took pictures, we were experiencing a truly novel scope of the downtown Minneapolis cityscape. It was the urban concrete you'd expect, juxtaposed with a surprisingly wild and woodsy shoreline.

During one wide stretch of the river near the University of Minnesota, we fought some stiff headwinds and significant chop. The crashing water was beating me up every time my bow broke through the whitecaps. I was getting soaked and worn out, doing everything I could to try and keep up. My son, with Earl in his lap, seemed to be doing just fine. He had a lead of fifteen minutes. Or was it thirty years? It was a good challenge for me, but I was nonetheless relieved when we got to a calmer and more protected stretch.

We then paddled between the wooded, steep riverbanks through Mississippi Gorge Regional Park. Making sure we missed the massive pilings, we paddled beneath the Lake Street-Marshall Bridge, an arch bridge connecting Minneapolis and St. Paul. There's an old line, "How do you get from Minneapolis to St. Paul? Cross the Lake Street Bridge and turn . . . your watch back twenty years."

Two river miles later, we approached our third lock and dam, referred to as Ford Dam. This one's official name, surprisingly, is Lock and Dam 1. I will later discover the USACE lock and dam numbering system is not as easy as 1, 2, 3. There are twenty-nine Mississippi locks and dams numbered 1 through 27. There is a 5 and a 5A. There is no number 23, as the numbers skip from 22 to 24. There is also no number 26 because that is named Mel Pierce. Number 27 is on a canal, skirting the Mississippi's Chain of Rocks above St. Louis.

Locks and dams are complex, massive physical marvels. They are also complex, massive political entities. Their stakeholders can be found, and heard, at the city, county, state, regional, national, and international levels. As long as the river flows, the diverse river interests will grate against each other. These competing pursuits include the agricultural, environmental, recreational, navigational, geographical, political, health, ecological, artistic, hunting, fishing, and commercial.

The border wars are the bloodiest, even on the Mighty Mississippi.

We passed beneath the Ford Bridge and locked through Ford Dam. This dam opened in 1917, and in the 1920s, a hydroelectric plant was added to power the Ford Motor Plant, which sat atop the St. Paul riverbank in Highland Park from 1925 to 2011. At its peak, Ford pushed nearly three hundred thousand Ford Ranger trucks onto our streets per year.

A mile downriver, we came ashore at our exit point, Hidden Falls Park (UMR 846.5). Our car was still there. I didn't realize it then, but this would be the first of many, many times that I would feel the relief of seeing the car still there, intact, at the downriver takeout.

Joe and Earl pulled me ashore and helped me up and out of my orange plastic cell. I still didn't know how to get in or out of my boat. That would come later.

We headed back to REI with the rental. An hour later we left the outfitter with the orange kayak still strapped to the top of my car. It was no longer a rental. I was now the owner of this end-of-season, closeout recreational kayak. The Dagger Blackwater 11.5 was mine for $350.

It was Saturday night, and I was already making plans for my next adventure. Sunday was a few hours away. It seemed like a good day to get *my* boat back on the Father of Waters.

Eight river miles on an autumn afternoon. Three boys. Three generations. Huck Finning down a timeless river. Locking through and locking in some timeless memories. I believe another passion just discovered me.

2

MY BOAT

Fall 2005

SEPTEMBER 18, 2005 (UMR 846.5)

The next day I was back at Hidden Falls Park in St. Paul with my newly purchased kayak. There was no one to push me on or pull me off the river this time. I was by myself, and I was planning my first solo adventure, a six-mile downriver paddle to Harriet Island, just across from downtown St. Paul.

I managed to get in the boat and launched from shore without too much trouble, but I was glad there were no witnesses to my awkward maneuverings. Even though the river runs through urban St. Paul, the landscape, when viewed from the river, is woodsy and rural. It's just the river, the shoreline, and trees. Oh, and people. It was a perfect fall afternoon, so the river and its shores offered a variety of recreational options. People were picnicking, swimming, fishing, boating, hiking, and biking along the riverside trail. I took pleasure in watching a man throw a stick into the water for his river-soaked dogs to fetch. Norman Rockwell could have filled yards of canvas from my vantage.

Just two miles into my trip, I paddled past the confluence with the Minnesota River. It's worth noting that from an elevated bike trail, one can see the larger, newly merged river with two distinct colors flowing side by side. The Minnesota, a dirty agricultural river, is the brown muddy one, and the Mississippi the much cleaner of the two. It's at least a mile before the two rivers lose their individuality and mix.

Past the confluence, I floated by a paddlewheeler heading upriver with a boatload of tourists enjoying the fall colors river cruise from Harriet Island. The travelers took my picture. With my orange kayak and yellow vest, I like to think I blended in with the autumn splendor. We shared a few waves back and forth, and a cool moment hung in the air as the two boats went their separate ways.

After a couple of hours on the river, my destination, Harriet Island, came into view along with other familiar St. Paul landmarks. The 1st National Bank building loomed high, and the Ramsey County jail sat just above the waterfront. The jail, decommissioned two years earlier, was built feet above the river, tucked into St. Paul's trademark limestone bluffs. The cells were known for their spectacular floor-to-ceiling views of the river and all its traffic. I made note of the irony of locking through on my first day of kayaking and checking out a local lockup on my second.

I paddled up to some steps leading from the river to my exit point and gingerly climbed out of my kayak. I was standing on Harriet Island! Mission accomplished.

I didn't know it at the time, but I would later go back to Harriet Island to watch a one-man play of Mark Twain with readings from his book *Life on the Mississippi*. The play was performed on the Centennial Showboat by Don Shelby, a popular Twin Cities TV anchorman and renowned Mark Twain impersonator. It was followed by a special river cruise on the *Jonathan Padelford*, a Twain-era sternwheeler. The play was great, but the river cruise was most memorable as I got to spend a few moments trading river stories with Don Shelby. He had doffed his Mark Twain disguise and was talking of his river passions, including his firsthand experience of rivers around the world and his extensive book collection about them. There I was, still a rookie paddler, trading river stories with "Mark Twain," aka a big TV news celebrity.

I mentioned to Don that I had been kayaking the Mississippi over a series of day trips and hoped one day to paddle all 670 Mississippi River miles in Minnesota. Don was most encouraging and generous with his own river stories. As he bid me farewell, he strongly recommended I jump into *Life on the Mississippi*.

I did—both the book and the river.

3

DAY TRIPPER

Fall 2005 to 2009

Over the next few years, I continued to take my one-day paddle trips, trading in my time usually reserved for golf for journeys on the river that spanned anywhere from five to thirty-five miles. These were typically solo paddles, working my way north or south of the Twin Cities, each time stretching farther and farther from my home base. Some trips were planned, some were spontaneous, and a few were truly memorable.

OTSEGO (UMR 885.0)

Near Otsego, Minnesota, just forty-five miles upriver from St. Paul, my son and I were enjoying our day of paddling. We had no cares. It was just the river and us, until it wasn't. One moment we were paddling down the middle of the river, and the next we had run aground. The river had abandoned us! In water that was barely ankle deep, we were forced to pull our boats along the sandy river bottom for several lengthy stretches of un-navigable, not-so-Mighty Mississippi. We were surprised that we could run out of river after it had been building up for 460 miles from its headwaters! Who knew?

HISTORIC RIVER TOWNS

I claim, along with many others, that Minnesota enjoys the best section of the entire Mississippi River. Its 670 miles (one-fourth of the entire river) include the headwaters and the miles below where the Mississippi transforms from a step-across stream with reed-filled wetlands to a waterway that runs through many lakes. It flows commerce free for almost five hundred miles until it hits the Twin Cities. From there to the Iowa border, the river serves the interests of everyone from industry's captains to recreationists and adventure seekers. From my own learning-on-the-fly yakker's perspective, Minnesota's Mississippi River offered the best proving ground for honing my skills. It allowed me to start in a paddler's kindergarten and matriculate through postgraduate sessions. Minnesota, not without its own dangers and challenges, is probably the safest paddling state on the way to the Gulf. The tows are small, with a max of fifteen barges, and the waters are clean. Below St. Paul, the river is graced with a string of charming, historic river towns.

On the Lower Mississippi River, one can paddle for days without seeing a town. They are off the river, hidden behind the thousand-mile-long levy system. In Minnesota, there are 160 river miles from St. Paul to the Iowa border, and there are towns strung along the river's shoreline like diamonds on a necklace. My early day trips included visiting these jewels, one day at a time. In descending order my waypoints included St. Paul, Hastings, Red Wing, Lake City, Wabasha, Winona, La Crosse (Wisconsin), Genoa (Wisconsin), and finally the river photo op of the iconic sign designating the three borders: Minnesota, Wisconsin, and Iowa.

The geography below St. Paul fit both my recreational and educational interests. The paddling distance from one town to the next was perfect for a day tripper, and the longest drive was two and a half hours, from Genoa to St. Paul. I could get down and back in the same day.

HASTINGS (UMR 814.0)

It was a wonderfully sunny summer day, and I was on the river with a variety of folks, all out enjoying the Sunday afternoon. Paddling toward Hastings, I had to lock through Lock and Dam 2, the first one downriver from the Twin Cities. Locks were still a new thing for me, so I cautiously paddled in and pulled forward as instructed. Entering with me was a high-powered waterskiing boat, converted for this day to a party boat and packed with a crew of well-oiled revelers. The skipper brought his five hundred horses to an idle right next to me. It was an odd match, one guy cautiously working his way down the river, and a group of sunbaked parrot heads partying Margaritaville style. As we acknowledged each other, the skipper smiled and hollered a friendly reminder to me: "Remember, when we leave here this is a no wake zone."

It was a timely reminder, not about the no wake zone, but about our purpose. This whole deal is about having fun. The big doors opened, and the big boat pulled out slowly, and then, in an instant, it was gone. But I was still smiling.

RED WING (UMR 792.0)

It was late afternoon, and I was heading from Hastings to Red Wing. The weather was wearing me down as the wind picked up under the darkening sky. The waves had turned into a chop accompanied by whitecaps, and I was in the wrong type of boat. My small, open-cockpit, recreational Dagger Blackwater was not feeling very recreational. As I approached Lock and Dam 3, I was getting soaked working through the peaks and valleys of the river. There were no other boats around, so I would be the only one locking through.

I would learn later that each lock and dam has its own phone number, and a boat can call to announce its arrival. At the time all I knew was that I had to pull on a rope hanging alongside a concrete wall at the lock's entrance to announce my intentions. That was the tricky part. With the rough seas, it was not just a challenge, it was scary trying to approach the wall to reach the rope. As the river crashed into the concrete wall, the waves bounced off the wall and into the next set of incoming waves. My overmatched boat, commanded by an underprepared pilot, was careening about in the violent river as I made several attempts to reach the elusive rope. Finally, with rope in hand, I announced my arrival. But there was no response to my signal. I started to panic. Was I stranded in the entry way? Did the lock master know I was there? And then, mercifully, the lock's stoplight changed from red to yellow to green. I was on my way.

I would subsequently learn more about the watery dynamics I had encountered. According to the laws of physics, my angst at the entryway was caused by a phenomenon called "reflection." A wave reflection is a wave that's characterized as a disturbance or variation that propagates energy between two points. The direction that the wave is traveling between the two points is called the direction of propagation. When any kind of wave meets a barrier or boundary between two materials, it may bounce off and begin moving in another direction.

Before my episode at the entry, I had always associated the term "reflection" with a quiet, peaceful time of self-discovery. As I paddled into Red Wing, I was glad to have this moment of self-discovery safely behind me.

LAKE CITY (UMR 774.0) TO WABASHA (UMR 759.5)

Downriver from Red Wing is Lake City, nestled on the shore of Lake Pepin, which is the longest lake on the Mississippi. The city lays claim to the title "birthplace of water skiing," but today it's known more for its sailboat traffic. There are more sailboats on Lake Pepin than any other place on the Mississippi, a fact affirmed by the T-shirts for sale at a local bar that say: Lake City—A Drinking Town with a Sailing Problem.

Due to my fledgling status as a paddler, I decided to skip Lake Pepin for the time being and instead launched my kayak downriver at Camp Lacupolis (UMR 764.9). This would be a short, five-mile paddle to Wabasha (UMR 759.5), where I could visit the National Eagle Center. Two miles into the trip, Wisconsin's Chippewa River flowed into the Mississippi, which I later learned dumps up to sixty thousand cubic yards of sand and silt each year into the main channel of the Mississippi River. That's six thousand dump trucks worth of sand and silt annually.[2] Just downriver from the tributary's entrance, I encountered the USACE's massive dredging equipment. The huge floating vacuum cleaner and its crew had a full-time job maintaining the river's nine-foot navigational channel. This particularly sandy section of the river is marked by the never-ending, Sahara-like sand dunes piled high on Wisconsin's dairy land.

I discovered the river's sand is a hot topic in the area. US Congress members, the city of Wabasha, state legislators, and the Minnesota Farm Bureau were all embroiled in opposition to the USACE's plan to deposit fifteen feet of dredged sand on the property of a nearby fourth-generation farm, thereby burying it. Lawyers, engineers, and US senators were involved. Warren Zevon's song title fit the occasion: "Lawyers, Guns and Money."

After five miles of paddling through a political hotbed, I arrived at the peaceful town of Wabasha, and the National Eagle Center. It's a non-profit center that focuses on educating the public about eagles and provides close-up encounters with eagles they have rehabilitated. The eagles were interesting, but the staff's preoccupation with the upriver dredging was the center of attention. "Do you know how many of our tax dollars are going to that dredging project?" No one in Wabasha, even at the National Eagle Center, was burying their head in the sand.

---

2. Brian Todd, "Crews Dredge Mississippi River After Late Snow, Spring Rain," *U.S. News and World Report*, June 15, 2019, https://www.usnews.com/news/best-states/minnesota/articles/2019-06-15/crews-dredge-mississippi-river-after-late-snow-spring-rain?context=amp.

WINONA, MINNESOTA (UMR 725.0),
TO LA CROSSE, WISCONSIN (UMR 697.0)

During his 1805 Mississippi River exploration, Zebulon Pike scouted out the river valley from atop Winona's famed landmark, Sugar Loaf. I had also scouted out my next leg of the Mississippi River from this same sentinel that served yesterday's traders and explorers. This paddling leg of the journey offered both good weather and good paddling. The most noteworthy challenge was the land transportation.

The logistics of a solo trip were always the same: you would end up with your vehicle at one end of the trip and the kayak at the other end. The interest of my friends and relatives in my big river adventures was waning as I went further in debt with favors owed. How many times could one ask for a shuttle to a put-in or takeout spot? And as my travels carried me farther away, the shuttles became longer, too.

In Winona, I hid my boat in some bushes in a riverside park, then drove my vehicle to La Crosse, Wisconsin, so it would be waiting for me after a twenty-eight-mile river tour. But how would I get back to my boat? I needed help. Two centuries earlier, when river explorers Lewis and Clark needed help, they found it from one of the locals, a Shoshone woman, Sacagawea. With luck, one of the Wisconsin locals, a cabbie, came to my rescue and helped me get back to my kayak waiting in the weeds in Winona. Sacagawea was never paid for her services. My guide received $100 plus tip.

LA CROSSE, WISCONSIN (UMR 697.0),
TO GENOA, WISCONSIN (UMR 680.0)

Another day trip in the early years included paddling from La Crosse to the tiny town of Genoa (with the accent on the o), Wisconsin (pop. 253). I arrived in town by paddling under the railroad tracks and Highway 35. Once in this riverside village, I saw a big building from a different generation called the Big River Inn.

In preparation for the trip, I had called the Big River Inn to inquire about possible lodging, and their cancellation policy because what I was doing was weather dependent. The hotel's proprietor responded that it was no problem because everyone who stayed there was doing something weather dependent.

The Big River Inn, with all its charm, sat right on the river. Over the years, it had served countless hunting and fishing parties. The big, old, wood-frame structure was not part of any nationwide hotel chain. It represented a different era, with yesterday's amenities. Upon my arrival, Harold the proprietor suggested I park my kayak at his house, "Just to be sure everything is okay in the morning."

Morning arrived and everything was okay. In fact, it was more than okay. Harold insisted he escort me to a suitable put-in place on the river and he helped me load my gear into the kayak, all while we carried on a wonderful conversation exchanging some of our life stories. In my future river trips, I made sure I routed my journey through Genoa, with two more stays at Harold's Big River Inn.

Part II

YEARS: 2010 TO 2014

Lake Itasca, Minnesota, to Burlington, Iowa

River Miles: 760

Kayak: ~~Open-cockpit recreation~~
~~Dagger Blackwater 11.5 ($350)~~
Wilderness Systems Tsunami 140
Touring Kayak ($850)

4

TINA WAS RIGHT!

Spring 2010

After five years and almost two hundred muddy Mississippi river miles under my boat from Otsego, Minnesota (UMR 885.0), to Genoa, Wisconsin (UMR 680.0), I was now a self-proclaimed river man. With this newfound status, I embarked on a robust research process to discover just what I was wading into. My research included films, expositions, and books—lots and lots of books. Maybe my bibliographical approach was different than any Louisiana Coonass River Man might take in nurturing an understanding of river life, but it was my approach. I spent many more hours lost in my books than I did in my boats.

During the years of my river travels, I learned I did not have to be on the river to be with the river. The river was always there. As I pored over maps and charts, researched where I was going or where I had been, walked along it, drove over it, and read about it, it was there. The spirit of poet Joyce Kilmer's "only God can make a tree" line in his poem "Trees" rings true with rivers also, but that hasn't stopped thousands "of fools like me" from describing them.

I have read my share of river books.

There is a smorgasbord of stories of boat trips on rivers. There are big boats, small boats, steamboats, showboats, coal, gas, wind, sail, and paddle-powered boats. My favorites include Mark Twain's *Life on the Mississippi*, Jonathan Raban's *Old Glory: A Voyage Down the Mississippi*, and William Least Heat-Moon's *River Horse: A Voyage Across America*. I have read multiple books by each of these three authors, amounting to thousands of pages. I have also read thousands of pages by a best-selling hometown murder mystery writer, John Sandford. At a local book signing, Sandford offhandedly mentioned that he had paddled the entire Mississippi. As he was signing my book, we talked briefly about our shared Mississippi River paddling experiences, and I asked if he would add a short description of the river with his autograph. He obliged with, "The Mississippi is long, long, long going down." The beauty of brevity.

I discovered in all my research one prevalent theme. It is best expressed in the afore-mentioned song "Proud Mary," where Tina Turner sings about the people living on the river. River life is not only about commerce or sport—it's about people.

I personally was not looking for this message, and I did not welcome it. As one disposed to introversion, I was embracing my kayaking journeys as a time for reflection amid nature's gifts. I envisioned a Walden-on-the-water approach. Who needs company when you have the river and all it has to offer? No, I was not buying the social aspects touted in the books. I liked my solo sojourns.

I could not have been more wrong.

My own personal story took a sharp turn early on, morphing from life on the river to laugh on the river. Tina was right! It really is all about the people. Enter the cast of characters.

HENRY J. CREPEAU, LAKE ITASCA, MEMORIAL DAY 2010

I met Henry through a business group. He was a highly successful, button-down broker at Merrill Lynch, an investment and wealth management firm. He used to joke, "I have the biggest office, on the highest floor, in the tallest building in the city of St. Paul." Henry liked high places and sported a very impressive adventurer's résumé to match. He had looked down on the world from the slopes of Africa's Mt. Kilimanjaro, Asia's Mt. Everest, and Europe's Mont Blanc. When he was not scaling some icy peak, he could be found, or not found, grabbing a handful of throttle, hanging onto a two-wheeled Beemer, stitching a line across the continents of the world.

Henry was a self-described Buddhist-Christian, and he honestly believed he was the luckiest man who had ever lived. His globe-trekking sojourns stemmed from his mantra "do it while you can."

I knew of Henry, but only from a distance. I was impressed by, and somewhat jealous of, his exploits. Luckily, I got to know Henry a little better when he approached me at a business gathering with an invitation to kayak the Mississippi River from Lake Itasca to Lake Bemidji. His invite went something like this: "I know you like kayaking and I think we should go on a trip. I have checked some maps and it should take us three days to get from the Mississippi headwaters to Bemidji. I've got all the camping gear." At that time, my kayaking was limited to day trips, and I had not been camping for forty years.

I asked about his kayaking skills, and Henry responded, "I've never been in one. Is a helmet required? A lot of what I do requires a helmet." That was good enough for me.

To prepare for our trip, we spent a couple of hours on a practice paddle on the river near South St. Paul. In that short time, we discovered an abandoned marina in St. Paul Park and were mesmerized by a beautiful flock of American white pelicans soaring and circling on a lazy afternoon. We were off to a good start.

We secured a MN DNR *Water Trail Guide* that included a series of Mississippi River maps that would prove to be invaluable. Of the ten states in which the river flows, Minnesota is the only state that offers a map with such detail, including campsites, portages, water access, and marinas. The map series covers the river from the headwaters to Hastings, Minnesota, for a total of 534 river miles.

We scheduled Memorial Day weekend 2010 as our trip to adventure land. We discussed our trip, we glanced at the maps, and, as timing would have it, we discovered that a kayaking movie, *Paddle to Seattle: Journey Through the Inside Passage*, was showing three days before our trip at the aptly named Riverview Theatre. It was billed as an action, adventure, comedy, documentary, and travel piece about two friends, Josh Thomas and J. J. Kelley, spending ninety-seven days together paddling 1,300 miles of the Inside Passage. We attended the showing and were surprised that one of the two main characters was present and, after the movie, talked to the audience about their adventure. When the theater cleared out, Henry and I approached the speaker, explained our upcoming trip and our novice status, and asked for any advice. He gave us excellent counsel: "Before you leave your house, take the time to practice packing your kayaks with all your gear. That way you will know if it all fits. Good luck to you guys!" It was pure wisdom. I would not have thought of that.

ITASCA STATE PARK, MINNESOTA, SATURDAY, MAY 28, 2010 (UMR 1347.0)

It was about a half-mile walk from the Itasca Interpretive Center parking lot to the river. It took several trips to lug our boats and gear to the head-waters. On the way, we read a plaque about Henry Schoolcraft coming upon the "true head" (*veritas caput*) of the Mississippi. And for a while,

Henry Crepeau jokingly became Henry Schoolcraft. After portaging the boats and gear, all we had to do was load the kayaks, take a picture, and shove off. We loaded what we could into the kayaks and trudged the other half of our gear that would not fit back to the cars. Why didn't someone warn us about that rookie mistake?

We entered the water heading downriver, or at least downstream. We paddled one-third of a mile before our first portage, the County Road 38 culvert. For the first thirty miles, the Mississippi heads straight north, or at least as straight as this river gets. We encountered four miles of rapids (Class I) below Vekins Dam. Although the rapids were small, I nearly experienced my first capsize when I got my open-cockpit kayak half-tipped and lodged sideways in the rocks. Sixteen miles downriver we crawled up the Coffee Pot Landing to enjoy our first shore lunch. Of all the campsites we visited, I liked the name Coffee Pot the best.

After two more miles, the river changed dramatically. What river? The river had disappeared, and we found ourselves surrounded by thick, watery reeds that rose three feet above our heads. I had read of one kayaker who had fastened a mirror to his paddle to use it as a makeshift periscope. The DNR *Water Trail Guide* warned: "The Mississippi enters a large wetland and finding the channel can be a challenge in low water conditions. This stretch is nearly four miles long. River reading, and compass skills are necessary to navigate through the wetland areas. In most cases follow the downstream flow."

Lost! I have never felt as lost as those moments when we were closed in by what seemed to be an endless fog of reeds. I was glad I was not alone. We discovered that we could detect the faintest hint of a current by watching which way the underwater reeds were bending. Our novice navigating worked, and we found our way out of the reeds and onto the actual river.

Looking back, I can say I am glad for challenges like that one, and I am glad I had a partner. Since then, I have talked with other S2S paddlers who had to start their trip miles downriver from Itasca due to low water making this section unnavigable. It is never the same river. We were fortunate to get the full experience.

As we paddled, we learned how to manage the rocky riffles, snags, beaver dams, and the never-ending turns. The waters were clear, and we could see lots of fish below us and turtles diving in as we approached. It was a great afternoon.

As the day began drawing down, we looked for a decent spot to camp for the evening. The best we found was a slightly sloping patch of tall grass with barely enough space for our tent. As we set up our camp, I noticed that

Hours from Lake Itasca, where did the river go?

my professional Wall Street stock trader and paddling companion was now trading upticks for wood ticks. We slept with our heads on the upslope. In the middle of the night, we were hit with a thunderstorm. It's tough waking up to inches of water pooling inside the foot end of the tent. Henry mentioned something about not recalling this tent having a leak or two.

The day arrived bright and sunny. It was a good morning for drying things out. As we climbed out of the tent, we discovered hundreds of dew-covered spider webs glistening in the day's first sun. My traveling companion was an accomplished photographer and occupied himself capturing the dreamcatcher-like images. Finally, back on the river, Henry got a great shot of me in my kayak, a stream of droplets from my paddle reflecting the early morning sunlight. I had the picture framed and hung it in my hallway. It took a few years for me to walk past the picture and notice—for the first time—that I was paddling with my paddle upside down. Kayaking is a learning process.

We passed Iron Bridge Landing (UMR 1299.2). The bridge was removed years ago, but it is here, according to the Mississippi Headwaters Board, that the river's official designation of "wild" changes to "scenic." We knew this not by our observation, but by what is reported in the *Water Trail Guide.*

The last challenge was crossing Lake Irving and finding the underpass to Lake Bemidji (UMR 1284.5). Crossing under Highway 197, we found ourselves on the shore of the lake. We exited from our boats and congratulated each other on exploring the first 62.5 meandering Mississippi River miles together.

Relieved to find our vehicle as we had left it, we unpacked the kayaks, loaded our gear, fastened the boats on the roof rack, and drove back to Itasca for the other vehicle. As we left our takeout point, we planted the seed that this would be our put-in point on a future trip.

5

THREE RIVER BLUES

Spring 2011

GLENDIVE, MONTANA, MAY 2011

It had been one year since Henry Crepeau and I slogged and paddled the first sixty-two miles of the Mississippi River, and in two days we were going to push off to see what the next sixty river miles would bring. In that time, I had learned that the planning and anticipation of a trip is part of the deal. Checking maps, schedules, weather reports, acquiring new gear, and lots of talking about a trip and its own unique challenges was consuming. For this outing, the unknowns were two big lakes, Cass Lake and Lake Winnibigoshish.

I was two days away from loading my kayak onto the banks of the Mississippi in Bemidji, Minnesota, yet standing on the banks of the wrong river, two states away. Actually, I was not on the riverbanks because the raging Yellowstone River had flooded the banks and was now wreaking havoc on a major portion of the countryside surrounding Glendive, Montana, where I had been working for the last month.

My drive from Glendive to Williston, North Dakota, tracked alongside the swollen Yellowstone until it joined up with the flooded Missouri River. The road then followed alongside the "Big Muddy" into Williston, where I boarded Amtrak's eastbound Empire Builder back home to St. Paul, Minnesota. It was a night train that would deliver me back home in time for breakfast. I crawled into my sleeper and tried to doze, but I kept thinking about the upcoming kayak trip and what I had left to do for final preparations.

First it was the flooding Yellowstone, then the flooding Missouri, and now in the middle of the night, we ran into the flooding Red River. The floods had closed some tracks. Because passenger trains must yield to the track-owning freight trains, we were diverted several times, waiting on sidetracks. We were rerouted around Fargo, North Dakota, because the tracks were under water. Instead of a breakfast arrival, I got to St. Paul just in time for supper, nine hours behind schedule. The entire day that I had reserved for checking gear and packing was reduced to one hour. I jumped in my car and drove the four hours to Bemidji, Minnesota, meeting up with Henry at midnight. We agreed on a sunrise wake up, and I finally fell asleep. After confronting the Yellowstone, Missouri, and Red rivers, the Mississippi would be there for me in the morning.

LAKE BEMIDJI, MEMORIAL DAY 2011

Last year's takeout was this year's put-in. Lake Bemidji (UMR 1284.5) derives its name from an Ojibwe word, Pemidjigumang, meaning "river that crosses the lake." We hugged the eastern lakeshore for two miles before spotting the somewhat hidden exit to the river itself. Four miles later, we arrived at Stump Lake campsite, the river's northernmost point.

At this point, the Mississippi River flows to within one hundred miles of the Canadian border. There are 1,650 miles separating our country's northernmost border, Canada, and our southernmost border, the Gulf of Mexico. This river is our nation's most natural bisector. It draws a line covering almost 95 percent of our country's nearly even north-south cleavage. There are twenty-six states that are to the east of the river and twenty-four states to the west. The Rocky Mountains also divide the country but are skewed to the west and stop short of the southern border. The sociopolitically created Mason-Dixon line is a north-south divider but is skewed to the east and has a history of shifting over the years. The federal government has also recognized this natural border created by the Mississippi River and now uses it to assign the first call letter to radio broadcasting stations. The letter K is assigned to states falling to the left (west) of the Mississippi, and W is assigned to those right (east) of the river.

As Henry and I paddled, the river was getting wider, but was still very narrow. Nine miles downriver, we met our first portage of the day. It was two hundred yards around the Otter Tail Power Company Dam. Built just over one hundred years ago, the dam's original purpose was to supply electric power to the city of Bemidji. Today it provides less than 1 percent of the city's power. I would later learn, as my travels brought me down the ten different states through which the Mississippi flows, that each one of the locks and dams has been the subject of fiercely held debates by varying interest groups, authorities, and agencies. Each dam is embroiled in politics from the local to national level because every dam creates positive and negative impacts, both upriver and down.

In our early preparations, Henry and I had reviewed the challenges of the two foreboding lakes on this stretch. More than a few people had drowned crossing "Big Winnie" due to mid-lake sea changes. Our planning talks were laced with anticipation but also sprinkled with a palpable dose of anxiety.

Henry had noticed an alluring feature within the first big lake we would encounter, Cass Lake. In the middle of Cass Lake there is Star Island. In the middle of this island sits Lake Windigo. A lake in an island in a lake! No wonder Minnesota is the "Land of 10,000 Lakes." Our plans included camping on Star Island the first night. It would require paddling twenty-three miles the first day, which was very doable in good conditions.

"In good conditions" was the operative phrase. Unfortunately, it was not the accurate one. After several heavy thunderstorms, we found ourselves somewhere between Wolf Lake and Lake Andrusia. We had not made the best of time, and it was late in the day. We were cold, soaked, and tired.

We came upon a modest riverside fishing resort and asked the owner exactly where we were. Based on his description, we calculated that Star Island was out of reach for the day. "By any chance, would you have a cabin available for one night?" The owner replied, "I do have one. I'll have to charge you $100 because my wife will need to clean up afterward." As we pulled the kayaks ashore, I whispered to Henry that I had set my limit at $500. But our good fortune continued. The owner prepared hamburgers and fries for us that, at the time, were the best I had ever tasted. We landed a hot meal, warm clothes, and a cozy bed. It was a surprisingly nice ending to a tough paddling day.

Over the next two days, Henry and I followed the Mississippi River as it flows through the two big lakes. Both Cass Lake and Lake Winnibigoshish are within the boundaries of the Leech Lake Indian Reservation (Gaa-zagaskwaajimekaag). This reservation forms the land base for the Leech Lake Band of Ojibwe, one of six bands comprising the Minnesota Chippewa Tribe.

CASS LAKE

As morning dawned, we were rested and ready to paddle the twenty-five miles to our next takeout, the westernmost shore of Lake Winnibigoshish.

Cass Lake was our first challenge. En route across the eight-mile, open water stretch, we took a slight side trip to investigate Star Island, with its very
own, hidden, interior lake. As we approached, we were met with thick,
dark clouds of tiny, biting insects. There were thousands of them. We were
outmatched, unable to get close to the island. As we retreated, we imagined
approaching this island at sundown the previous evening, miles from shore
and totally exhausted. Our $100 lodging fee proved to be a stroke of luck
and a great investment.

We experienced good paddling conditions as we crossed Cass Lake
and covered the twelve miles of river between the two big lakes. Our river
time discussions involved the next day's daunting task of paddling somewhere between fourteen and twenty miles across Winnie. The degree of
difficulty would depend upon the lake, the weather, and how much we
wanted to "cheat," pursuing a straight line across the lake. We had read the
Water Trail Guide's caution: "Do not paddle across Lake Winnibigoshish.
A slight breeze can produce large waves across it. If you must paddle, do
so only in warm weather and stay within swimming distance of the shore."
The warning seemed straightforward, and a bit scary. There are many tales
of Winnibigoshish playing the role of widow maker. The lake's name
comes from the Ojibwe meaning "dirty water." There was good reason
the next challenging stretch had been stuck in my mind since we pushed
off days earlier in Lake Bemidji.

By early evening, we had reached the western shore of Big Winnie.
We discovered a nice, flat wooded area that served as a great campsite. We
later learned that our camping area was known to the locals as Grandpa's
Camp. It was nestled amid the trees of Bowstring State Forest. Our campsite was peaceful and offered a great view of the wondrous lake. It provided
a perfectly serene ending to our day's adventure.

Or so we thought. As we got settled on the shore, we noticed two truck
campers backing through the woods to find a good spot, just a stone's throw
from our tent. A lot of hollering, cursing, and barking orders accompanied
their efforts to back the trucks through the trees. Once positioned, the hollering and cursing continued as our new neighbors popped tops and partied.

"Accept the things you cannot change."

Although the sun had not yet set, Henry and I tucked in early. It was
then that I discovered the result of being rushed with my packing two days
earlier. I did not have my air mattress, and the ground was hard as a rock.
It was only ten o'clock, but Henry had already been snoring for two hours
while I tried to cope with my situation. I was resentful that Henry could sleep
through our neighbors' commotion. Little did I know, it would get worse.

Pop, pop, pop, bam! The fireworks exploded just feet from our tent. Our neighbors, well stocked with pyrotechnics, celebrated loudly into the night. At least I was no longer envious of Henry. Now we were both wide awake. Life on the Mississippi.

It was fitting: serenity to calamity and—eventually—back to serenity. We awoke to a spectacular sunrise.

As Mark Twain wrote in *Life on the Mississippi*,

One cannot see too many summer sunrises on the Mississippi. They are enchanting. First there is the eloquence of silence, for a deep hush broods everywhere. Next, there is the haunting sense of loneliness, isolation, remoteness from the worry and bustle of the world. The dawn creeps in stealthily; the solid walls of black forest soften to gray, and vast stretches of the river open up and reveal themselves; the water is glass-smooth, gives off spectral little wreaths of white mist, there is not the faintest breath of wind, nor stir of leaf; the tranquility is profound and infinitely satisfying. Then a bird pops up, another follows, and soon the pipings develop into a jubilant riot of music.[3]

First light on Lake Winnibigoshish (Photo by Henry Crepeau)

---

3. Mark Twain, *Life on the Mississippi* (New York: Barnes & Noble, Inc., 2010), 174.

I could not have said it better myself.

Henry's photographic talents captured the memorable moment. I look at the image of that sunrise every day as my computer monitor comes to life, depicting a lone American white pelican starting its day immersed in varying ribbons of red, gold, and orange.

LAKE WINNIBIGOSHISH

The partyers slept in while we marveled at the mirror of a lake, broke camp, and deliberated our navigational options. Our straightest line was fourteen miles, which routed us right through the middle of the lake. Heeding the caution (do not paddle across Lake Winnibigoshish), we opted for a southeasterly route that would be about sixteen to eighteen miles of paddling. Some may disagree, but I think kayaking requires more tenacity than bull riding. In bull riding, you try to stay on the bull for eight seconds. In kayaking, you try to stay in your boat for eight hours.

We met the journey ahead with both optimism and anxiety as we pushed off for our day-long paddle. This was a big lake.

Henry was a good traveling companion, keeping the mood light as we mixed our paddling with traveling tales. Henry recalled one specific mountain climbing experience on Mont Blanc that required a year of advance preparation. For twelve months prior, he established a regular routine of climbing up and down the steps of the IDS building (a fifty-story Minneapolis skyscraper) with a weighted backpack.

He talked of his climbing team approaching the summit in challenging weather, and the lead guide having "the dreaded conversation" with Henry and his climbing partner, who had been struggling in the near impossible weather conditions. The guide approached the pair and directed them in a most serious tone, "You have got a decision to make." In those few words the message was loud and clear. As close as they were to Mont Blanc's peak, they needed to turn back because of time, weather, and the real danger of being stuck on the mountain should they continue. It was a tough moment. Despite having invested countless hours and thousands of dollars, and getting so close to the summit, the team retreated. Henry's philosophical reflection was apt: "Nothing's up there but ego."

Henry stressed his adherence to a strong belief in safety first. I learned that as part of his wear-a-helmet, stay-alive approach, Henry also pays $300 every year for his Global Rescue Membership. "They will evacuate me by helicopter if needed," he said. "I did decline to pay extra for the optional hostage negotiation package."

Consistent with the safety-first theme, I brought up one of my favorite sailing platitudes. "When is it time to reef the sails? The moment the thought first enters your mind." Alternately, an old salt would frame it, "If you are asking whether it's time to reef the main, it's already past that time." You do not want to be caught scrambling with the mainsail in the middle of the storm.

We got the opportunity to employ this mariner's advice while crossing Winnie. Not with sails but with our rain gear. As we saw the thunder clouds in the distance, we chimed, "Time to reef the sails." Our reefing consisted of finding our rain gear (on deck or in the hatch), doffing our personal flotation devices (PFD), and carefully donning the rain gear and life jacket, all while keeping track of the paddle and not capsizing in the waves of Winnie.

I would come to learn that this is a routine process for the experienced kayaker, but we were still quite green in our paddling skills. In fact, we were greener than we knew at the time. We got to practice this procedure twice as we experienced firsthand the big lake's sea changes, as cautioned in the *Water Trail Guide*.

After a few storms, stories, and thousands of paddling strokes, we passed Plug Head Point, another favorite name of mine, and arrived at Winnie Dam and Recreation Area (UMR 1227.4). This dam was commissioned amid controversy by Congress in 1881. According to the Minnesota Department of Natural Resources *Water Trail Guide*, an Ojibwe Lake Winnie resident, Sturgeon Man, had argued to the US government, "No white man knows the damage that will be done to us." He was right. The dam raised water levels about eight feet, wiping out Ojibwe cemeteries, villages, and crops. Compensation was provided to Sturgeon Man's descendants 104 years later in 1985.

We pulled our boats out at the dam and drove back to Bemidji to collect the other car. We congratulated each other on being among the uncelebrated few who have experienced the Mississippi River from its step-across-creek beginnings to its passage through Bemidji, Cass, and Winnibigoshish lakes. Our sixty miles of outdoor classroom had provided up close and personal lessons in topography, ecology, history, politics, and people—from the warmth and hospitality of the fishing cabin owner to the noisy shoreside revelers. The paddling was challenging, and the company was great.

Driving home I recalled the last five days that covered the Yellowstone, Missouri, Red, and Mississippi rivers, and Winnibigoshish and Cass lakes. I was still a novice paddler, but I was less of a beginner than I had been five days ago. I felt a sense of accomplishment. I also felt a wood tick crawling on the back of my neck.

6

WHAT A DIFFERENCE A DAY MAKES

Summer 2011

With the challenges of the miles-long maze of tall, view-blocking reeds in the Itasca headwaters and the day-long paddle across deadly Lake Winnibigoshish now safely in my memory bank, it was time to face my fears one more time and check off the last of Minnesota's biggest challenges: Lake Pepin. It is twenty-two miles long and two miles wide. It represents the widest point of the entire Mississippi River. Due to my level of kayaking knowledge, or better stated my level of kayaking ignorance, I was underequipped for the task ahead of me. I was still paddling my first kayak, an 11.5-foot, open-cockpit, recreation kayak.

It was a howling, gray, and blustery day as I drove the sixty-five miles from St. Paul to my put-in spot near Old Frontenac. The boat ramp was in a nice, peaceful riverside park, but that was the only peaceful aspect of the day. The cold morning brought a headwind that was kicking up whitecaps on the huge lake. "Well, if I'm going to do this, I'm going to do this." Tucked into my open cockpit, I pushed off.

There's an old pilot's adage, "I'd rather be home wishing I was flying, than flying wishing I was home." It works for paddling, too. As soon as I was paddling in the turbulent waters, I changed my mind and headed back for the safety of the shore. Just turning around in the flowing river was all that I could handle. After a few minutes, I was gratefully back on solid ground.

In hindsight, the river was probably navigable that morning. The combination of my novice paddling skills, the wrong type of boat for those waters, and my inexperience with any turbulence added up to me being "glad I was home, wishing I was paddling." I had lived to fight another day.

Two weeks later, I tried again. It was a beautiful summer day, and I arrived for a second time at the ill-fated launching spot at Lake Pepin. This day was different. The river had calmed down from my last visit, and there was a mild, steady tailwind. I still had the wrong boat for these waters, but because of a recent acquisition, I was not focused on my boat and its deficiencies. I was the proud owner of a new toy: a kayak sail.

The popularity of Lake Pepin on that summery Sunday was validated by the hundreds of people getting their boats out of the marina and onto the water. Boats under power and sailboats of all sizes were crisscrossing the entire twenty miles. I pushed off and was thinking how wise I had been to abort the mission from this very spot just fourteen days earlier. Between the pilot's adage and Henry's safety-first rule of adventuring, I was proving to be a good student.

My new sail was designed just for kayaks. When unfurled, it resembled a big umbrella on its side, with a plastic window insert so I could see where I was going. It was not built for tacking but was designed for downwind runs, or possibly a reach with the right wind.

Searching for the most favorable wind and current, I found myself paddling down the middle of the lake. I had seventeen miles to cover, and I was doing it in style. With a consistent and moderate tailwind, it seemed like a perfect place to try out my sail. I hoisted my mini spinnaker and settled in. Well, to be accurate, I didn't really settle in, because although I didn't need to paddle due to the wind power, I did need to use my paddle for a rudder, and I still had to manage the sheet for my sail. I was fully occupied, but it was a nice break from the normal paddle routine.

As I traveled down the lake, I was approaching a sailboat regatta in progress, so I doused my sail and held back as I approached the racers. The sailboats were coming from my portside and crossing in front of me, heading toward a big orange race marker, just off my starboard. Having been in a few regattas myself, I realized that the boats would round the marker and then head to starboard on their upwind tack. I quit paddling so the racers could pass in front of me before they headed up the lake. It was quite a moment. I had an up-close, front row seat as I watched these thirty-five-foot, $100,000-plus toys jockey for position. Captains yelled orders and barked rights-of-way to their competitors as they rounded the mark, barely feet from one other. I was now on the inside of the racecourse triangle, as the ships headed north. As the last one passed in front of me, I resumed paddling down the lake.

The serenity of that moment did not last. The colorful, straining sails and the screaming skippers were not tacking upwind after rounding the mark. They were circling back, doing a 360-degree turn around the mark, and I was right in the middle of their racetrack. Two huge sailboats were bearing down on me in my underpowered, plastic peanut. It was going to be close—uncomfortably close. I not only remember the size and imminence of the sailboats, but I also recall a sailor's face, and even his teeth, as he hollered, with panic in his voice, "You've got to get out of here!"

In an instant, my easy, breezy afternoon turned into a very real, very present nightmare. I paddled as fast as I have ever paddled, watching over my shoulder as the racing boats sliced through my wake, missing me by feet.

The recovery took a while. My heart rate, breathing, and sweating were all out of control. But I made it! My adrenaline was the proof.

According to Merriam-Webster, adrenaline is a stress hormone produced within the adrenal gland that quickens the heartbeat, strengthens the force of the heart's contraction, and opens up the bronchioles in the lungs, among other effects. The secretion of adrenaline is part of the human "fight or flight" response to fear, panic, or perceived threat. It's also known as epinephrine.

Although these words fall short in capturing the true essence of adrenaline, our bodies can experience the entirety of it in any given moment.

Of course, I was safe, and the fury of the moment was over, but the images of the yachts bearing down on me, the skipper's teeth, and his voice all crowded my senses. Yet as I breathed through all the mess of the mayhem, new feelings found their way to the surface of my emotions: It was deadly! It was wonderful! I am alive!

I didn't know it then, but there would be more of these life-affirming moments awaiting me downriver. I know this kind of excitement is not the reason I kayak; that's more for the whitewater X-gamers. But the moments of intense, full body adrenaline are a positive by-product. Sure, I know I'm alive, but sometimes I need to feel it.

The rest of Lake Pepin was a nice, slow paddle. I stayed close to the shore and got off the river in a safe marina at Camp Lacupolis Resort (UMR 764.9), near Reads Landing.

The Itasca headwaters' maze of reeds, Cass Lake, Lake Winnibigoshish, and Lake Pepin: Minnesota's fearsome foursome had been put to bed. There would be other fears to face, in due time.

7

SAFETY FIRST

Spring 2012

For the first few years of this river adventure, I had completed many solo day trips and, with the help of my explorer partner, Henry Crepeau, I had managed a couple overnight camping and paddling trips. My next leg of this years-long quest was to undertake a solo overnight trip. It would be a two-day trip covering sixty-one river miles, starting in La Crosse, Wisconsin (UMR 697.0), and ending just past Lock and Dam 9 in the town of Prairie du Chien, Wisconsin (UMR 636.0).

I had connected with a young man who worked at a canoe rental shop in Prairie du Chien. We had never met before, but we were able to make plans over the phone. He agreed to shuttle me and my kayak from my takeout spot back to my vehicle where I had put in the previous day. We locked in a time and place where I would meet him on the bank of the river in Prairie du Chien.

During the first day, my paddling progress had been slower than planned and the question loomed: Was I going to meet my shuttle driver on time the next day? It was going to be close. River time.

Of course, I had learned the virtues of a safety-first mindset from Henry. But I also knew that safety has many enemies, one of which is a schedule.

For the night on the river, I camped on an island and planned for an early start. As I dozed off, I realized that if I didn't make it to our meeting point on time, I could be stranded somewhere on the banks of the Mississippi in the middle of western Wisconsin with a kayak and fifty pounds of gear. No one dies in that story, but there is also no magic plot twist that reunites me with my vehicle sixty miles upriver. I decided that I needed to be on the river the next morning before sunrise.

I've never found breaking camp to be an easy or efficient process. Taking down and packing my tent, clothes, food, paddles, and PFD can be cumbersome enough without going through the motions in the darkness of night, in the diminished circle of light afforded by my headlamp. Somehow I fumbled my way through and was in my kayak and on the water an hour before the day's first light. I felt confident my in-the-dark efforts would allow me to catch my shuttle on time.

Although it was an eerie time of day, or night, the river was smooth for paddling. I had been straddling Iowa and Wisconsin in a section of the river that was strewn with hundreds of sloughs (sounds like "sloos") that were interlaced with the river's main channel. I realized these streams, marshes, and swamps ran tandem and at times were indistinguishable from the river. After a short while of paddling in the dark, with my headlamp revealing just a few feet of pathway, my kayak hit a mid-river sandbar. I seemed to be on a teeter-totter, balancing precariously on this sandy underwater fulcrum. Careful not to tip over, I eased off the sandbar and pondered my predicament.

Idyllic, misty morning straddling Wisconsin and Iowa

At some point, I had gotten off the main channel and was heading down an unnavigable cul-de-sac slough. It was still dark, and I was alone— so very alone. This was another of those moments when the pilot's adage applies: "It's better to be home wishing you were flying. . . ." Flying or boating, it is the same thought. I wished I were home.

As I retraced my route, now paddling upriver, the sun's first glimmer provided enough light for me to spot a buoy marking the main channel. I backtracked to a point where I could get back onto the actual river, and I was headed for home, or at least a designated spot down the river. My concerns about arriving on time eased a bit when I paddled up to Lock and Dam 9, the one dam I had to pass through, at just the right moment. I arrived just as the lock doors were swinging open to lock through another pleasure craft. A few miles later, I was off the river, my gear was packed, and my ride appeared.

It was a pleasant ride following the river back to my vehicle. My teen-aged shuttle driver was a paddler and a good conversationalist. We enjoyed trading river stories. It was a big relief knowing another leg of the river was checked off and that I was able to safely look back on the experience of night paddling. As my journey progressed, I would continue to paddle down the river and up the learning curve.

8

HUNDREDS OF TICKS AND ONE BEAR

Spring 2013

My plan was to head back up to northern Minnesota. I invited Bob Verchota, a friend and professional associate for over thirty years, to join me on a two-day paddle from Lake Winnibigoshish (UMR 1227.0) to a stretch below Grand Rapids, Minnesota. Bob was a likely candidate because he lived and worked in Bemidji, Minnesota—the first city one arrives at after entering the Mississippi's headwaters—and he was an avid outdoorsman and athlete with expertise ranging from hunting, fishing, and paddling to hockey and golf. Bob's email response to my invitation was lengthy, with a rather dark tone:

> Your top to bottom journey is a huge undertaking and having lived in the town calling itself the "headwaters" of the Mississippi, I have had a regular diet of talk at the local boat shops about all the paddlers who start and most of who may get to Minneapolis/St. Paul, the few that make it out of the state, and the far fewer who actually finish in the Gulf of Mexico. I lived in St. Louis for a couple years and heard the nightly news of missing boaters and drowned partyers—their bodies recovered days later, 20 miles downstream, hung up in some raft of trees along the bank or against a bridge. And in those southern stretches you have other dangers like snakes, gators, and locals who may find single travelers an interesting diversion.

With the fine print of "common side effects" so stated, Bob agreed to jump in and explore the next river section with me. Once on the water, this true outdoorsman's shadier views of river travel dissipated and were upgraded with wonderful descriptions. After our trip, Bob wrote of his recollections. Here's a sample that he has allowed me to share:

The first part of this section of river is about 20 miles down to the Schoolcraft State Park. It's beautiful. It alternated from 10 yards wide with deep flowing water to 40 yards wide and slower stretches with grass flats, sandbars, rushes, and cattails growing high enough to obscure the surrounding landscape. Sometimes all you could see was river, rushes, and sky. Banks of the river varied from the large flats with willow and rushes to steep inclines of eroded sand with vegetation and trees on top. Birch and pine were dominant on the taller banks and often a white or red pine was spotted, serving as a perch for eagles and osprey. Fish were common along those sections with sandy shallows. Beaver and muskrat were there, along with kingfishers, ducks, and jays. Redwing black birds seemed to be everywhere.

Our first day proved to be a nice, easygoing paddle on a nice, easygoing river. We took in the flora and fauna and spent the hours reconnecting and catching up on each other's lives. As evening approached, we found a grassy field suitable for pitching a tent. We prepared our dinner by pouring boiling water in a tinfoil bag of some dehydrated pasta. The meal was not noteworthy, but the wood ticks were. As we headed into our tent for the evening, we armed ourselves, each with an empty plastic water bottle to serve as a holding cell for the annoying Arachnida. I am not sure if there were more ticks or more expletives. By morning, each of us had dozens of the little pests bottled up. We would continue to feel the ticks crawling on us, or imagine the ticks crawling on us, in all kinds of private places—for days!

As we ate our oatmeal breakfast, there was a splash in the river about fifty yards upriver from our campsite. We saw a black bear swimming across the river. We were glad it was swimming to the other side, but we were also alarmed that he had been on our side, and so close.

On our second and last day of paddling, we got on the river early and paddled to Cohasset (UMR 1182.0). We spotted a restaurant in sight of the boat ramp. It was a chilly and drizzling morning, so we decided to get off the river and enjoy our second breakfast. No camp oatmeal this time; we enjoyed bacon and eggs and hot coffee. With our energy levels renewed, our bones warmed, and more ticks removed, we were ready for the big push to Grand Rapids. As we left Cohasset, we paddled through the Bass Brook State Wildlife Management Area. Our MN DNR *Water Trail Guide* describes this area as "protecting cultural sites dating to Dakota occupations more than 3,000 years ago."[4]

---

4. Minnesota Department of Natural Resources, *Mississippi River—A Water Trail Guide: Vermillion River to Palisade* (St. Paul, MN: The DNR Information Center, 2010), Section 3.

Just five miles farther, we approached the Blandin Paper Company Dam. The *Water Trail Guide* described a 1,200-yard portage right through the town of Grand Rapids. Not too appealing. The Blandin Paper Company, in addition to damming up the entire river, also offered another option to getting downstream of the massive dam. On shore just above the dam was a telephone with instructions to call for assistance. Within minutes of our phone call, a man showed up with a truck, shuttled us around the dam, and deposited us safely back on the river. It was like Uber on the Mississippi!

Bob and I paddled to our takeout spot at the Blackberry Landing (UMR 1167.0) and were met by Bob's family who shuttled us back to his home. It had been a good trip. We covered sixty miles, made it through good weather and bad, had some great conversations, and got up close with creatures great (one black bear) and small (hundreds of wood ticks).

9

NO MAN EVER STEPS IN THE SAME
RIVER (BAR) TWICE

Fall 2013

I met Dan Meer, the owner of Clear Waters Outfitting Company (and shuttle service), at Wilson Park in St. Cloud (UMR 925.0). I transferred my boat and equipment to his truck, parked my vehicle on a side street, hoped it would still be there in three days, and headed for Crow Wing State Park. As if reading my mind, Dan asked if I would like to scout out the river and the rapids in Sauk Rapids, just a mile upriver from the park we just left. It was a section I would need to encounter in three days.

Dan coached me as we looked down on the rapids from a safe headland. "As soon as you cross under the bridge, head way over to your left; then after the first set of rapids, immediately get over to the right so you miss that big boulder. Once you're past that, you should be alright."

It seemed simple enough from a hundred yards away. But those rapids, described as "Class I-III, Caution: scout before proceeding" in the Minnesota DNR's map series, would not leave my mind for the next three days. Dan, with his years of river experience, seemed to think it shouldn't be a problem. His advice was drilled into the planning and problem-solving parts of my brain, as well as my amygdala, where fear and anxiety reside.

It was a pleasant, one-hour shuttle ride. I learned about Dan's background, how he started his family's outfitting business, and highlights from his own adventures, both on the river and off.

It was sunset when we arrived at Crow Wing State Park (UMR 990.3). We shook hands and Dan headed back home, leaving me alone with my boat, my pile of gear, and a thick cloud of hungry mosquitoes. I got to try my new mosquito net hat as I scrambled to set up camp.

After collapsing in my tent, escaping the wrath of the blood-sucking legions, I was ready to conk out.

Kaboom! KABOOM!

Feel-it-through-your-whole-body explosions were detonating in my new backyard. I discovered at that moment Camp Ripley Military Reservation is very active in armament training. For an hour, there was a nonstop barrage of shells exploding. The river, no more than one hundred yards wide at the park, was the only separation between my temporary shelter and the front lines of Ripley. My son would later tell me each time I heard an artillery shell explode, the cost represented more than the value of any of his cars. Maybe he should drive better cars.

No songbirds would greet me the next morning. I was awakened by the predawn resurgence of artillery fire. It was a strange juxtaposition: hundreds of earth-rattling shells exploding nonstop and the peaceful, pastoral setting of a river meandering through the wooded countryside. War and peace.

The next night, I got off the river at Fletcher Creek Boat Launch (UMR 969.2). Finding no suitable campsite, I set up my tent in a parking lot about ten yards from a "No Camping" sign.

Morning came early, triggered by gunshots. I was perplexed. How could that be? I was more than twenty miles downriver from Camp Ripley. But these explosions were different. They came from civilian firepower saluting the duck hunting season. They began one half hour before daylight, and wouldn't you know, I didn't see a duck all day.

Next stop: Little Falls. As I horsed the heavily loaded kayak up the grassy bank to face a portage around the Little Falls dam, I was surprised by the warmest welcome from a man known locally as the Can Man. "Want some help with your kayak? I've got a four-wheeler with a trailer." We loaded the boat on his trailer and drove to the next put-in. "Your boat will be safe here. Can I drive you someplace for lunch?" I enquired if the Black & White Diner was still in business. En route to the eatery, we passed a huge cage of cans for recycling. The Can Man explained his moniker came from his volunteer harvesting of every can in sight.

The Black & White has always been a favorite of mine. I was hungry, and it did not disappoint. I can't explain why, but the patty melt, fries, and Coke qualified as one of the top two meals I had on the entire adventure. It was the right fuel, at the right time.

The Can Man brought me back to shore, and I was off for the Blanchard Dam (UMR 952.9). I had called the MN DNR previously to get a scouting report of this stretch of the river. The DNR ranger cautioned me about this next portage. "It's a long, tough one, up and down over two railroad grades. Do you know what you're getting into?" I said "No, I don't, but that's why I'm doing it." It smacks somewhat smartass, but it was true. I was getting comfortable with discomfort.

"Up and down two railroad grades" sounded easier on the phone than the actual exercise. These were steep, slippery hills, one right after another. This portage was described in the river guide as three hundred yards, but it was at least a mile. A DNR ranger admitted to me a few years later that some of the stated portage distances may have been rough estimates. This one proved to be very rough. It took me four trips to portage my boat with all the gear. I had to hump it over the hilltop train tracks and then trek a tough, woodsy trail. Halfway through my first pass, I hoped there would be a spot—any spot—to set camp, because I was going to be spent when this was over. But it would be hours before I dropped my gear at a makeshift campsite below the dam.

With my tent pitched and my gear stowed, I sat down on a big, smooth log to recover from the brutal hours invested in my journey. On the log I found evidence that I was not the first to pass this way. Etched in the smooth surface was the briefest summary of an earlier sojourner's sentiment: "Fuck that portage."

Tucked in for the night, I took the day's inventory. It started with the rude awakening by the predawn reveille of the duck season opener. Once on the river, it was a peaceful, downhill paddle as the Mississippi connected Minnesota's forests to its prairies. In Little Falls I was welcomed, and spoiled, by the city's volunteer ambassador, the Can Man, with a patty melt that added technicolor to my life at the Black & White. Below the Little Falls Dam, I had passed the river's confluence with Pike Creek. A couple miles further down was the site of the now submerged 1805 winter fort of Lieutenant Zebulon Pike, a noted Mississippi River explorer who is also known for a certain Colorado mountain top. Another five river miles brought me to the portage of perdition. And I was now camped within a stone's throw of the Blanchard Dam, which is the largest hydroelectric dam on the Upper Mississippi. With the powerful but lulling sounds of the rushing river, it made for a most peaceful way for a traveler to fade out. Life was good.

The following morning, rested from the Blanchard Dam portage, I got off to an early start and paddled toward the next portage twenty miles downriver. The early morning sky was an uninterrupted blue, and the river was calm. It was a perfect day in central Minnesota. As I paddled around a bend, I came upon a doe and her fawn standing on the riverbank, their inverted reflection displayed in the mirror of the river. I stopped paddling and let the river carry me closer. It was a quiet, peaceful moment for just the three of us. The serenity was lost when the fawn suddenly slipped and fell into the water. Thrashing and splashing cut through the silence, as the fawn struggled back to shore. A moment later the doe and her wet baby were reunited, and all was well with the world once again.

After a half day of paddling, I pulled off the river into the muddy bank just above the Sartell Dam (UMR 928.8). The portage was listed as three hundred yards in the Minnesota DNR map, but I wondered what the true distance was based on my experience the day before with the upriver portage from hell. I decided to make the initial pathfinder trek a light one, so I grabbed the paddles, PFD, and a couple of small bags. Rather than a rugged hilly path through the woods, I discovered this to be a more urban experience as I walked through the parking lot of the River Boat Depot Bar on a sunny Saturday afternoon.

A voice from the shadows of the bar's screen porch hollered, "Where'd you come from?" Finally realizing it was directed at me, I replied, "From Brainerd." What had been a voice became a guy walking toward me. Soon he was up close and personal, and checking out my gear. As he inspected my paddles he said, "You're a kayaker. I'm a canoe guy myself. The first time I took my son to the Boundary Waters, he was ten years old. Now he's thirty-three and we just finished up another trip this spring. Great, isn't it! Where you headed?" His nonstop chatter accompanied me all the way to the end of the portage. Heading back toward the bar, I asked if he was just sitting in the bar and would he like to make $20? "Oh, you want me to help carry some stuff? Sure!"

I realized it was probably not the Lewis and Clark approach, but I welcomed the help. After our third half-mile trek together, he invited me into the bar for a drink. "What beer do you like? You want something with a bite?"

"Diet Coke's fine. My drinking days are thirty years behind me," I said. He understood and we entered the "Boat's" slice of Americana.

Out of the sun and into the cozy confines of the riverside watering hole, we joined ten other patrons spending down their Saturday afternoon at the horseshoe-shaped bar. I learned that Steve Fabel, my temporary Sherpa, was an engineer from nearby—and aptly named—Cold Spring. The locals were right out of central casting. "Is that a Tilley? I've got one, too," queried one friendly sort, gesturing toward my head. We extolled the hat's features, lifetime guarantee, and secret compartment, surmising its ability to pass unscathed through an elephant.

A woman celebrating a mid-life birthday happily announced her daughter was taking her to a Bonanza Steak House the next day as a birthday treat. The patrons touted the bar's cheeseburgers and recalled one river paddler, Harry, who stopped on his way through and couldn't get enough of them. Ten minutes later a new customer entered. A moment passed and the new guy, unprodded, brought up Harry again. "Harry loved those burgers! He stayed for three days, camping out in a woman's front yard. I bet he ate twenty of them before he passed through."

I asked Sherpa Steve about the rapids awaiting at the Sauk River confluence. He said they could be a challenge, agreed with the "stay to the left" strategy, and thought I would probably be alright. I offered him the $20 I had promised for the packhorse service, but he stubbornly refused. "Pay it forward," he ordered. I have since learned to appreciate Steve's advice more than I ever imagined. His words continue to remain with me, and over the years they have unknowingly helped scores of people in need. Thanks for the gift, Steve. I'm happy to say I'm still paying for it.

Steve walked me down to the river, we took a picture, and off I went. I had two miles of paddling and anticipation before I finally got to face my lingering fear of the past few days. The Sauk Rapids are reported to be the largest rapids on the entire Mississippi. I had the sense a class III challenge was ahead.

The Minnesota DNR's website defines Class III rapids as "Difficult rapids with high, irregular waves capable of swamping an open canoe." My advance reading prepared me for waves up to four feet, along with strong eddies, strainers, and powerful currents. Kayak control in the tight spots would be the name of the game; I just hoped I had the right stuff.

Like Caesar crossing his Rubicon, I was now irrevocably committed. I paddled under the final bridge just above the Sauk River confluence. I recalled my Clear Waters Outfitting scout Dan Meer's advice from a few days earlier: "As soon as you cross under the bridge, head way over to your left; then after the first set of rapids immediately get over to the right so you miss that big boulder. Once you're past that you should be alright." Now, on the river, as I looked to the left, I saw lots of white water; and then I noticed two swimmers just standing waist deep in the river, but way over on the right descending bank. At that moment, the right side looked a lot safer than the left. Was there enough time to ferry to the safer side? Change of plans. I stroked as best I could to reach the other side as the swift current was driving me downriver.

As I approached, the two men gave me a look that was both bemused and concerned. From their front row seats, they awaited the drama, or mayhem, that was about to play out. "What is this crazy kayaker getting himself into on this side of the river?"

As I got nearer, I realized, too late, that I was on the wrong side of a very turbulent stretch of four-foot rapids, strewn with bone-crushing boulders. The river delivered me into the breach. It was white waters, white knuckles. You don't get to count down from three before you commit. The river has taken care of that for you. Try to hit the best spot. Paddle! Focus! It's loud, wet, and I'm spinning out of control. In an instant I could see the two swimmers, but this time I was looking upriver with my kayak heading through the rest of the rapids backward.

Now I look back at my ride as a poor man's copy of Teddy Roosevelt's experience, recounted in Candice Millard's *The River of Doubt*, as he describes an unchartered tributary of the Amazon as "black, . . . boulder-strewn rapids (that) turn the river into a roiling cauldron."

As the river calmed, I realized I was through the Sauk Rapids, I was upright, and my takeout spot was just a mile downriver. In one sunny Saturday afternoon, I had gone from the River Boat Depot Bar's cast of characters talking of Tilley hats, paddling, and paying it forward, to escaping the largest rapids on the river. Once again, I realized, I am alive! It was quite an afternoon.

Off the river, I experienced the familiar relief that my vehicle was where I had parked it. It took ten minutes to drive back to the River Boat Depot Bar. I was looking forward to reporting back to Steve, and my other new barroom BFFs, of my adventures with the river and rapids.

As I entered the bar, I didn't see Steve. In fact, I didn't recognize anyone. It was a new bartender, and a new crowd. This much older group looked as if they were settling in for their Saturday night dinner.

No man ever steps in the same river (bar) twice.[5]

Days later, I did send pay-it-forward Steve a note thanking him and telling him that I had made it to St. Cloud. He replied:

Dennis,

Good to hear from you! It was my pleasure to give you a hand. I enjoyed meeting you. The crowd at "the boat" is different from daytime to nighttime. I'm glad you didn't capsize, the rapids there can be pretty tricky.

Good to hear you're getting more paddling in. With the project I have going on at work it's looking like I won't be able to get my son up to Quetico this year, but we should still be able to get a BWCA trip in before he starts back at school.

Happy paddling!
Steve

---

5. Heraclitus, 535 BC: "No man ever steps in the same river twice, for it's not the same river and he's not the same man."

10

DRIFTING OFF IN THE DRIFTLESS AREA

Spring 2014

With the melting snow and longer days, I found myself heading to the "driftless area" to launch my kayak into a flooded Mississippi River. The driftless area is a region that the glaciers skipped as they scraped across the Midwest ten millennia ago. The area covers parts of Minnesota, Wisconsin, Illinois, and Iowa.

I had called the Minnesota DNR to get a more knowledgeable perspective on paddling on a flood-level river. The DNR ranger was most helpful as he schooled me on high-water paddling. "First off, I can't tell you not to go. But here are some things to consider before you decide. Go check out your intended route closely. Drive to the area and check out the river from a bridge crossing the river. Remember, it is not just the question of can you paddle in the high waters, it's can you get off the river. Watch out for strainers, those partially submerged trees that can trap you with the river pushing you under. Also paddle with someone else in these high, fast waters. You do not want to be doing this by yourself."

He added, "On a personal note, I will also say that paddling a fast river can be fun and very exciting."

Following *some* of his advice, I paddled the fast, swollen river between Iowa and Wisconsin along a stretch dotted with numerous islands with sandy shores, ideal for taking a break or camping for a night. That is, they would have been ideal, under different river conditions. I was not experiencing those conditions. I could hear the DNR ranger's words: "Remember, it is not just the question of can you paddle in the high waters, it's can you get off the river."

President John F. Kennedy made famous the phrase, "A rising tide lifts all the boats."[6] A corollary could be "a flooding river sinks all the islands."

The river islands were still there, spaced so conveniently for one passing through, but their sandy beaches were gone. The flooding river had overtaken all the shoreline and riverbanks. The rising river had climbed up trees, making them appear as telephone poles sprouting out from the water. There were hundreds of uprooted trees the river had deposited up against bridge abutments, docks, mile markers, and other river structures.

No, the islands and mainland shoreline were no longer available for spending the night. As the sun dropped, my anxiety rose. Paddling a flooded river in the dark was not a viable option. Would I be homeless in the driftless area? I finally spotted a narrow slice of grassy high ground, barely suitable for my tent. It was about forty yards wide and straddled the rising river and some railroad tracks.

In the last light of day, I pulled ashore and set up camp near the high ground of the tracks. I was glad to be off the river and ready for bed. As a light sleeper, I mentally prepared to be awakened in the night by a tow's sweeping searchlight scanning the river shores, as had happened so many times before.

However, on this night, I was awakened not by a sweeping beam, but by a small, distant dot of light that continued to grow, along with an accompanying sound. What had started as a speck of a spotlight became blinding, and the low rumble became deafening. The lumens and decibels were off the charts. Roaring toward me was a Midnight Special, pulling a mile's worth of screaming steel as it thundered through, mere steps from my tent.

Doing the math, a mile-long train, roaring by at a mile a minute, will result in a high-adrenaline moment of one minute. As the train shook me for those sixty seconds, the roaring, shaking, and looking-at-the-sun brightness burned a lifelong hole in my sensory memory. That moment, from its buildup with the first flicker of light to the quiet return to nature's night sounds, was repeated two more times that night. It was not only an awakening, it was another life-affirming experience.

Thirty years prior, my son and I had scored great tickets to the Indy 500. We were seated on the first turn, twenty rows up from the track. At the very beginning, we were simply in awe of the speed the pace car kept as it led the drivers around the famed oval. Then the starter waved his

---

6. President John F. Kennedy, "Remarks in Heber Springs, Arkansas, at the Dedication of Greers Ferry Dam," 1963, https://historynewsnetwork.org/article/73227.

green flag. The air exploded as thirty-three cars floored it into a different dimension. Sight, sound, smell—all senses redlined in an instant. I've never forgotten. It continues to be the most memorable sporting moment in my life, and that includes the moment when I, as a baseball geek teenager sitting in the right-field bleachers, witnessed Minnesota Twins Julio Becquer hit a two-outs, bottom of the ninth, full-count, pinch-hit, walk-off, grand slam homerun. The ball landed in the stands a few feet from me.

A crowd of twenty thousand going crazy as a homerun baseball crashes into the stands. The thrill of a racetrack holding four hundred thousand spectators. A series of night trains screaming through a campsite. It is wonderful those adrenaline moments stay with us for a lifetime.

Part III

YEARS: 2015 TO 2018

Clarksdale, Missouri, to Pilot Town, Louisiana

River Miles: 1,400

Kayak: ~~Open-cockpit recreation~~
~~Dagger Blackwater 11.5 ($350)~~

~~Wilderness Systems Tsunami 140~~
~~Touring Kayak ($850)~~

P&H Capella 173 Sea Kayak ($2,000)

11

INTRODUCTION TO MIKE CLARK, BIG MUDDY

Spring 2015

Face your fears. From the moment I first dipped a toe in the Mississippi River at Boom Island there has always been some degree of anxiety associated with my paddling life. Initially it was, "Can I keep this boat from capsizing? Can I navigate through a lock?" Followed by "Can I take a trip by myself? What about all the barge traffic? What about Sauk Rapids? How is my little boat going to fare on Lake Winnibigoshish and Lake Pepin?" They are huge lakes!

As I put in more hours on the water, my paddling skills improved. If one starts at the top, the Mississippi can be a good teacher. From a step-across creek to a meandering stream, to a small river, to a lake. These are graduated steps. I had logged my share of hours and miles. I had surprised myself by paddling all the way into Iowa.

As the water got bigger, so did my boats. I started with a $350 used Dagger Blackwater 11.5-foot open-cockpit recreation boat. This worked out well, but I learned afterward that it was the wrong boat, and dangerous, for what I was doing. That was not the boat for Big Winnie, Sauk Rapids, or Lake Pepin. I had advanced from my open-cockpit rec boat days to a touring boat, an $850 used Wilderness Systems Tsunami fourteen-foot with a cockpit and skirt. I liked this boat, but as the river got faster and wider, I felt I was underequipped.

Throughout my riverine adventure, I relied on a local gem of an outdoor store for gear and advice, Midwest Mountaineering. Over the years, two of the store's representatives, Jeremy and Brian, had taken a special interest in helping me. Jeremy, with his coaching and gear expertise, pushed me up my kayaking learning curve. Brian developed a personal interest in and curiosity about my numerous Mississippi paddling trips and steered me to my next boat: a $2,000 used P&H Capella 173 sea kayak. It was more

57

boat and more money than I could ever have imagined when I took my first paddle strokes just a few years back. My paddle now cost more than my first kayak.

The river kept rolling and my goals kept growing. At one time my goal was to paddle the entire Mississippi River in my home state, Minnesota, which equates to 670 miles. Done. I had traveled through the entire set of *Minnesota Mississippi River Water Trail Guides* and was now studying the *US Army Corps of Engineers (USACE) Upper Mississippi River Navigation Charts*. I had paddled into Iowa and Wisconsin, but I could not help peeking ahead to Illinois and Missouri. St. Louis was such a big, sexy, scary, river-town goal. If I could make it to St. Louis, I could be a real river man.

I needed to address the immediate fears linked with my next travel plan. "Do you know what you are getting yourself into?" Below the last dam on the Mississippi—the Mel Price Lock and Dam—the river turns into a wild, undammed river. Upriver from St. Louis there was the Chain of Rocks. Every book I read about S2S travels included some discussion of how to get over or around this rocky barricade. I understood there was a ten-mile, commercially clogged canal that side-stepped the notorious rock dam. There was also the confluence with the Missouri River. What happens when the country's two biggest rivers collide? And waiting at the end of this plan was the St. Louis riverfront itself, the most industrialized, barge-filled section of the river I had faced yet. I needed help.

Where would one find a Mississippi River guide? In Mississippi, naturally. Somehow, I got connected to John Ruskey, chief visionary officer and founder of Quapaw Canoe Company based in Clarksdale, Mississippi. He referred me to Mike Clark, aka Big Muddy, founder of Big Muddy Adventures in St. Louis, Missouri. If one is going to be a river expert, what could be a better headquarters than a place that's a few paddle strokes from where the country's two largest rivers come together?

We vetted each other by phone and a plan was established. Weeks later, I drove to St. Louis. I made a quick stop at the National Great Rivers Museum in Alton, Illinois. From there, I had to cross the Mississippi on the Clark Bridge as I journeyed to see Mike Clark. How fitting. On the bridge I had a close look at the river. We had endured a rainy spring and the river was high and fast. This was now a river that was bigger than anything I had paddled. And this was not even on my list of things to fear, like the Chain of Rocks or the St. Louis harbor.

I arrived at Mike's Kanu House, located just off the river outside of St. Louis. Kanu House serves as a waypoint for all sorts of river paddlers. My welcoming tour included a review of a variety of boats ranging from a voyageur canoe to regular canoes and kayaks, along with assorted river life supplies and equipment. An introduction to Dolly, a giant but gentle Mastiff guard dog, and a steak dinner prepared outside on an open fire completed the orientation.

The next morning, Mike drove me seventy-five miles upriver to my put-in at UMR 273.5, just below Lock and Dam 24 in Clarksville, Missouri. On the way we joked about Mike Clark, driving to Clarksville, and Louis and Clark, which sounds a little like Dennis and Clark. He gave my kayak a shove and I was off into the big river in Clarksville. I would rendezvous with him a few days later so he could guide me through the last lock and dam, Mel Price, and points south.

CLARKSVILLE, MISSOURI

Launched with the help of Mike Clark's push off, I was heading south. Back on the river again, I noticed the *USACE Upper Mississippi Navigation Charts* offered an amusing sidebar of riparian nomenclature. Two miles into my trip (UMR 271.0), I passed Eagle Island. Seven miles later, I paddled safely past Dead Man's Island (UMR 263.5). Just seventeen miles below Eagle Island, I passed another Eagle Island (UMR 254.0). How many Eagle Islands do we need? Another few miles downriver (UMR 246.0), I found a campsite near another island, named from an earlier era, Jim Crow Island.

It had been a long day, and it was the first night I camped solo on this bigger, wider, faster river. And then, in a wink, it was the next day.

The Mississippi morning sky was smeared by a full palette of reds, oranges, yellows, golds, and blues. I was alone, I was awake, and I was ready for whatever the day would bring.

I paddled past the mouth of the Cuivre River, a French word for either copper or musical brass. In the same stretch, I passed Hat Island, and just a half mile below I passed Peruque Island, a name whose French origin means "wig." It seemed fitting that the wig would be just below the hat. That's what happens when one is paddling. If there is something new to play with—whether it's a French wig under a hat, or a green buoy just barely visible, or a red one racing toward you—you're not just paddling. The next thing that was not just paddling was a man on the deck of his cabin, perched on a high spot on the Missouri riverbank. We were close enough to acknowledge each other, and he asked if I had had my morning coffee in a most welcome-to-this-great-morning tone.

The smearing of the Mississippi River morning sky, UMR 246.0

I accepted the invitation and moments later, he and I were enjoying our morning brew on his deck. He was around fifty and it was obvious he was enjoying life in his posh, well-appointed, more-than-just-a-cabin river dwelling, replete with a river-gazing, high-powered telescope. Set on a prime piece of real estate, he was placed perfectly to enjoy the river traffic coming and going around the bend. It was obvious by the trappings that he was successful in his occupation, but our morning's discussion focused on two things: river trips and auto racing. He was in the last stages of preparation before testing his skills maneuvering his sports car through the turns of the racetracks of upper New York state. I was "straightenin' the curves" at four miles per hour in my kayak, and he was trying for triple digits.

We hit it off and could have talked all morning. If you meet a stranger on an airplane and talk for hours, you still arrive at your destination on time. On a self-propelled river cruise, every minute you are talking on land is a minute you are not cruising on the river. We enjoyed a great early morning together, and an hour later I had to be on my way. As I was leaving, he strongly recommended I stop for lunch at Kinder's Restaurant & Lounge. "Mention my name," he said. "They all know me there." He said it was just a few miles downriver, right at the Golden Eagle Ferry, in Golden Eagle, Illinois (UMR 228.5). Two Eagle Islands, now an Eagle Ferry.

A little later in the day I received an email from my breakfast host with his posting to a New York auto racing website. He was announcing his impending arrival at the racetrack, but he also mentioned his early morning meeting with Dennis Van Norman, who was kayaking down the Mighty Mississippi. Hey! Who knew my fifteen seconds of cyberfame would be in Albany?

I had awakened to a glorious day and, buoyed up by the wonderful, serendipitous visit with a comrade adventurer, the paddling came easy. A couple of hours later, I spotted the recommended restaurant heralded by a billboard-sized sign, "Kinder's Restaurant & Lounge—On and Sometimes in the Mississippi—Best Catfish & Chicken Around."

The hospitality I experienced from my coffee-drinking, race car–driving new friend upriver seemed to carry over to this "On and Sometimes in" oasis. I decided if it's the best catfish around, I'd better go with that. It was the first of a score of times this northern boy would sample the ubiquitous staple offered from Missouri all the way to the Gulf of Mexico.

"On and Sometimes in the Mississippi," Kinder's Restaurant and Lounge

I would discover that catfish, like French onion soup or crème brûlée, is prepared differently every place you try it. My catfish taste-testing adventure proved to be an ongoing highlight.[7]

GRAFTON, ILLINOIS

Before leaving for this leg of the trip, my friends Cindy and Jeff Redmon told me that Cindy's brother, Tom Davidson, lived in Grafton, Illinois, at the confluence of the Illinois and Mississippi rivers. Cindy had mentioned my trip to her brother, and it was suggested I stop and meet him on the way down.

Grafton was two days paddling from my put-in and it gave me time to adjust to this larger, higher, and faster river. During my acclimation process, I recalled a useful paddling tip. Remember, this boat is designed to stay afloat. Just do not interfere with its function.

I pulled into Grafton in the late afternoon and met a couple on the marina dock while waiting for Tom. This couple was curious about my trip, and with a hint of envy said they sure wished they could be doing just what I was doing. It was a variation of the same conversation I'd have with strangers all along the river.

Moments later, Tom introduced himself and we headed off to a nice catfish dinner at a local river's edge restaurant. Tom was an economics professor at nearby Principia College, home of the National Rugby Champions, the Thunder Chickens, and alumnus Robert Duvall, of Tender Mercies fame. After dinner, Tom toured me around Grafton and gave me a totally different perspective of the Mississippi River as we drove to his college campus, perched high above the river on the area's tallest bluff.

As the river naturally occupies the lowest terrain of an area, it is sprinkled throughout its run with majestic bluffs offering spectacular high points for viewing. Much like my riverside conversations with wannabe kayakers, I was learning that in most of the towns I visited, locals were always happy to show off their town's scenic highlights. Following the day-long view from two feet above the river, confined to my kayak's shell, the chance to see miles of this sprawling riverscape from the blufftop offered a welcome new perspective.

---

7. Note: I was sorry to learn that the 2019 Mississippi flood waters demolished Kinder's Restaurant and put them out of business, at least for a while. It sounds as if the Kinder's people are rebuilding and looking forward to a reopening. It will be a grand reopening, I am sure.

As the sun was getting lower, I thanked Tom for the perfect evening, snapped a photo, and climbed back in my kayak for the next leg. This would be a short one. I pushed off from the Grafton marina and headed a few paddle strokes, and a few minutes, into the middle of the river to set up camp on Island No. 526.

It had been a rainy spring, but I had enjoyed good weather from Clarksville to Grafton. The good weather changed as the new morning offered a much wetter outlook. It poured the entire following day. This would be the only time of my entire trip that I would be weather bound, inside my tiny tent for the next twenty-four hours. Realizing I was under house arrest for the day, I decided to do a little writing. For every trip I had always packed a writing pad, and on every trip, I found I never had any time to write. I was always spent at the end of the day. Now I had the entire day. I gathered some thoughts and put pen to paper. To my dismay, my pen ran out of ink after two lines. It was my only pen. Oh well, I still had my thoughts.

The next morning the good weather returned, and I was to rendezvous with my guide, Mike Clark, eighteen miles downriver just above the last lock and dam. No number on this one, just Mel Price.

ON THE ROCKS IN ELSAH, ILLINOIS

Just an hour downriver from Grafton I discovered Elsah, Illinois. The daily newspaper of Alton, Illinois, *The Telegraph*, reported: "Elsah, the tiny town that hardly seems to have changed in the past 150 years was named the state's top scenic spot by voters taking part in the Illinois Top 200 project. . . . Elsah still looks much the same as it did 150 years ago—cozy homes and gardens tucked into a small valley along the Mississippi. The entire village is on the National Register of Historic Places."[8]

I found Elsah, Illinois (UMR 214.0) by accident. Looking for a place to take a break, I turned my kayak off the river by following a small tributary under the Great River Road and realized I had discovered a time machine. Elsah, a village of seven hundred hearty souls, was a quick paddle into the past. Set slightly off the river traffic's path, it was a place that would be easy to miss. The village with its buildings from a century and a half past

---

8. "Elsah, Great River Road Take Top Spots in Illinois Top 200 Voting," *The Telegraph*, May 14, 2018, https://www.thetelegraph.com/news/article/Elsah-Great-River-Road-take-top-spots-in-12913020.php.

was a peaceful, scenic, and quaint place, but there was one moment that was most memorable for the paddler passing through.

The riverbanks under the Great River Road bridge were topped with large rocks two to three feet in diameter. As I paddled into town under the bridge, I noticed a baby fawn huddled in a cozy spot among the rocks. It was the smallest deer I had ever seen. Born that spring, the fawn was the size of a medium-size dog, maybe twenty-five pounds. It watched as I paddled past. This babe was still camped in its spot as I paddled out to the river an hour later. The moment presented a mystery. How did this peanut get in the middle of the rock field? Where was its mother? Would it be okay? Should I have done something?

"On the rocks" baby fawn in Elsah, Illinois

MEL PRICE LOCK AND DAM

Paddling downriver, I arrived mid-afternoon at the Mel Price Lock and Dam. This proved to be a milestone in my travels because the Mel Price was not only the largest, but it was also the last lock and dam on the Mississippi River. I pulled ashore on the right descending bank, onto a boulder-filled field of revetment.

LOCKS AND DAMS ON THE RIVER

As I waited to reconnect with Mike Clark, I appreciated the significance of this moment in time and space. I had made it to the Mississippi's final lock and dam. As I traveled down the Mississippi, I had encountered numerous and diverse dams. Some were nature's design, constructed by beavers, but most were built by man. My research revealed we are a dam-building country. Over the past century we have led the world in blocking our rivers and streams with our dams. The US Army Corps of Engineers lists at least ninety thousand dams over six feet tall.

Each of the Mississippi's lock and dam complexes, from the first one in Minneapolis to the last one in Alton, Illinois, has a lockmaster, a traffic light, and a mooring rope. Sometimes I was the only one locking through and sometimes there was a crowd.

When locking through, the issue was always timing with the commercial traffic. The barges have priority, whether they are heading down the river or up. The longest wait I encountered was two hours, but it was at a place where I could get out, get a sandwich, and watch the barge train move through.

On a previous trip, during a break from paddling one evening, just above a lock and dam, I met a river man who owned a nearby campground on the Wisconsin side of the river. He mentioned there was no good place to pull off the river for miles, and he invited me to camp the night with the other RV campers on his property. As a group of campers sat around a fire pit, we talked of the river and the upcoming locks and dams. My host suggested that because of the recent high waters that I might try paddling over the dams' spillways instead of dealing with any locking through hassles like waiting for tows. He assured me it would be an easy, time-saving option.

The next day I tried the new approach. A spillway is a section of the dam adjacent to the lock. It is a concrete slide for the water to pour over the dam structure. As I approached my first spillway, it was as if my rollercoaster car was just arriving at the top of the first big hill. I had committed, so all I could do was hang on for the ride. But I didn't just hang on; I paddled like crazy to keep the kayak pointing downriver as I shot into the water below the dam. There was that adrenaline again. So I did it again on the next dam.

One note to the spillways. Years later, I was talking with a man who was an engineer with USACE. The spillways came up in our conversation and he mentioned there is a fine, I think he said $200, if one is caught going over the spillway of a dam. He gave me a brief, but friendly, lecture on the dangers of the river just below a dam. If one should capsize below a spillway, you can be sucked in and trapped in the hydraulics of the river. The dynamics of the river do not fare well for the paddler. Lesson learned. I have sworn off spillways for all future trips.

The paddling plan was for me to rendezvous with Mike Clark, and he would guide me through the massive Mel Price lock, safely navigate through the confluence of the country's two most powerful rivers, and then deal with the dreaded Chain of Rocks, depending upon the river's water level. At low level, we would face the options of the ten-mile industrial canal that skirts the rock dam or a portage around the rocks. With the river at a higher level, we could possibly shoot right over the rocks. In my research I learned that the Chain of Rocks, in structural geology terms, is an anticline, that is, a type of fold that is an arch-like shape and has its oldest beds at its core. This would be the less-heralded arch in St. Louis.

From the riverbank I reached Mike by phone. There were some logistical issues to deal with, so Mike suggested I proceed through the last lock, the largest lock on the river, and meet him on the Missouri shore just below Duck Island. This revised approach meant I would paddle through the Missouri-Mississippi confluence on my own, which had been one of my fears. Mike's words, "You should be just fine," were less than reassuring. He is the guide, I thought, but he had seen me on the river just once, when he pushed me off in Clarksville.

From the shore I phoned the lockmaster, gave him my location, and asked when a good time would be to lock through. He gave me the all-clear and I was off. I was proud of my increasing knowledge of locks and dams and their usually helpful lockmasters. Mike Clark had suggested that as soon as I exited the lock to bear to the right if possible and take the small river channel winding around the west side of Maple Island. This is a nice, peaceful stretch of a couple miles that avoids the commercial congestion at the downriver entrance to the huge lock.

This backwaters channel was a welcome relief from the typical river commerce. It was narrow, quiet, and woodsy. I was back in nature, when out of nowhere, there was a giant explosion of water a foot away from my stern. My heart nearly jumped out of my chest. The serenity of the moment was blown to bits. A flying Asian carp had rocketed itself from its marine depths to within a few feet of my kayak. It was an adrenaline rush! Reading about this fish did not prepare me for the personal and rude introduction I experienced.

I discovered it was quiet paddling if I stayed in the middle of the channel, but I was running the flying fish gauntlet whenever I ventured close to the shoreline. So I stayed in the middle lane.

THE CONFLUENCE OF THE MISSISSIPPI AND MISSOURI RIVERS

Back on the big river, I was just a mile above the confluence of this country's two largest rivers. The wet, rainy spring had the Mississippi flowing at high water and the Missouri at just below flood level. At this point on the map, the Mississippi has been running for 1,250 river miles. The Missouri, from its origin at the confluence of the Jefferson, Madison, and Gallatin rivers in the Rocky Mountains area of southwestern Montana, has been building up steam for over 2,300 river miles. In the previous year, I had visited the source of the Missouri River at Missouri Headwaters State Park and was curious, and somewhat tentative, about experiencing how the rather mild Rocky Mountain stream transforms itself on its route to its Mississippi merger. Because the river is the boss, one cannot pause and ponder at any one point. There is no stopping. The river will deliver you to your destiny. It just keeps rolling along. The confluence was fast approaching me. I could see the chaos ahead.

In *Life on the Mississippi*, Mark Twain recalls Louis Jolliet and Father Jacques Marquette's description of the confluence of the Missouri and Mississippi rivers as "a torrent of yellow mud rushed furiously athwart the calm blue current of the Mississippi, boiling and surging and sweeping in its course logs, branches, and uprooted trees." As to the mouth of the Missouri, "that savage river which descending from its mad career through a vast unknown of barbarism, poured its turbid floods into the bosom of its gentle sister."[9]

---

9. Mark Twain, *Life on the Mississippi* (New York: Barnes & Noble, Inc., 2010), 8.

Three centuries later, I offered my own description on heading into the breach of this modern-day maelstrom: "Holy Fuck!" Bless me, Father . . .

The Missouri was just below flood level and made up the right half of the new river. It presented itself as a wildly moving surface of watery hills and valleys strewn with thousands of trees, logs, and assorted flotsam. I had not paddled in anything close to this. Mike's earlier words, "You should be just fine," had no application here.

Remember, this boat is designed to stay afloat. Just do not interfere with its function.

I would do my best to let my kayak follow its intended role. The task: stay calm and absorb the roiling rollercoaster action as the never-ending next wave smashes relentlessly over the boat's bow and my kayak skirt. I did not know it at the time, but one cubic yard of water weighs over 1,700 pounds.

Paddling downriver, the current takes you with the waves, logs, and trees, all going in the same direction. But now as Duck Island raced by on my starboard, I had to ferry across the raging Missouri half of the river to reach the shore and turn myself over to my trusted guide. Past the point of no return, I bobbed and weaved through the St. Louis–bound uprooted forests, trying to get enough lateral movement to not overshoot the intended landing zone. There were about a dozen fishermen on the riverbank all watching with some amazement as I delicately approached through the four-foot waves and debris. Upon reaching dry land, I was congratulated by the anglers for putting on the mini thrill show. "You won't catch me doing that!" one of them exclaimed. I was welcomed by the group, but one person was missing: Mike Clark.

River time.

I explained I was expecting to meet my guide at this spot. While waiting, we talked of fishing, kayaking from Itasca, and if the four-foot snake slithering by on its way to the river was poisonous. The consensus was yes. Fifteen minutes later, a welcomed face appeared. It was Dolly, the guardian mastiff. She brought Mike Clark along with his canoe. The three of us visited briefly with the fishermen and then we were southward bound. The Chain of Rocks awaited, just four miles downriver.

THE CHAIN OF ROCKS

One advantage of the river being so high, Mike said, is that we would be able to zip across the Chain of Rocks, forgoing the portage or canal alternatives. As we approached the challenge, Mike would follow me, just in case something happened. It was a fast, downhill ride over the rocks.

In my river book readings over the years, all the references to the Chain of Rocks had built my anxiety to a significant level. It all dissipated in a matter of minutes. It was a fun paddle over the watery anticline. Check off the first of the St. Louis arches.

I was glad to shoot the chain. The swift, high river provided us with the easiest option for a clear path downriver. Little did I realize that what the fast water gave us today, we would have to pay for dearly in the morning.

Just a mile downriver, we arrived at our takeout spot, Mosenthein Island (UMR 188.0). It had been a long day. Starting in Grafton, at the confluence of the Mississippi and Illinois rivers, I had finished off the last Mississippi River lock and dam, encountered my first flying Asian carp, experienced and survived the excitement of the Missouri and Mississippi rivers' confluence, been momentarily stranded on a remote shore, linked up with my guide, and skipped over the Chain of Rocks. I was ready for sleep. As I was pitching my tent, Mike had other plans. He built a campfire and prepared a delicious meal of pork chops and potatoes. It was wonderful!

Having reached the confluence of the two big rivers, I was now in Lewis and Clark territory. Two centuries earlier, the Corps of Discovery expedition traveled the Mississippi River between its confluence with the Missouri River in St. Louis and, two hundred river miles downstream, the confluence with the Ohio River in Cairo, Illinois. I was looking forward to comparing notes with two of the country's most honored explorers.

THE ST. LOUIS HARBOR

I awoke to Mike serving a full breakfast of bacon, eggs, and a pot of cowboy coffee brewing in the campfire coals. As the saying goes, "An army marches on its stomach." We made our plan for the St. Louis harbor area, which was about five miles downriver. Again, Mike and Dolly would stay behind me in the canoe. I mentioned I had a marine radio and offered it to Mike to use in the harbor area. I was a rookie as far as marine communication goes, and I was going to be busy enough just paddling.

Still miles upriver from the city, Mike pointed out the Gateway Arch. This structure is the world's tallest arch and the tallest manmade monument in the Western Hemisphere. I snapped a photo of the 630-foot-high masterpiece, but from my vantage point it looked tiny. Mike proved to be an excellent river docent as he subsequently described three key bridges spanning the industrialized St. Louis waterfront.

The first of the three bridges was the Stan Musial Veterans Memorial Bridge (UMR 181.2). It is the newest large-span bridge across the Mississippi, and it opened in 2014. It was to be named the Veterans Memorial Bridge but was renamed to memorialize the St. Louis Cardinals hero Stan Musial after his death in 2013. The bridge is affectionately referred to today as the Stan Span.

Just a mile downriver is the Martin Luther King Bridge (UMR 180.2). The bridge opened in 1951 as the Veterans Bridge. The name was changed in 1968 after Dr. King was assassinated. It seems like the veterans' bridges get their names changed when someone famous dies.

Downriver from the Martin Luther King Bridge spans the Eads Bridge (UMR 180.0). Opening in 1874, this bridge has major historical significance as it was the first large-span bridge to cross the river, and it hosted the first railroad to cross the Mississippi, allowing trains to venture into the new West. An engineering marvel in its day, the bridge was designed and built by self-taught engineer James Buchanan Eads, who had earned his reputation after building several ironclad gunboats for the Union in the Civil War. The Eads Bridge was the first bridge he had ever built.

St. Louis certainly earned its title as the Gateway City, and the history of the bridges and the country's western movement was interesting, but I had bigger fish to fry. I was facing twelve miles of busy, industrial waterfront. The river, squeezed into a concrete channel with endless terminals and docks, was racing along creating three- to four-foot-deep troughs filled with trees, logs, and who knows what other debris. Unlike the raging river at yesterday's confluence, today's paddle included heavy commercial river traffic. Above the Mel Price Lock and Dam, a towboat can push fifteen barges, collectively known as a tow, three wide and five long. Now, in this undammed river, the tows can manage up to forty-two barges, six wide and seven long.

This was not fun. I was dodging and maneuvering around the trees and logs, while getting slammed by the nonstop waves. Each wave would engulf me and then release me.

Somewhat to my surprise, my kayak was doing its part. As tense as the moment was, there was a feeling of success and accomplishment every time the bow of my kayak reappeared from the serial submersions. I was working with the boat!

Moored barges lined the sides of the river, making it impossible to pull over or stop. I was taught pulling in upriver from a moored barge can lead to death. Tows and barges were all over. My strategy was to stay close to the right descending bank, parallel to the moored barges, and out of the main traffic. As I paddled close to the moored barges, a towboat came out from a terminal just downriver from my intended route and turned upriver toward me. The parked barges were on my right, and the oncoming tow, with its powerful wake, was bearing down on my left, leaving little space in between.

This was not good. A few thoughts flashed in the moment. I recalled my daughter Kelly's somewhat joking protest before every one of my trips: "Don't go. You will die." I was also glad Mike Clark was following me to fish me out if needed.

The gap was closing. No exit on starboard. A tow, with its turbulent wake, approaching on port. Stay calm, Dennis. Remember, this boat is designed to stay afloat. Just do not interfere with its function. At that moment, the towboat suddenly veered toward the center of the river, leaving me some breathing room.

I had dodged a bullet but was still white knuckling my way through the waterfront. Two hours after entering the city's commercial zone, I passed the River City Casino and Hotel (UMR 171.7). It was two hours and ten river miles from the Stan Span that I finally was able to pull over and look behind me for Mike and Dolly. When we regrouped, Mike said he saw the predicament I was getting into with the approaching towboat. He called to the tow captain on my marine radio alerting him to the orange kayak approaching. Mike reported the captain's first response, "Oh, shit!" was followed by a quick evasive maneuver that was very timely and welcome. I learned later that on a towboat's radar, a kayak looks just like a log. And we were in a sea of logs.

America's great poet T. S. Eliot was born and raised in St. Louis and makes a couple of apt references about the river in his *Four Quartets*:

> I do not know much about gods; but I think that the river is a strong
> brown god—sullen, untamed and intractable . . .
>
> The river is within us, the sea is all about us . . .
> It tosses up our losses, the torn seine,
> The shattered lobsterpot, the broken oar . . .
> Often together heard: the whine in the rigging,
> The menace and caress of wave that breaks on water . . .[10]

---

10. T. S. Eliot, "The Dry Salvages," in *Four Quartets* (London: The New English Weekly, 1941).

I was glad to have the "menace and caress of the wave that breaks" behind me. We stopped for a quick shore lunch downriver and discussed our paddle through St. Louis. Mike admitted the high-water conditions were more challenging than usual.

Once out of the industrial waterfront, with its concrete channel and commercial traffic, the river seemed a lot tamer. It was still a little beyond my comfort zone but much more manageable than the river running through the city. I mused about how much farther I wanted to take this journey. St. Louis could be a very natural stopping point.

We paddled the last few miles to our takeout at Cliff Cave Landing (UMR 166.7). It had been a few days and another hundred river miles. This stretch had some people and moments of interest. It also had its boring, time for thinking, paddle, paddle, paddle moments. The Gateway City and the river proved to be exciting. The river was the memorable part, and because it demanded my full attention, my glimpse of the Gateway Arch came from miles away. I was too busy to notice when I paddled right in front of it.

I stopped at the arch on my drive home. It was a nice view of the river from 630 feet high. From where I stood, I spotted the tiny orange kayak strapped on top of my vehicle, parked next to the river. Perspective.

After doing the tourist thing in Gateway Arch National Park, I headed for home. As I crossed the Clark Bridge, the river did not look as fierce as it had at the very same spot a few days earlier. What was it Heraclitus said 2,500 years ago, about stepping in the same river twice?

12

STUCK IN THE GATEWAY CITY
Summer 2015

It was summer in St. Paul, and I woke to KFAN radio's guest comic of the morning, John Mulaney.

"I was a very nervous kid, I was anxious all the time when I was younger, but what's nice is that some of the things I was anxious about don't bother me at all anymore. Like, uh, I always thought that quicksand was going to be a much bigger problem than it turned out to be. . . . I used to sit around and think about what to do about quicksand."[11]

Weeks had gone by, and it was time. Today was the day I'd head southbound to "Saint Louie." There is something very satisfying about getting packed, strapping the kayak on the rooftop, and getting an hour on the road before you see the sun's first hint in the eastern sky. It's the best time of the day, and it's the best way to start a trip.

I had a ten-hour drive to meet up in St. Louis again with river guide Mike Clark, Big Muddy. He was putting me up at Kanu House for the evening before my river launch. Unlike the sexier through paddle where one puts in at Itasca and takes out in the Gulf of Mexico three months later, my piece-by-piece approach was requiring a lot more road trips. This was my second trip "through the Cedars"—Cedar Rapids and Cedar Falls, Iowa—en route to St. Louis.

St. Paul to St. Louis is not a fun drive, but I was armed with James McPherson's audio book *Battle Cry of Freedom*. As the cover proclaims, "This is historical writing of the highest order." It is. As a born and bred "Yankee," I was not that well versed on all things Civil War. This was about to change as I planned several kayaking forays south of the Mason-Dixon Line.

---

11. John Mulaney, "New in Town," KFAN FM 100.3 Sports Radio, Minneapolis–St. Paul, MN: iHeartMedia, 2015.

The ninety-day river sprints from source to sea are a lot faster and cheaper than my way, which included many country-spanning road trips. My sum journey stretched out over thirteen years, offering a taste of the Mississippi River, bite by bite. I would not have done it any other way. In ninety days, you get to experience the river. In a dozen years, you get the landscape, the cities, towns, history, people, their accents and their stories, and, lest we forget, the river.

The Mississippi River is America's River. It is as American as apple pie and the Fourth of July. It *is* America. It is the punchline of a kid's first joke: "What has four eyes (i's) and can't see?" It is the first grader's singsong mnemonic aid for learning how to spell their first long word: "M, I, double S, I, double S, I, double P, I." It has signaled the start of a million hide 'n' seek games: "one-Mississippi, two-Mississippi, three-Mississippi. . . ." It is an artist's river. It is a working river. It is an author's river, a poet's river, a singer's river.

As the river cuts its circuitous route through the country in its many facets and forms, the river's music also makes its own meandering, top-to-bottom path. On the top end we find *Prairie Home Companion*'s Pat Donohue celebrating the river's peaceful and serene source, Lake Itasca. He picks his way through in his soothing but bluesy rendition of "The Other End of the Mississippi River Blues." Drop twenty degrees latitude and we take in the Delta's own Tina Turner as she belts out her rough and raspy "Proud Mary," recalling a poor woman's river experiences in the "Big Sleazy." Paul Robeson, Andy Williams, and Johnny Cash are just a few other names who have celebrated the Mississippi in their music. In researching Mississippi River songs, I learned of a Mississippi River author, Dean Klinkenberg. It is reported that Dean has catalogued 1,027 Mississippi River songs.

My odyssey was a river adventure with a dry land bonus. I would come to cherish the land portion as a separate enterprise. The water and the land are two distinct phenomena.

It was early evening when I arrived at Mike's Kanu House. His neighborhood is just blocks from Ferguson, Missouri, which achieved national notoriety for its racial tensions in the previous year. Mike was not home when I arrived, but he had instructed me to enter the house and feed Dolly. Luckily, Dolly, the guardian of Kanu House, remembered me from our earlier trip, so we got along nicely. I fell asleep promptly after a long day on the road.

I awoke when Mike got home about midnight, and we discussed the plan of an early launch with me driving to the put-in at Cliff Cave Landing (UMR 166.7). Mike would retrieve my vehicle and pick me up 112 miles downriver at the takeout in Cape Girardeau a few days later. Wanting to get an early start in the morning, I left Kanu House in the dark, drove through urban St. Louis, and arrived at Cliff Cave Park at 7 a.m. only to realize the park gates did not open until 8 a.m.

I was a little jittery waiting for the gates to open, and it wasn't from the morning coffee. My apprehensions arose from reflections of the previous trip when Mike and I exited the river at this point. Cliff Cave Landing is thirty miles below the Mississippi and Missouri rivers' confluence, and those thirty miles had included a lot of white-knuckle kayaking through the city of St. Louis's waterfront. For me, the Mississippi now presented a huge, untamed, undammed, wild experience all the way to the Gulf. In those last thirty miles, I had been aided by the guidance of one of the best river men around. But this was to be my first solo trip on the new industrial-strength river.

The gates opened. Cliff Cave Park is a large park, rich with history. During the eighteenth century, French fur trappers operated a tavern here for traders traveling the Mississippi River and the cave was used as a beer cellar. Now the park has modern facilities equipped with a parking lot about a quarter mile from the river. Though the surroundings were nice, there was not a good place to launch a boat due to the water level and a very rocky shoreline.

Probably under the influence of Mike, or rather his sobriquet, Big Muddy, I had geared up for this trip with a pair of up-to-the-knee Chota wading boots. I looked like one of the trappers who stopped here for a cold one two hundred years earlier. The task at hand was to get the kayak down to the river and find a suitable place to launch. As luck would have it, there was a couple out for an early morning walk, and the man asked if he could help me with my boat. People on the river are happy to give.

One on each end, we walked the kayak and paddle the quarter mile. Near the river, we both foraged through the trees, mud, and rocks looking for any place to launch the kayak. There was a small creek running to the river. We were on one side of the creek, elevated about four feet above the opposite side. The other side looked flatter and possibly presented better launch site options. Our plan was I would jump over the creek to the lower, smoother side, my new helper would push the boat across, and then he would follow.

In my new Chotas, I took a running leap, cleared the creek, and landed on the other side. But I did not stop there. I just kept going—down. I was in mud up to my crotch. The trapper was trapped. My new friend exclaimed, "That's not good!"

I could not move. The man with me was going to go around the creek to the other side to see if he could help from there. I asked him to throw me the kayak paddle before he left. There I was, stuck, alone, three feet deep in mud. Then a funny thing happened. As I was taking inventory of my predicament, John Mulaney's words came to mind: "I always thought that quicksand was going to be a much bigger problem than it turned out to be." I was able to see the humor in my sticky situation.

Back to my plight. After repeated, failed attempts to move any part of my lower body, I decided on a new tack. I disassembled the paddle and laid the two paddle blades close together and fashioned a little "shelf" in front of me. I was able to lean from my waist onto the shelf and pry myself, ever so slightly, upward. Continuing with this new crabbing technique, I moved my paddle fulcrum forward, inch by inch. Eventually I was able to crawl in the mud to the safety of dry land. What seemed like hours was probably thirty minutes.

Moments later, I joined up with my new friend. We lamented our efforts but also shared a few laughs. He eyed my mud-caked body and said, "I suppose this puts an end to your trip."

What kind of trapper did he think I was? I had not yet even started.

We found a launching spot—it was not ideal, but it would work. I thanked him. We took a photo and parted ways. I then returned to the parking lot and changed into some clean, dry clothes that I dug out from my camp gear. I put my soaked, mud-caked Chotas in the vehicle and proceeded to make several portages down to the river.

It was a dicey, craggy launching spot tucked into some sharp and slippery rocks. I was able to load my gear and eventually I carefully eased my kayak into the river. Hours after pulling into the parking lot, I was paddling again. It felt wonderful being safe at home, alone on this untamed, undammed, wild Mississippi.

The river was big, and the day was beautiful. Once on the river, I was able to focus on the next buoy and keeping proper distance from the heavy barge traffic. I had checked the navigation charts, and now it was a matter of staying afloat and paddling. I recalled the Minnesota DNR Ranger's question, "Do you know what you are getting into?"

I still did not.

A day of paddling consists of waking, breaking camp, checking charts, paddling, looking for a spot to take a break, paddling, avoiding tow traffic and their haystack wakes, wing dams, eddies, and looking for a spot for lunch. Then it's paddling, thinking, getting bored, getting jolted to attention by a whirlpool or boil, searching for that next buoy, stopping for an afternoon break, and one last paddling set that includes a self-debate about how far you can paddle and still have a chance to find a suitable takeout spot with time to unload and set up camp before darkness.

It is not just a float down the river.

It takes a lot of work to move down the river at three to five miles an hour. The nights, however, are special. In your tent, you are a few feet from the Mighty Mississippi, hearing the river sounds, seeing the tows' search lights sweeping the water and land, listening to the owls and coyotes, watching the moon shadows. There is no Hilton that can match these moments.

Dawn broke. Fifteen miles downriver was the town of Herculaneum, Missouri. As I have repeatedly discovered throughout my journey, there are numerous river towns whose names have been filched from cities spread all over the globe. The original Herculaneum was in Italy. Was, because that town met its demise in the first century, buried in ash when Mount Vesuvius blew.

Another fifteen miles went by, and I passed Penitentiary Point on the Illinois side. I did not stop, but I am still curious about its name. The next waypoint was Ste. Genevieve, Missouri (UMR 124.0). Approaching the city, one must be on the lookout for the crossings of the Sainte Genevieve–Modoc Ferry, which the locals have dubbed with the coolest name, the French Connection.

As mentioned earlier, the river tenders a lot of time for thinking. As I passed Ste. Genevieve, not the most common of names, I thought of one of my favorite aunts, also named Genevieve. Catholic families often named their children after the church's saints. Genevieve was the patron saint of Paris. My aunt Genevieve, Gen for short, had a large family and later in life the kids referred to her as the "Gentle General." I asked my cousins how she got that handle. Gen, true to her political beliefs, had written to President Clinton to enlighten him on how things should be. She signed her critical letter Gen Wempe. Days later she received a letter from the White House. To her surprise and delight, Gen had received a personal response from the president himself. The letter began, "Dear General Wempe . . ." and that is the origin of aunt Gen's Gentle General moniker.

More thinking, more paddling, more thinking.

It may have appeared the trip was going well. There was good weather and reasonable tow traffic, and I was making decent time. However, I was having a couple of issues. I started to develop a paddling rash under my right arm that was irritating. I also recalled a golf tournament I had planned to participate in, for which I might not get back in time.

I approached Chester, Illinois (UMR 109.6), the city best known for being the home of the mythical mariner Popeye the Sailor Man. It was also home to the second oldest prison in Illinois, Menard Correctional Center, sitting right on the riverbank. My planned destination, Cape Girardeau, was still fifty-five miles downriver—two days. My paddling rash was bothersome, and I was losing interest in the trip, not to mention my golf addiction was rearing its ugly head. Checking the *USACE Navigation Charts*, I found Grand Tower thirty river miles away.

As I paddled through the day and approached Grand Tower (UMR 79.9), I decided to bail completely out of the Cape Girardeau plan, settling for Grand Tower. But I still had to deal with the logistics of getting back to my car. Mike was planning to pick me up in two days in Cape Girardeau, and now I was hoping he could fetch me the next morning at Grand Tower.

A simple phone call could fix that, I thought. But sometimes the simple things are not that simple. I had no bars, no service. "Quicksand" delayed my trip's start, and a lack of cell phone service was thwarting my finish.

There was a large, sandy beachhead that looked like a good spot to take out. As I pulled the boat ashore, I noticed a group of serious motorcyclists. Revving their Harleys, they were getting set to leave the area. I flagged down one of the last couples. They, decked out in their black leathers, and I, sporting my orange floatation vest, presented a clash of cultures. I asked if they might have a phone with service. They happily obliged and I made my phone call.

"You wanna beer?" they offered.

"No thanks, my last one was quite a few years back."

The biker responded, "Oh, they wanted me to do that. What was the name of that place I went? The place with the initials?"

The lady rider replied, "You mean AA?"

"Yeah, that's it. I got there and listened to their ideas. It sounded like they wanted me to quit. Well, that was enough for me. I am not a quitter! I don't drink that much anyway. What have we had today? I think we just had a six pack here at the river."

"We had a few on the bike," replied the woman.

He countered with, "And then the ones we had in the bars."

I thanked them for their hospitality, phone, and the brief visit. We snapped a quick photo, the Hog growled, and they were off.

The sandy shore led to a ten-minute walk to a private campground, Devil's Backbone. It sits on a blocky cliff, Devil's Bake Oven, with the beach nestled below. With names like that, I felt lucky to be settled in. My campsite was directly across from Tower Rock. On the Missouri side, this sixty-foot promontory offers some historical significance. The earliest European inhabitants were river pirates who used this as an ambush site. Meriwether Lewis mentions this spot in his journals, stating that rivermen who passed the rock would celebrate in a way similar to sailors crossing the equator, by raising a drink of spirits.

Trappers and traders hoisting one at Cliff Cave Park, pirates and the Corps of Discovery explorers raising a drink of spirits at Tower Rock. This leg of my journey had been bookended and celebrated by some of this country's iconic river men. My new Harley friends were keeping the tradition alive. What a country!

It felt good crawling into my tent that night. Yes, I had cut my original plan short by a day, but I did get in another eighty-eight river miles. I also learned more about what this big, untamed, undammed river is all about below the Missouri confluence. And I did it all by myself.

Big Muddy would pick me up in the morning. Being trapped in the Mississippi mud in St. Louis seemed like a long time ago. I slept well.

13

THE BLUZ CRUZ

Spring 2016

MEMPHIS, TENNESSEE

It was snowy in Minnesota and my kayak had been in storage for several months. The last kayaking season was a defining moment for me and for my Mississippi River interests. My kayaking started out slowly, as merely a breather from a raging golfing addiction. Golfing 140 rounds a year in a state that has only a seven-month season could be viewed as out of balance.

I felt that my kayaking had now achieved passion status. I am particular as to what constitutes a passion in my life. Reader be warned. These next few words may drift off into more of a philosophical or psychological bent, but it is part of understanding my approach to kayaking. For something to be deemed a passion of mine, there are four criteria, and all must be met.

1. If it is worth doing, it is worth doing poorly. Look at the variety of activities in which people of all skill levels are enjoying themselves such as skiing, golfing, and tennis. There are a lot of bad tennis players who are not being denied their enjoyment just because they do not have a backhand.
2. You will do it in any type of weather. For the avid practitioner of a desired activity, there is no such thing as bad weather, just bad clothes. These people are firm believers in layering. They are not just fair weather fans.
3. You will do it with others, and you will do it by yourself. A person likes the activity for the activity itself. Because one cannot find someone to do it with them will not stop the person from the activity that they enjoy.

4. You will persevere, even when it gets tough. There will be a time when you say to yourself, "I hate this, and I am never doing it again." But you know you will. Golfers and marathoners come to mind.

In my life's doings, I believe it is important to understand one's taxonomy of activities. There is a distinction between my passions and my addictions. With my passions, I will pursue them because I like doing the activity. There is an inherent feeling I get from pushing off from shore and finding a rhythm after those first few paddling strokes. It feels good.

When it comes to my addictions, I will participate in an activity—like golf—because it is a day that ends in "y." I may not necessarily want to do it. I just need to do it. I golf because that is what I do. The alcoholic model probably applies here. But enough of Freud, Jung, and Plato. Let's get back to paddling.

My kayaking had brought me farther than I had planned, both in distance traveled and skills acquired. With my time on the water, I had become an average or intermediate paddler. In the past season, I had advanced geographically to Grand Tower, Missouri, about one hundred miles downriver from St. Louis. Now it was still winter, but I was thinking about kayaking, and debating whether I would continue my Mississippi sojourn. The size and temperament of the river below Memphis was a question and concern of mine. It was that fear factor once again. In my forays through St. Louis, I had experienced some comfort and confidence in having Mike as my river guide.

Snowbound in Minnesota, a plan came to mind. If I could find someone in Memphis to accompany me for a ten- to twenty-mile paddle in the Memphis area, I could accomplish two things. I could learn in safe conditions what the Lower Mississippi had to offer, and I could briefly escape the Land of 10,000 Frozen Lakes. If one paddles on the Mississippi long enough, a few names always surface. Three big names are Mike Clark in St. Louis, John Ruskey in Clarksdale, and Dale Sanders in Memphis. Dale Sanders is not just a river man, he's a world-class, worldwide adventurer. I had read about Dale in several sources, and I had determined if anyone knew about kayaking the Mississippi in the Memphis area it would be him.

I called Dale, introduced myself, explained that I wanted to escape Minnesota's winter, and said I had an interest in learning about the big river in Memphis. I was exploring the possibility of coming down to Memphis to kayak for a couple of days and wondered what he thought. Dale explained it was thirty degrees in Memphis and they were experiencing a very cold winter. My idea was not practical. We did chat for quite a while about our travels and adventures and agreed to keep in touch.

This was not the first time my plans did not pan out. Unfortunately, I was still stuck with a nagging anxiety about the Lower Mississippi and how my skills may or may not match up.

Plan B was serendipity. My Memphis-in-the-winter plan morphed into Vicksburg, Mississippi, in the spring. Shortly after my brief connection with Dale Sanders, I found two new pieces for my Lower Mississippi puzzle. Enter Adam Elliott, with Quapaw Canoe Company, and the annual Bluz Cruz paddle race.

The announcement read:

> Join the fun at one of the great races along the Lower Mississippi River! Bluz Cruz 2016! Blue Cruz is the classic 22-mile race ending up on the Yazoo River in downtown Vicksburg. Begins at 8:00 a.m. on Saturday, April 30th at Madison Parish Port, LA, and ends in Vicksburg, MS at the river front.[12]

Up until that time I had not heard of river races for paddlers. I had done my share of running 5Ks, 10Ks, marathons, and even a couple triathlons, but had never been in a paddling race. My road racing was during the 1980s running boom, and there were lots of races and lots of runners. I was not fast, but the races were good experiences to measure my performance against myself and a few of my friends. My goal was not to win but to do.

I had mentioned the idea of a paddling race in Vicksburg to a golfing crony, Steve Larson, who happened to be a Civil War history buff. Steve recalled his trips to Vicksburg, and he enlightened me about the significant role Vicksburg played in the war, the siege of Vicksburg, and the strategic impact of gaining control of the Mississippi. Although it was not part of my original plan, I found myself getting caught up in an aspect of our country's history that I had not pursued previously. This conversation marked the beginning of an entirely new interest that I was developing, our country's Civil War.

Vicksburg was far enough south that I would be able to test out the Lower Mississippi to see if I was up for continuing this river ride to the Gulf. I signed up for the Bluz Cruz. Forget Graceland, I was headed for the Deep South.

---

12. John Ruskey, *The River Connects Us All: Lower Mississippi River Dispatch No. 344* (Clarksdale: The Rivergator, 2016), https://www.rivergator.org/wp-content/uploads/2021/04/Lower_Mississippi_River_Dispatch_No_344.pdf.

VICKSBURG, MISSISSIPPI

About the same time that I committed to the Bluz Cruz, John Ruskey, the founder and owner of Quapaw Canoe Company, connected me with an associate river guide of his, Adam Elliott, who was a river guide in Natchez, Mississippi. Adam was also participating in the Bluz Cruz. Through phone calls and emails, Adam and I planned the next leg of my river pilgrimage. After the Bluz Cruz, Adam and I would continue from Vicksburg through Natchez and on to the Old River Control Structure (ORCS).

St. Paul to Vicksburg is 1,050 miles, and it's a long road trip. I noticed as the latitude changed, so did the menus and accents. Biscuits and gravy, catfish, and "y'all" were de rigueur. The southbound string of river towns offered historical waypoints of the first magnitude. Hannibal, with Mark Twain, Huck Finn, and a white-painted fence; St. Louis, the Gateway Arch, Lewis and Clark; New Madrid, epicenter of the county's three largest earthquakes east of the Rockies; and Memphis, with Graceland and the intersection of King and King streets to honor both Rev. Dr. Martin Luther Jr. and BB.

Arriving in Vicksburg, I located the Bluz Cruz headquarters and picked up my instructions and race number. I found lodging across the street from the Vicksburg National Military Park. I decided to unwind after the long drive by tracking down the Clear Creek Golf Course and sneaking in a quick nine. I then delivered my kayak to the race's starting point in Madison Parish Port, Louisiana, where I was met by lots of paddlers with "y'alls" to match.

Although I did not enter the Bluz Cruz as a serious competitor, I did awaken on race morning with prerace jitters. On the bus that took us to the Louisiana start line, I met a contemporary of mine, Linn Hartman from Drasco, Arkansas. He was part of John Ruskey's crew on the Quapaw Canoe Company's voyager canoe, Grasshopper. He mentioned that he had been planning a canoe trip on the Mississippi for only sixty-five years. We had a wonderful chat, two seniors who would soon be splashing in Old Man River with a crowd of Gen X, Y, and Zers. As we approached the staging area on the bus, someone said they saw an alligator lying in the mud. I looked, but no gator. I did, however, mentally file "gator" as another thing to fear on the big river.

Final instructions were announced. The only thing left before we began the race was to carry our boats through fifty yards of shin-deep Louisiana mud to get on the river. A drone circled above, filming the colorful flotilla, as ninety-three paddlers schooled around the start line. There were canoes, kayaks, tandems, quads, the super serious surf skis, peddle boats, a special category named "pool toys," and a stand-up paddleboard. Dwarfing this aquatic assemblage was John Ruskey, at the helm of Grasshopper, the ten-person voyager canoe. I spotted Linn Hartman on the boat, geared up and manning a strategic paddle. I also bumped into Adam Elliott and his paddling partner, Brooks Harrington. This was our first face-to-face meeting after numerous calls and emails. We wished each other luck and agreed to meet at the finish. The gun sounded, and we were off!

The Lower Mississippi was large, but we had favorable conditions. Paddling down the middle of a wide section of the river, I recalled Loretta Lynn and Conway Twitty twanging away about the Louisiana woman and the Mississippi man, and how they were going to meet across that wide, alligator-infested Mississippi River. This was not the white-knuckle experience from the St. Louis industrial waterfront. The instructions were simple. Paddle twenty miles and take a left up the Yazoo River to the finish in Vicksburg, Mississippi. As the race progressed, the boats got strung out, and as they entered the Yazoo River, they created a three-hour, distinctive marine review.

Official Bluz Cruz records will show the first paddler finished in 2:18 and the last crossed the finish line in 5:21. I snuck in at 3:35, a six-mile-an-hour pace. My middle-of-the-pack finish was predictable, but I did get one unexpected perk. Out of ninety-three paddlers, I had traveled the farthest to participate, and I had finished in forty-sixth place. Do the math: I was in the top half of the class.

At the finish there was food, a great little band, awards, and lots of positive people. I shared lunch with a USACE representative. I should have gotten continuing education credits for all that I was learning. I met and shared stories with Linn Hartman, John Ruskey, and Adam Elliott. Adam and Brooks had won their class, which increased my confidence in my guide for the next several days. Adam and I finalized our plans to continue onward the next day to Natchez and points south.

That evening, I found a restaurant that overlooked the river. I relaxed and took inventory. It was a lot of work driving more than one thousand miles each way. There were hotels, meals, and logistics—all to paddle a score of Mississippi River miles. Then I realized it was not work, it was growth. Experience is the toughest teacher, and the lesson comes after the test. I took the Lower Mississippi test, and I graduated in the top half of the class. Some of my fears were fading like an early fog burning off with the morning sun. This was fun.

Two weeks after I got home, I received an email from my bus ride partner, Linn Hartman:

> Hope you had a good trip down to Natchez. Enjoyed meeting you at the Cruz. It was good fun. Would be interested in keeping in contact as you continue down river to the Gulf. I continue to fabricate a front rowing system for my 15-foot Grumman. Might save a kink in the neck. Hope all is well. Keep in touch.

I called Linn recently to see how he was doing. As timing would have it, Linn was excited because the very next day he was getting in his very first kayak with his daughter. How cool is that? Just a few years ago my son was pushing his old man, trapped in a plastic kayak, into the Mississippi River for the very first time, and now my new Bluz Cruz buddy's daughter was talking her dad through his first kayaking strokes down in Arkansas. One can never overlook that special moment when the kid becomes the parent's teacher.

14

VICKSBURG, THE KEY CITY, TO NATCHEZ, THE BLUFF CITY

Spring 2016

With the Bluz Cruz now on my résumé, it was time to take the next bite. After the race, my guide-to-be, Adam Elliott, and I drew up a plan for our trip south. In taking on the river piece by piece there is always the logistics of putting in and taking out, with the accompanying issue of ground transportation. We planned that I would drive the seventy-five miles from Vicksburg to Natchez, meet up with Adam and Brooks, and leave my vehicle in Natchez. Brooks would drive Adam and me, with our boats, back to Vicksburg. We would launch from Vicksburg (LMR 437.0) and head toward the ORCS (LMR 304.0). Brooks would retrieve us and bring us back to Natchez, and I would drive north 1,100 miles. Some might say the planning is the boring part of the entire exercise, but it's vital.

Our planned launch date, following the Bluz Cruz, got weathered out, so I stayed in Vicksburg and took a tour of the Vicksburg National Military Park. It was time well spent. There were tombstones, bunkers, and lots of cannons, each with information of their origin stamped on the business end of their barrels. My visit exceeded any history class that I had ever sat or slept through.

In the Civil War, Vicksburg was the keystone to which side would control the Mississippi River all the way to New Orleans. In May 1863, General Grant and his troops surrounded the town and proceeded to starve out its citizens and Confederate soldiers. The siege lasted forty-seven days. On the Fourth of July, Vicksburg gave in. According to the Vicksburg Convention and Visitors Bureau, for the next eighty-one years, the town did not celebrate the national Independence Day holiday. This changed after World War II, when President Eisenhower gave an inspirational speech in Vicksburg. The town didn't totally concede. They called the holiday the Carnival of the Confederacy until 1976.

The star of the show in this national park proved to be the salvaged Union ironclad warship USS *Cairo*. The USS *Cairo*, named after Cairo, Illinois, was built under the direction of James Eads. Remember Eads? Because of his shipbuilding heroics, building seven ironclad warships in one hundred days, he was awarded the contract to build the first all-steel, train-ready bridge across the river connecting St. Louis and East St. Louis in 1867. Today, the Eads Bridge is the oldest bridge spanning the Mississippi.

The USS *Cairo* was commissioned in January 1862. In June 1862, she enabled Union forces to occupy Memphis by capturing the Confederate garrison of Fort Pillow on the Mississippi. I am not sure what image of strength was implied by the naming of this fort. In December of its first year of service, the USS *Cairo* met its demise on the Yazoo River seven miles upriver from Vicksburg.

A Union crew member gave this account:

Just as we were training on the battery we were struck by a torpedo, which exploded under our starboard bow so that the water rushed in like the roar of Niagara. In five minutes, the hold was full of water and the forward part of the gunboat was flooded.

The author, along with an officer, were the last two to leave the sinking ship:

By jumping into the "dinghy" which was manned by two sailors. . . . We moved off just in time to escape being swallowed up in the seething caldron of foaming water. . . . Nothing of the *Cairo* could be seen 12 minutes after the first explosion, excepting the smokestacks, and the flag staff from which still floated the flag above the troubled waters.[13]

The crew member who penned this account was George Yost. He was the youngest of the crew at fifteen years old!

What I discovered at the Vicksburg National Military Park was this was not just a Civil War history lesson. I learned I was right in the middle of it all. I had paddled under the Eads Bridge in St. Louis and, the day prior, I had paddled my kayak up the Yazoo, just seven miles from where the USS *Cairo* met her fate. Memphis and Cairo were my future ports of call. The tour in the park turned out to be a very welcome rain delay.

Leaving Vicksburg, I headed for Natchez, about seventy-five miles south. Thirty miles down Highway 61, I came to Port Gibson, another

---

13. George R. Yost's Journal, Vicksburg National Military Park, n.d., https://www.nps.gov /museum/exhibits/vick/cario_today/torpedo2.html.

Mississippi River town. Entering the town I noticed a welcoming sign, *Port Gibson—The town too beautiful to burn*. According to the City of Port Gibson's website, the Union Army's General Grant spared the town from being destroyed because of its beauty. It was indeed a charming town, and as I drove through the tiny burg I noticed, both ironically and sadly, right on the main street, there was a house that had recently burned to the ground, leaving only an empty plot of ashes.

Just a few minutes down the road, in the middle of nowhere, I came upon a big, old, wooden building with a small sign on its side: *Old Countr Store Est 1875*. Who knows how long the "*y*" had been missing? There were a few cars parked that piqued my curiosity, so I pulled in to take a look. The Old Country Store had started almost a century and a half ago as a mercantile store, but somewhere along the way it had been converted to a restaurant. It still resembled an old mercantile, but signs proclaimed the "World's Best Fried Chicken." It was a Sunday afternoon and the after-church crowd, in their Sunday best, were filing in. So I joined them.

Arthur Davis, the proprietor and host, welcomed us to the huge buffet that had every Southern entrée and side a Northern visitor might imagine. Once we were seated with our feasts, Mr. Davis, better known

Old Country Store south of Port Gibson, Mississippi

as Mr. D, grabbed a mic and talked about the Country Store's history. He said his "grandmama had passed down a one-hundred-year-old recipe for the world's best fried chicken, and that she bought the store 'for a song.' Because she bought it for a song, I've got one for you." With that introduction, the proprietor turned entertainer strolled from table to table serenading each customer with a wonderful version of "You Are So Beautiful." After singing, Mr. D made the rounds, encouraging each of us to try the dessert. I couldn't decide between the peach or cherry cobbler, so he suggested, "get them both, and why not add a slab of ice cream?"

The Southern Sunday spread, with the accompanying vocals, made for a special afternoon. And I was all by myself. Wanting to share this moment with somebody, I noticed two women, contemporaries of mine, seated nearby.

Because I am disposed toward introversion, I have developed and rehearsed a few lines to start a conversation. Spoiler alert: There are no big secrets being revealed, just a few "cue cards" I use to get things rolling. For instance, if I want to talk with an "ink and iron" type, I may start with, "Is there a story behind that ink?" I think people like to talk about their tattoos. (Sidebar: My friend Richard said to me, "Hey Dennis, your tattoo line got me in trouble with my family. I was out to dinner with my wife, my son, and his wife, and I asked the waitress, "Do you have any tattoos?" They all went crazy!" I responded, "That's not the way it works, Richard. The person has to have a *visible* tattoo, otherwise it's creepy.")

If tattoos are not an option, I usually fall back on two garden-variety conversation starters: "What's your name?" and "Where are you from?" Yes, these are my two big openers. Either of these will most likely elicit a brief, one-word answer, so I have my follow-up questions. When I hear a person's name, I always ask how it is spelled, or I offer my own guess as to the spelling. If it's a Sara(h), I respond, "with an *h*?" It helps me remember the person's name, and it also gets them talking.

My follow up to "Where are you from?" is to mention a factoid about their city that I might know, or an observation if I've been there, or something sports-related if they seem like the type.

With the two fellow female diners at the Old Country Store, I decided to keep it simple. I leaned toward their table and asked, "Where are you two ladies from?"

"We're from Canada, Edmonton," one of them said.

Having never been to Edmonton, my mind raced. What did I know about their city? The only thing I could think of was Wayne Gretzky, and the one thing I knew about Gretzky happened twenty-eight years earlier.

It was all I had, so I went with it. "How could the Edmonton Oilers trade the Great One to the Los Angeles Kings?" I asked. That was all it took.

"That Peter Pocklington! Don't get me started!" one of them moaned. The other woman joined in, both clearly sports fans. They ranted on the hockey team's owner who, at the time of the trade, the citizens of Edmonton had hanged in effigy. The owner's traitor-esque trade of Canada's treasure to glitzy Hollywood would never be forgotten, nor forgiven. At the time of the trade, one member of Parliament had proclaimed, "The Oilers without Gretzky is like apple pie without ice cream, like winter without snow, like Wheel of Fortune without Vanna White!"[14]

The pair of Canadian women carried on as we left our tables. We tracked down Mr. D for a photo op and brought the conversation outside. The topic of Number 99 being shuffled off to Hollywood morphed into the three of us being in the Southland, here and now. One of the women mentioned many years ago she and her son had taken a tour of the South, including Memphis, Natchez, Vicksburg, Nashville, and New Orleans. "We stopped here, and I thought it was a special place, so I wanted to bring my friend." An introvert's four-word cue card "Where are you from?" had led to a delightful exchange.

My day had started with a tour of a national Civil War park, learning horrific details of how America had been torn in two. Now, 150 years later, in history's shadow of the bloody battles, two countries could be seen hugging it out on a Sunday afternoon in a dusty parking lot of an old country store. It was a serendipitous confluence of two nations, each enjoying the other's company, wishing each other well and safe travels, everybody smiling. It was a special moment as they were off to explore the Southland and I was headed to Natchez. It's not just about the river. It's not just Americana. It's about the people.

14. Noreen Rasbach, "Canadians Stunned by Gretzky Trade," *UPI*, August 10, 1988, https://www.upi.com/Archives/1988/08/10/Canadians-stunned-by-Gretzky-trade/1356587188800/.

15

NATCHEZ TO ANGOLA PRISON

Spring 2016

The next morning, I met up with Adam and Brooks in Natchez, and we drove the boats back to Vicksburg. We took the Natchez Trace Parkway, a 450-mile scenic drive that roughly follows the "Old Natchez Trace," which was a historic foot trail that served as a lifeline through the Old Southwest for boatmen, settlers, soldiers, American Indians, slaves, and slave traders.

After making final reconnection plans, we said goodbye to Brooks and put in on the Yazoo River. The Bluz Cruz finish line was our starting point. As we pushed off from the landing, I was curious how the next few days would go, curious about the river, but also curious about this new guy with whom I was going to be spending every mile and every hour for the next few days. I had talked with Adam on the phone in the preceding weeks, met him briefly at the Bluz Cruz, and spent the past couple of hours with him from Natchez to the Yazoo. Now we were on our way, headed down the Mississippi River.

Adam was in a canoe and proved to be a strong paddler, which I knew from his award-winning performance at the race two days earlier. He was also a good paddling partner. There is one convention about pace that is sometimes employed in running groups: the lead runner is responsible for the last runner. Adam was aware of my pace and kept us comfortably linked.

Adam, at thirty-six years old, was my son's age. He was a true Huck Finn nature boy who had a penchant for turtles and owls. He owned and operated a full-time carpentry contracting business that was augmented by his part-time river guiding venture. I would come to learn that he excelled at both. As I learned more about the river way down south, I was also learning about the people way down south. With just two people

Adam Elliott (*left*) and author (*right*) on boat landing in Natchez, Mississippi (Photo by German tourist Suzanne)

paddling for hours at a stretch there is a lot of time to talk. Two cultures, two generations, learning about each other and about this all-connecting, nation-spanning river.

In his Mississippi Southern drawl, Adam was a storyteller. He talked of his solo paddling trip from Itasca to the Gulf. It involved a minimal amount of planning. He just did it. In eighty days.

We paddled and camped and the next day we struck camp and paddled some more. Adam knew of a hideaway restaurant in Lake Bruin, the Fish Tail, that was originally on an oxbow of the river, but due to the Mississippi's meandering, the restaurant was now high and dry about a mile from the riverbanks. We pulled our boats into the brush, climbed the levee, and hiked the dirt road to lunch. The menu's offerings were a foreign language to this Yankee. With my guide's coaching I enjoyed a representative sampling of the Southland's luncheon fare.

Novelist Joseph Conrad, consistent with his nautical bent, penned in *The Mirror of the Sea*, "Nowhere else than upon the sea do the days, weeks and months fall away quicker into the past." Taking license to substitute river for sea, I found myself living Conrad's sentiment. Time is lost in the wake of a thousand paddle strokes. Hours spent under the sun's long summer arc offer time for thinking, talking, and having one more buoy rush up to meet you. Long days on the river are reduced to just a few memorable moments.

As our paddle strokes provided the rhythm, Adam created the lyrics as he talked of past river memories. One included his meticulous, on-the-river calculations of how many Jeep Wranglers could fit in a river barge. Another included the recollection of river guiding a group of male and female architects from Switzerland who were fond of nighttime skinny dipping sessions. Hearing this story, I took pride in contributing the moniker of the "Swiss Miss" connection to describe this special international relationship between the Mississippi guide and his Swiss clientele.

A river guide's toolkit should include the requisite yarn-spinning talent needed for passing the endless paddling hours. Adam was fully equipped. Adhering to the truth-in-advertising principle, his garrulous art form was self-described early in our adventure. "You have to understand, my stories will be long, but they often don't have a point." I didn't realize it at the time, but my river odyssey would include the two of us spending hours, days, and weeks exchanging some interesting and some not so interesting tales as we paddled toward our future memories.

The next morning, Adam and I were breaking camp, getting ready to head down the river. As we finished our early morning coffee, we heard a loud thrashing in the nearby trees and then a big splash. We could see a doe disappear into the woods, but what was more surprising was the large buck jumping into the Mississippi. It was heading toward the middle, where the river's current was most powerful.

There are a few things I have a hard time imagining. Examples include how a 747 can fly, how a pair of train engines can pull a mile-long train, how an ocean liner can cross the seas, and how a deer can swim. Deer have huge bodies with skinny legs and tiny hooves. How can they paddle with such seemingly inefficient tools?

The buck kept paddling toward the opposite shore, more than a mile away. We watched in amazement as the buck moved toward the swifter current. As it got closer to the middle, it was being swept downstream at a faster clip. We watched as just the deer's head remained visible as it was carried downriver at a quickening and sickening pace. It was not a pleasant moment. I wrote the deer off as it was carried faster and faster down the Mississippi. We could see the tiny speck of the buck's head. But we could tell it was still paddling—more downstream than across—slowly ferrying itself to the far shore.

He eventually got to a slower current and emerged safely on the other riverbank, quite a distance downriver from his starting point. We felt a massive sense of relief. But what had instigated the river crossing? Was it something the doe said? Of course, we'd never know. However, if there's one thing I do know, it's that paddling is about patience, and that buck had it.

NATCHEZ, MISSISSIPPI

We approached Natchez, the consummate "Life-on-the-Mississippi," steam boatin' river town. History and topography have turned Natchez into a tale of two cities. Atop the bluff overlooking the river is the well-to-do plantation and azalea set, Natchez-on-the-Hill. At the river's edge is Natchez-Under-the-Hill, where all the action is. I mean was.

Taken from the river town's marketing verbiage:

> Known as Natchez-Under-the-Hill, this area of Natchez was described by numerous nineteenth-century travelers as one of the rowdiest ports on the Mississippi River. Here docked the keelboats and the flatboats, and, beginning in 1811, the steamboats. Taverns, gambling halls, and brothels lined the principal street. Here, rumor has it, the only thing cheaper than the body of a woman was the life of a man. Enslaved people were also sold at the landing at Natchez-Under-the-Hill. It

was this landing that attracted early flatboat men from the North, who floated down the Mississippi River, sold their goods and their boats and trekked homeward on the 450-mile bandit-plagued footpath called the Natchez Trace.[15]

Adam and I paddled into town and missed all the Under-the-Hill excitement by two centuries, but we did stop at the Magnolia Grill for lunch. It was evident this was Adam's hometown as soon as we walked in. He was greeted by both patrons and staff. The riverside restaurant proved a welcome respite from the MRE (meal ready to eat) camp fare. We stopped next door at the Silver Street Gallery & Gifts. I introduced myself to the proprietor, Gail Guido. I had previously read of Gail's exploits on the Atchafalaya River with John Ruskey. There's that name again, John "The-Mississippi-River-Connects-Us-All" Ruskey. Gail's gallery also featured several John Ruskey paintings. We talked of her trip down the "Atchaf," and my interest was piqued.

After the prim and proper gallery, I took a few steps forward and went back two hundred years to check out the Under-the-Hill Saloon, reportedly the oldest saloon on the Mississippi and a watering hole where Jerry Lee Lewis performed. "The Killer," who grew up just across the river in Ferriday, Louisiana, would cross the river for regular performances at the saloon. As a fan of the Killer, I was impressed with a "tribute section" staked out in the saloon touting wild man Jerry Lee and his rock and roll, rockabilly, honky tonk, and blues renditions. I learned later there was a combination Jerry Lee Lewis Museum/Drive-Thru Liquor Store just twelve miles away in Ferriday. I'd have to catch it next time.

Leaving Natchez, Adam and I met two women on the landing who had just arrived from Germany and were in the middle of their international Southland tour. We visited briefly. They mentioned that in Germany canoes were called kayaks, or was it the other way around? A picture was snapped, and we were on our way. A few weeks later Adam received a message and a picture:

Hi Adam!

I'm back in Germany and I thought you might want to have the picture I took of the two of you. How was your trip? I hope everything went well. Take care.

Susanne

---

15. Friends of the Riverfront Natchez, "Natchez Under-the-Hill," accessed July 21, 2022, https://for-natchez.org/underthehill.html.

The days and miles passed, and we found ourselves approaching our takeout point, just beyond the ORCS. Prior to reaching our final destination, we had to pass a twenty-two-mile stretch that was dubbed on the USACE river charts with a most sinister collection of appelations: Glasscock Cutoff, Dead Man's Bend, Widow Graham Bend, and Coochie Discharge. Following that eerie Four Horsemen of the Apocalypse, we approached still another not-so-happy waypoint. It was one more riverside prison: Louisiana State Penitentiary.

This prison, otherwise known as Angola (named after the African country that was the origin for the majority of our country's slaves), is the largest prison in the United States. According to Wikipedia, the super slammer houses 6,300 inmates, both men and women, ranging from minimum security to death row. Its eighteen thousand acres of riverfront property are the size of Manhattan Island, located on a Louisiana oxbow of the Mississippi River. In Neal Moore and Cindy Lovell's book *Down the Mississippi*, they mention that Angola Prison has its own zip code, 70712. As Adam Elliott and I paddled past, we crossed wakes with the Angola ferry. I was much happier being in my boat than theirs.

We headed toward Shreve's Cutoff, named after Captain Henry Miller Shreve. Captain Shreve, in addition to being the first to captain a steamboat on both the Ohio River and Mississippi River to New Orleans and back, also played an instrumental role by skippering the steamboat *Enterprise* to New Orleans, supplying Colonel Andrew Jackson with timely, critical munitions in the victory of the Battle of New Orleans. Shreveport, Louisiana, is named in his honor. We exited the Mississippi just below the ORCS and headed toward the Lower Old River boat ramp (LMR 304.0).

The ORCS, built in the 1960s, is a massive, manmade, concrete and steel structure designed to control the flow of the Mississippi River. I was surprised to learn that the Mississippi, left to the forces of nature, would eventually jump the tracks of its current route to New Orleans and spill its guts into the Atchafalaya River, ending up in Morgan City, Louisana. Not wanting to leave NOLA high and dry, nor flood Morgan City, lots of engineers, lots of agencies, lots of time, and lots of money resulted in a massive diversionary structure being built for the country's largest river.

Approaching our takeout spot at the Lower Old River boat ramp, we paddled right into an unexpected and fortuitous moment. As we rounded our final bend, we saw a towboat, the *Twyla Lure*, moored near the landing called the Mud Hole. During our trip, Adam had been communicating with a tow captain that he knew. He was Michael Coyle, captain of the *Twyla Lure*. We were invited to come aboard for a tour.

Our docent was the galley chief, Janette Sturma, a most hospitable woman, who toured us throughout most of the boat. There were a few off-limit areas only because of fresh paint. The *Twyla Lure* was making final preparations for preening at the upcoming Towboat Week in Grafton, Illinois, and she did not want to smudge her make up. Who knew?

Some references will define the contemporary idiom "in one's wheelhouse" as "the part of a batter's strike zone most likely to produce a home run." Our tour led us to the real deal: the *Twyla Lure*'s wheelhouse. This is the true origin of the current phrasing. Captain Mike took over this part of the tour. We were obviously "in his wheelhouse." Better than a corner office, it was a workspace with a 360-degree view and walls of windows, redundant radar screens, spotlights, compasses, navigational equipment, communications devices, and charts. Like kids in a candy store, both Adam and I took turns taking a spin in the stately but comfortable skipper's chair.

Captain Mike fit the image of a riverboat captain; he was experienced, calm, and helpful. He explained the importance of paddlers having marine radios and communicating with the towboats. "Without the radio communication, a kayak can look like a log on the radar screens," he said. Unfortunately, I already knew this firsthand.

The *Twyla Lure* was a workhorse whose job was hauling limestone rock on an established route from Ste. Genevieve, Missouri, to the Mudhole near Angola, with occasional longer runs to the Big Sleazy, New Orleans. The captain and the crew were looking forward to the upcoming "towboat convention" to show off their boat. As we were leaving, reveling in the pilothouse-to-fantail walk around, we passed by the galley and saw a crew of real river men settling into a splayed-out mound of fresh crawfish piled high on the table. Our tour guide and head chef, Janette, was obviously the crew's favorite.

Brooks was waiting with the truck as we paddled up to the Lower Old River boat ramp. We loaded the truck and were on our way. As we traveled the kudzu-bracketed back roads to Natchez, we reviewed the days on the river, talked of our next trip, and relaxed. Back in Natchez, we said our "goodbye, y'alls," and I headed north.

What started as a rain delayed trip learning about the USS *Cairo*, a Yankee iron-clad boat, ended with me learning about another iron-clad boat, the *Twyla Lure*, this one from Dixie. I'd had a few days on the water, accrued 130 river miles, and now I had 1,100 miles on the road ahead.

16

THREE KINGS: COTTON, BB, AND REV. DR. MARTIN LUTHER KING JR.

Fall 2016

The Vicksburg Bluz Cruz race and other lower sections of the river paddled in the spring had answered a few of my questions. How would my paddling skills fare in the Lower Mississippi? How much of this river did I want to take on? As an accidental adventurer, could I find and afford someone to join me in my disjointed and spontaneous journeys?

I noticed a slight dissipation of my anxiety over any mismatch between my kayaking experience and the skills needed to travel the Deep South via the Father of Waters. As my river miles increased, so did my curiosity to paddle and peek around the next bend. I was getting accustomed to the treats the river was doling out. From being part of the colorful flotilla heading up the short stretch of the Yazoo River to cross the Bluz Cruz finish line and paddling by the Angola Prison ferry, to touring Captain Mike Coyle's *Twyla Lure* towboat, these river gifts were rare but valuable.

Of course, there's a cost to these memorable moments. About 95 percent of a kayaker's time is paddling down an always growing, dangerously powerful river. It is numberless paddle strokes, against the wind and waves, from dawn to dusk under a slowly arching sun. It's watching out for the next boil, eddy, or tree lurking beneath the surface. It's paddling past one more in the infinite line of buoys, either green cans or red nuns. The kayaker's work, vigilance and boredom, is balanced with 5 percent of something new and unexpected. The tradeoff is a bargain.

I found myself wanting more of the river. Anticipating the next leg of this years-long journey had become part of who I was.

Adam Elliott and I each brought different things to our recently formed adventure-seeking team. Adam was a young, competitive paddler. He was a native of Mississippi. He was a keen observer of nature, and he was generous in sharing his wisdom of the wilderness with this city boy.

He had also already paddled from Lake Itasca to the Gulf. And I . . . well, I brought an eagerness and willingness to learn from a master.

As it turns out, the question, "Could I afford someone to join me on my adventure?" was answered easily. Adam and I negotiated a reasonable price. I would bring $125 per day and a few jokes. A day at Disneyworld costs more and the rides last but a couple of minutes. As far as affordability, my river adventure never really had a budget, probably on purpose. If it is a true passion, one finds the time and the funds.

My paddling had advanced to a level that allowed me to proceed to the next step. I wanted to do more of the river, maybe even all of it. Adam showed up just in time to get me from point A to B, C, and beyond. He was just the assist I was seeking. In his ever-helping spirit, Adam had arranged our next leg from Memphis, Tennessee, to Rosedale, Mississippi. It would be 155 river miles, and another thousand-mile road trip from St. Paul.

I pulled out of my driveway at 4:45 in the morning. It was now fall and I was heading south again, destination Benoit, Mississippi (pop. 423), just twenty miles north of Greenville. My former river guide, Mike, aka "Big Muddy," had offered me lodging at the Kanu House near St. Louis along the way.

I stopped in Hannibal, Missouri, and took a walk around the river town's touristy tribute to Mark Twain, Huck, Tom, Becky, and their haunts from one and a half centuries ago. While wandering the cobbled backstreets, I happened upon Planters Barn, an intimate theater offering a one-man show featuring riverboat pilot, humorist, and author Mark Twain himself. The playbills were hawking "international acclaim, playing to rave reviews." It looked great, but I was headed to another one-man show, "Meet Me in St. Louis," featuring renowned river man Big Muddy.

It was good to reconnect with Mike. His hospitality and outdoor cooking were welcomed by this peripatetic paddler. We ate, exchanged stories of the river, and I settled in with day one behind me. I got an early start the next day.

In the weeks preceding my trip, as part of my dry land learning about the Mississippi River, I read John M. Barry's book *Rising Tide: The Great Mississippi Flood of 1927 and How It Changed America*. As it turns out, 1927 was a big year for America. In the spring, Lucky Lindy left New York City in his tiny Spirit of St. Louis and fought to stay awake for thirty-three hours, finally parking his plane in Paris. He was the first one to do it solo. Later, in the fall, Babe Ruth parked his sixtieth home run, a mark that would last until the 1960s. These were my two references to 1927. I was surprised to learn that the biggest news story of the year in this country was not the Atlantic aviator or baseball's basher. It was the Mississippi River flood, and it was in Greenville, right where I was headed.

There was a connection with the 1927 flood and my trip to Benoit. In John Ruskey's words, "The Mississippi River connects us all." Hang on for the loop to close.

In our planning discussions, Adam had arranged for my lodging in Benoit. "I've got you staying with a friend of mine, Eustace Winn. He's got an antebellum mansion and a couple of shotgun shacks. You're welcome to one of the shotgun shacks for the night. I'll meet you there in the morning."

Two things about the invitation stood out to me: the name Eustace Winn and the term "shotgun shack." I found out that Adam's friend, Eustace Winn, was the namesake and a young branch of the same family tree as another Eustace Winn. In 1927, the year of the great Mississippi flood, the earlier Eustace was a resident of Greenville. He had ordered and built a Sears catalogue kit house just south of Greenville's levy. As the story goes, the brick chimney from the mail-order house held fast, anchoring the house as Eustace scampered to the second story to escape the wrath of the Mississippi as Greenville's levy burst. Eustace's Sears house was the only house left standing in the area below the levy.

There's that river connecting us all.

The other thing mentioned in the lodging invitation was the shotgun shack. This term was new to me. More dry land learning was required. I became enlightened through the grace of Wikipedia, which revealed a shotgun shack is a narrow house, usually no more than twelve feet wide, with rooms arranged one behind the other and doors at each end of the house. The "shotgun" in shotgun shack is thought to refer to the home's linear configuration. Quite literally, one could fire a weapon through the front door and hit a target in the backyard.

The shotgun shack is synonymous with the South and is a big part of the region's folklore and culture. Wikipedia reports, "it was the most popular style of house in the Southern United States from the end of the American Civil War through the 1920s" and that "superstition holds that ghosts and spirits are attracted to shotgun houses because they may pass straight through them, and that some houses were built with doors intentionally misaligned to deter these spirits."[16]

---

16. "Shotgun House," Wikipedia, last modified August 22, 2022, https://en.wikipedia.org/wiki/Shotgun_house.

On the road again, I looked forward to my personal introduction to the Delta's very own architectural iconography. My trip took me past miles and miles of Mississippi cotton fields. A variety of huge, colored bales lined the recently harvested fields. Near Coahoma, Mississippi, I made a point to pull off the road and discretely cut off a small stick of the cotton plant with a half-dozen cotton bolls attached. It still sits on a shelf in my office.

Upon reaching Benoit, I discovered in the middle of nowhere the Winn demesne. There was Eustace Winn's house, two shotgun shacks, and the centerpiece—a huge antebellum plantation mansion called the Baby Doll House, replete with the Doric columns, balcony, and covered porch. This Southern beauty regaled in its grand and gracious scale.

As planned, there was nobody home when I arrived. Across the expansive manor's lawn, I spotted the two shotgun shacks, side by side—a double-barrel shotgun? The long day on the road ended with a beautiful sunset, which I enjoyed as I paged through some local tourist booklets stashed in my shack. One article featured a unique Delta treasure, Doe's Eat Place, just down the road in Greenville. Had I known, I would have planned to stop for dinner on my way down.

Cotton field near Coahoma, Mississippi

Baby Doll House with Doric columns reaching toward a lazy Mississippi sky

Dawn arrived and I noticed both Eustace's and Adam Elliott's trucks parked by the Winn house. They invited me in for breakfast and I finally had a chance to meet my gracious host. Watching these two good ol' boys reconnect was special. And they thought I was the one who talked funny. You betcha! Eustace toured us through his house, which could have passed for a natural history museum with the assortment of artifacts, arrowheads, fossils, snakeskins, skeletons, and bleached animal skulls. Eustace's dog, Rocco, a high-spirited mix of pit bull and black mouth cur, served as our docent's trusty assistant.

After our tour, Adam and I conducted a final gear check, and we were off to our next launching spot, Memphis, Tennessee. It had been almost five months since Adam and I had stepped out of the river at the Mud Hole in Louisiana, and now we were getting set to step back in at Mud Island in Tennessee. I can understand some calling the Mississippi "The Big Muddy." It's a common mistake, but that particular nickname should be reserved for the Missouri River. My personal proof is when I had paddled past the point of no return and had to confront the confluence of the two monsters. The Mississippi was water, but the Missouri was a torrent of raging mud.

Mud Island in Memphis might connote a backwoods orientation, but it's in the center of the action. Our launching site, the Mud Island boat ramp (LMR 738.0), is part of Mud Island Park and rests directly below the iconic M-shaped Hernando De Soto Bridge connecting Tennessee with Arkansas. Just blocks away was the unique intersection of King and King, two streets each honoring a famous King—Dr. Rev. Martin Luther Jr. and BB. We were embarking from the base of the city's signature Memphis Pyramid, a 320-foot, modern-day glassy tribute to the pyramids of the original Memphis, an Egyptian city on the banks of another great waterway, the River Nile.

With all the planning, packing, and driving finally behind us, we were on the river again for the next four days, with 150 river miles rolling ahead of us. After twenty miles of paddling, the left descending bank turned from Tennessee into Mississippi. Goodbye, Tennessee Ernie, hello, Nina Simone. We were straddling Arkansas and Mississippi.

When on the river for days at a time, one is always taking a gamble on good weather. On our second day, a wicked thunderstorm blew up just before noon. As luck would have it, a possible shelter appeared right around the bend. It was Fitzgerald's Casino (LMR 695.5). As every river gambler can attest, you've got to "know when to hold 'em, know when to fold 'em." We folded 'em and unfashionably slogged into the gambling hall for lunch. We did not push our luck at the tables, but afterward we waited out the storm perched under a nearby bridge. River gambler's luck.

Returning to our riverine route on day three, we once again experienced another of John Ruskey's "the Mississippi River connects us all" moments. As we stroked our way down the river, Adam suddenly cried out, "Whoo, whoop!" His call was answered with a similar call. Adam, the guide, spotted everything before I did, and he had given out what I would learn is the Quapaw greeting call. The call was answered by none other than John Ruskey himself at Island 63 (LMR 640.0). He and a few of his Quapaw river guides were in the process of ferrying a class of fourth graders across the river in two voyageur canoes. We were invited to escort their huge canoes, each carrying the precious cargo of nine- and ten-year-old adventurers. I was paddling alongside the group of junior paddlers with all my gear, and I was skirted into my relatively tiny boat alongside their big voyageur canoe. The guide, Isaiah "Kayaker" Allen, asked his students if they had any questions for me. One curious little girl, looking at me tucked into my boat with my paddling skirt stretched over the boat's cockpit, inquired, "Are you standing up in there?" It was a good question.

Reaching the opposite shore, we were treated to an elaborate shore lunch as we traded river stories with John Ruskey, his Quapaw Canoe Company guides, and a band of inquisitive newcomers to the river.

The next day was our final day. At about noon, we spotted a remote outpost with an older man tracking our progress from the deck of his cabin (LMR 611.0). How remote was it? I checked a map later and discovered the cabin was just a few minutes from the town of Alligator, Mississippi (pop. 187). We paddled over for a visit. The man mentioned his cabin was built on a stretch of USACE revetment, and he was at their mercy, but the arrangement had worked out fine for the past twenty-five years. He invited us to bring our lunches ashore and join him.

We climbed the rock-armored bank, and ten minutes later we were at the cabin. Near the deck we noticed a very old, ten-foot-long piece of wood with unusually rusty hardware. Our host Mickey explained the river had deposited this unique flotsam on his bank, and after his research, he concluded that the shape of the wood, the hardware, and the square-headed bolts were a strong indication that this lumber was once part of a nineteenth-century steamboat's paddle wheel.

He graciously invited us to come up through his cabin and join him on the deck to eat and enjoy the view. A quick walk through his river outpost revealed spartan furnishings, the obligatory spyglass, and a few books. On the deck, Mickey was seated behind a small table and motioned us to

Part of 1800s paddlewheel?

sit down and enjoy the moment. I inquired about the thick book on the table. "I'm reading Tolstoy," he said. "*War and Peace?*" I asked, gesturing toward the table. "No, it's a biography," Mickey said. "I just finished a book on Chekhov."

We learned of Mickey's corporate sales career, his world travels, his interest in history including Russian authors and Delta riverboats, and his intellectual curiosity. We exchanged stories of the river, barges, and travels. Mickey mentioned that he had been to Minnesota just once, to Warroad. I had been to Warroad too. It is cold, remote, and known as "Hockeytown, USA."

Well spoken, well read, well traveled. Hail fellow well met. Little did we know, the river would take a sharp turn.

Asked how his travels landed him in the cold, remote village of Warroad, Minnesota, Mickey talked of his journey into Canada, the Great Lakes, and northern Minnesota. "One thing I remember about Warroad, there was one girl, she was probably ten or twelve years old; well, she had the best ass on her. I had seen her mother, and she had a normal ass, but this girl's ass! I still think about it."

The ensuing silence hung in the air.

"Mickey, we've gotta get back on the river, but can I get a quick picture of you and Adam before we go?"

Click. And we were gone.

What started off as a poor man's copy of Pierre-Auguste Renoir's *Le Dejeuner des canotiers* (Luncheon of the Boating Party) ended up with two guys paddling a quick escape from Mickey's backwoods, banjo-pickin' *Deliverance* on the Delta. (Mickey's last name has been omitted to protect the guilty.)

A few miles downriver (LMR 607.0) from Mickey's cabin, we were no longer in between the borders of Arkansas and Mississippi. As the river went southwest, the Arkansas border jumped the riverbanks and veered southeast, forming an oxbow-shaped state border south of the river. As can be seen on the USACE charts, the river's previous route had followed the Arkansas border, which runs directly through the crescent-shaped Old River Lake. Through this process of the river changing its course, known as avulsion, the Arkansas border circles back and cuts through the charmingly named Tar Paper Shack Lake before reuniting with the Mississippi River a few miles later (LMR 604.8).

This phenomenon of the river's meandering nature mingling with society's political borders can be lost to the paddler unless one spots a state border sign. In *Life on the Mississippi*, Mark Twain provides a more colorful description of the dynamic nature of Old Man River, as he describes "one of the Mississippi's oddest peculiarities, that of shortening its length from time to time. If you will throw a long, pliant apple-paring over your shoulder, it will pretty fairly shape itself into an average section of the Mississippi River."[17]

With only fifteen miles to our takeout at Rosedale, Adam and I found an airport runway-sized sandy beach inviting us to take a break. On the beachhead, we launched a kite Adam had packed and we watched as the afternoon breeze sent it soaring into autumn's cloudless, deep blue sky. Adam discovered in the sand a perfect skeleton of a gar's head that gave us a few moments of capturing some pics of the bony creature in various poses.

Across the river, on the Arkansas side, was the mouth of the White River. This much smaller tributary joined the Mississippi at a right angle, forming a watery "T." The significance of the ninety-degree angle was that it provided Adam and me with a great side show as we watched what seemed like a parade of tow captains maneuvering around each other at the tricky entrance to the big river. It was a tow boat rodeo. The turns were

---

17. Mark Twain, *Life on the Mississippi* (New York: Barnes & Noble, Inc., 2010), 103.

Adam Elliott piloting a kite in the Mississippi sky

challenging and required on-the-spot communications and cooperation between the pilots. As we listened in to the captains' jargon on our marine radios, it was apparent how much the captains rely on each other. We noticed this camaraderie, courtesy, and willingness to help each other, and us, throughout our entire journey.

Nobody blows a whistle to signify the break is over, but we both seemingly knew when it was time to start paddling again.

The last paddling leg went smoothly. We finished by navigating the final two miles up the busy Napoleon Cut-Off to reach the Rosedale Harbor, the boat ramp, and Adam's truck parked right where we hoped it would be. We loaded our boats and gear onto the truck and made our way past nearly a hundred trucks lined up to unload their newly harvested cotton and other crops at the harbor.

We had traversed 150 river miles in four days. Now we were off to Benoit for dinner with Eustace. Our host planned for us to visit Doe's Eat Place in Greenville, as featured in the travel publication from my first night in the shotgun shack. One of the reviews said you will find Doe's on the wrong side of town, but it's worth it.

Doe's Eat Place had survived a long and colorful past. Dominick "Doe" Signa's father originally opened a grocery store in the building in

1903. Papa's Store did well until the 1927 flood. After that, Big Doe Signa went into bootlegging to help the family get back on its feet. After several years he sold his forty-barrel still for $300 and a Model T Ford. Around 1941, Mamie received a partial recipe for hot tamales. She improved the recipe and began selling them. That was the beginning of Doe's.

As the restaurant's website reports, "At first Signa ran a honky tonk in the front part of the store. It was strictly for blacks . . . ironically, the 'carriage' trade arrived by the back door, like segregation in reverse. One of the local doctors began coming for a meal between calls. Big Doe would cook him up a steak and feed him in the back. Pretty soon the doctor brought another doctor, then a lawyer and before he knew it, Doe had a regular restaurant in the back . . . he eventually closed the honky tonk and focused on the eat place."[18]

Following custom, we entered Doe's through the kitchen. Before we got to the dining area, the chef demanded, somewhat politely, our order. "You want hot tamales before your steaks?" I was not aware that tamales were part of the Mississippi fare. Later I would learn more of the Mississippi hot tamale connection. River man and writer Boyce Upholt, in his article

(left to right) **Author, Adam Elliott, and Eustice Winn at Doe's Eat Place**

18. Doe's Eat Place, accessed August 30, 2022, http://www.doesbatonrouge.com/history/.

"Red Hot Tamales," describes, "The firmest evidence of the local hot tamale tradition comes from Robert Johnson himself. In 1936, his recording of 'They're Red Hot' describes a woman selling red hot, hot tamales. . . . Since then, the food has thrived, mostly in African American communities, with recipes passed down through generations."[19] In fact, Greenville is the self-proclaimed "Hot Tamale Capital of the World."

You do not go to Doe's without sampling the hot tamales. The steaks were huge and delicious, the bill was huge, our tabs were separate, and the service could not have been more Southern or more hospitable. The name of the place might be grammatically challenged, but the fare is gastronomically perfect.

Back at the Winn estate, Adam and I found our night's lodging in one of the rustic shotgun shacks. Adam grabbed the west end room, and I the east. It had been a long day followed by a huge steak, fries, and tamale feast. After a day on the river, exposed to nature's elements, I welcomed a good night's sleep in a comfortable bed.

Lights out came fast. In the blackness of the evening and the darkness of the room, I was sleeping peacefully when "Boom!!!" The entrance door, directly into my room, was blasted open with a shockingly loud crack. I then heard what sounded like footsteps on the wooden floor. Not able to see anything in the darkness, I was terrified and paralyzed. I just huddled in the bed and listened, wondering what was coming next. The footsteps came and went, along with some rustling sounds, and then came back again. There were no voices, just footsteps that continued for a while and finally stopped. Curled in a fetal position, I recalled my Google research on shotgun shacks and their ability to draw ghosts and spirits.

As a nonbeliever in ghosts, at least until then, I pondered my plight until I finally fell asleep again. As the sun came through the still-open door, I was awakened. Thankful that I survived the nighttime mysteries, I arose to take a quick inventory. As I looked outside, I noticed my neon orange cap had found a place on the lawn, fifty yards away from the shack. Next to it was my sweatshirt, some other clothing, and a pile of papers strewn about the yard. Going to retrieve my hat, I noticed the pile of papers turned out to be my book, *Old Man River*, by Paul Schneider, that I had left on the floor. The book had been chewed to pieces. I soon discovered the same teeth marks had perforated both my hat and sweatshirt. That was all the forensics needed. The suspect was identified as Rocco, Eustace's four-legged sidekick. Case closed.

---

19. Boyce Upholt, "Red Hot Tamales," *Meridian*, November 28, 2016, https://www.meridian.net/mississippi/2016/11/23/13733224/tamales-mississippi.

Shotgun house ransacked by Rocco

Leftover spoils of Rocco's ransacking

Before we were on our way, Eustace proudly toured us through the Baby Doll House, so named because it was where the 1956 Academy Award–nominated movie *Baby Doll* was filmed. The movie starred Carol Baker, Karl Malden, and Eli Wallach and was directed by Elia Kazan with help from the story's author, Tennessee Williams. Our tour included a review of many of the movie's promotional posters, pictures, and artifacts. Eustace had recently rehabilitated the 1858 mansion, and it was now a real museum, used for a variety of social functions including special events and, of course, Southern Belle weddings.

Baby Doll House, formerly the Burrus mansion, enjoys a rich and colorful history. Construction began in 1858, and Judge Charles Burrus moved in sometime during 1861. The mansion dodged a bullet during the Civil War as it narrowly escaped being burned to the ground by Yankee soldiers. This fortuitous fate occurred because of a previous college friendship between Judge Burrus and a Yankee commander, who gave orders to spare the mansion.

The promotional pieces describe the mansion's noted visitors over time. One notable visitor was Confederate Gen. Jubal Early, who hid at the home after Lee's surrender, before being secretly transported across the Mississippi River at night by Charles Burrus. There were also a few "George Washington stayed here" type guests said to have stayed at the home, among them being John Wilkes Booth, and the famous James brothers.

It was time to leave Eustace, Rocco, and this magical place tucked in the middle of nowhere on the outskirts of Benoit. Following the handshakes and "bye, y'alls," Adam and I both headed to Clarksdale, Mississippi. I had wanted to check out the "crossroads" of highways 49 and 61. This was the spot where Delta Blues legend Robert Johnson had supposedly made his Faustian pact to turn his guitar into a magical instrument. We rendezvoused at the devil's intersection, took a few photos, and we went our separate ways.

Eight hours later I was once again in Hannibal, Missouri. Good driving conditions and a rather spontaneous plan had brought me to the Planters Barn Theatre just in time to take in Richard Garey's long-running one-man show, *Mark Twain Himself*. I was intrigued by the theater, so I looked forward to an evening of indoor, relaxing entertainment.

The first half of the performance was a Victorian tea setting. Guests were served tea and cookies as Mark Twain mingled with the patrons, spinning local color yarns from the 1800s. After a while, Garey, as Mark Twain, motioned us all to take our seats in the tiny theater. The theater provided an intimate setting. We were only feet from the stage.

There were about fifteen of us, and Mark Twain had us all hooked from his first words. I remember it was just a few minutes into the show and our writer and humorist was describing his brief stint in the Confederate Army before going AWOL. The next thing I recall was the audience's spirited applause, and Twain taking his bows. The show was over, and I was embarrassed. I had fallen asleep for almost all of the show. I have been known to snore, and snort, at times when asleep. With only a few people in this friendly little gathering, I was trying to imagine how much of a disruption I had been to the audience and the actor. I have taught evening classes in college, and I know what it is like talking to a sleeping student. And Mark Twain was a lot more interesting than any of my lectures on compensation plans in the workplace.

Exiting the theater was another awkward moment. Earlier I had enjoyed a wonderful one-on-one conversation with Mr. Twain at the Victorian tea party. We talked of Hannibal and the river. We hit it off. Now he was camped at the exit taking in compliments and thanking everyone. How could I say I enjoyed the evening when he watched me sleep through most of his show? Maybe another time.

Driving home from Hannibal the next day, I had about eight hours to look both ways, that is backward and forward. This trip had been a kaleidoscope of events, some big and some small, some good and some weird. On dry land, there was a giant cast of characters: Big Muddy, John Ruskey, Mickey (yikes!), Eustace Winn, Adam Elliott, and Mark Twain himself. Then there was the river and what it offered the curious traveler. Eight days and 150 river miles of the 2,350 miles of the Mississippi—we had knocked off just a small stretch. That was the good news. There were plenty more small stretches awaiting me.

It was the end of September, and I was heading back to home to Minnesota, but I knew I wouldn't be there for long.

17

SOURCE TO SEA (S2S), THE ATCHAFALAYA RIVER

Fall 2016

I thought a lot about my week living on the big, wild Lower Mississippi River. St. Louis truly had represented the beginning of a new river. In addition to having the Missouri River explode into my Mississippi, the river was now unchecked by the locks and dams up north. I was curious about what future segments of the Lower Mississippi would offer. Not so much what treasures, but what life-threatening hazards lurked, both on and off the river. Throughout all my river travels, I heard one consistent point of view from those living any place on the river: "Be careful and be safe. The river is alright here, but it's dangerous downriver!"

I was concerned about the Lower Mississippi and its treacheries that lay in wait. I used caution in my next steps. I had skipped ahead to a somewhat controlled environment on the Lower Mississippi by entering the twenty-two-mile Bluz Cruz paddling race in Vicksburg, followed up with another 250 miles aided by the seasoned river-guiding services of Adam Elliott.

In reading, talking, and paddling my way down the river, my goals proved to be as fluid and meandering as the river itself. Even the concept of S2S crept in at times. I had read other paddlers' descriptions of their moment tasting the salt water of the Gulf at the end of their excursions. That was enticing and would surely be a moment to look forward to. But one obstacle in my mind en route to the sea was the stretch from Baton Rouge to New Orleans. Those 150 miles have been referred to as Cancer Alley, and they overshadowed all my previous fears of the river.

John Ruskey, river man extraordinaire, came to the rescue. As I pondered, I reviewed some of my research materials including *The Rivergator*, a comprehensive document designed specifically for paddlers on the Lower Mississippi. Over a period of years, John Ruskey, with the assistance of others including my guide Adam Elliott, had published the go-to guide for paddlers navigating the Lower Mississippi at high, low, and medium river levels.

The Rivergator seemed to be addressing my specific concerns of getting to the sea by way of the risky Cancer Alley thrill ride. In fact, it directly addressed my anxiety with the Baton Rouge to New Orleans route:

> Staying on the Mississippi you will soon encounter very dangerous river conditions through Baton Rouge, New Orleans and Venice (including poor campsites with toxic air and water conditions). You will have to paddle several hundred miles of choppy crowded water sharing the main channel with sea-going freighters, cargo boats, re-supply vessels, and endless fields of barges as they fleet up for the long-distance journey back up the river. Commonly known as "Chemical Corridor," but also described as "Cancer Alley," paddlers might want to add an oxygen face mask to their equipment list here and maybe a haz mat suit. Seriously. Some paddlers have gotten sick within this stretch when they ended up downwind of the wrong smokestack. You will be camping next to refineries, chemical plants, plastics manufacturing, and lots of coal-fired power plants. More toxins are dumped in the river here than any other piece of river in America. No more remote camping, no more swimming, no more quiet sections of river teeming with wildlife. This is a section of the Mississippi you paddle just to get through it.[20]

This did not sound like a lot of fun, but *The Rivergator* also proffered a persuasive case for taking a safer, more scenic route:

> Paddlers should consider taking the Atchafalaya River through its paradise of three distinct biotas: 1) the variegated bottomland hardwood forests, 2) the cypress/tupelo gum swamps, and 3) the marshy coastal plains. It also coincides with the heart of Cajun country. To be sure, it's not completely wild. To be sure, there are some pipelines and a few small refineries; there are a few oil storage and processing installations; there are a few small communities to paddle through and a few bridges to go under. But they are few and far between. There is very little sign of mankind, and a lot of forests, swamps, lakes, bayous and back channels. The sky is uncluttered by cranes and powerlines, and the stars are bright at night. Baton Rouge and New Orleans are a distant glow on the horizon after dark. There is very little commercial traffic, and no giant tows with big waves. Tows here are limited to 2x3 barges maxi-

---

20. John Ruskey, "Alternate Route to the Gulf of Mexico: The Atchafalaya River," *The Rivergator*, https://www.rivergator.org/riverlog-page/atchafalaya-river-atchafalaya_upper-2/.

mum. But there are a lot of hunters and fishermen. The Atchafalaya is populated with Cajun river rats and hunting camps, and so it is a lived-in kind of wilderness, kind of like the Barranca del Cobre region of the Northern Sierra Madres, or the Navajo country of the Four Corners, very similar to the Lower Mississippi in days gone by, which was also thinly populated along its banks by all types of pioneers and people living off the river and the land, but who had become part of the wildness by their harmonious lifestyle. Almost 1/3 of the Mississippi River is diverted here as a way of protecting the City and Port of New Orleans, creating the 4th largest and the shortest big river on the continent. Why not go with the flow, and take the Atchafalaya?[21]

Why not?

In the spring, Adam and I had discussed the Atchafalaya option as we paddled to our takeout at the ORCS. Now it was fall, and I was heading back to Natchez, prepared for one more round on the river, this time the Atchafalaya. As I approached Memphis, I called Dale Sanders and he invited me to stop by his place near Memphis so we could meet in person after our series of phone calls. Dale sports a world-class résumé of worldwide adventures and proved to be a most welcoming host. He greeted me with a big smile, a Santa Claus beard, and a positivity I felt from our first handshake.

He showed a genuine interest in my experiences with the river, and my future river plans. We talked of my planned trip down the Atchafalaya River and of his globe-trekking journeys. This man, the one-time world record holder for oldest person to paddle the Mississippi S2S, invited me to sign his paddlers "Wall of Fame." This wall was dedicated to the Mississippi paddlers and their brief messages and philosophies. I made my mark: "Source to sea via Atchafalaya. Started 2006. ETA 2017. Bit by bit, five days at a time. God bless you, Dale!!! 9/16/2016." I was now committed, in writing. It was an honor to join the names of all the others who had paddled through, creating their own Mississippi memories.

Our visit was brief, but as I continued southbound, I realized I had just met the fourth "president" of my Rivermen's Mount Rushmore. What a lineup: Mike (Big Muddy) Clark, Adam (First Man on the River) Elliott, John Ruskey, and now, a rough-rider for sure, Dale Sanders. How can a guy not get excited for the next leg of river time!

After arriving in Natchez the following day, Brooks shuttled Adam and me once again, this time from Natchez to the Lower Old River boat

---

21. John Ruskey, "Alternate Route to the Gulf of Mexico," *The Rivergator*, https://www.rivergator.org/riverlog-page/atchafalaya-river-atchafalaya_upper-2/.

Author (*left*) and Dale Sanders (*right*) at Dale's "Wall of Fame"

ramp at the Mud Hole, just below the ORCS. This was our put-in spot for the next five days in the Delta on the Atchafalaya River.

On the inside cover of his book *The Control of Nature*, John McPhee provides a masterfully written account of the relationship between the Mississippi, the Atchafalaya, and man's tinkering with both:

> In the natural cycles of the Mississippi's deltaic plain, the time had come for the Mississippi to change course, to shift its mouth more than a hundred miles and go down the Atchafalaya, one of its distributary branches. The United States could not afford that—for New Orleans, Baton Rouge, and all the industries that lie between would be cut off from river commerce with the rest of the nation. At a place called Old River, the Corps therefore had built a great fortress—part dam, part valve—to restrain the flow of the Atchafalaya and compel the Mississippi to stay where it is.[22]

Our chauffeur, Brooks, offered his bon voyage and we were headed downriver once again. In minutes we were at the Old River Lock. Thirty years ago, John McPhee described this particular lockage: "The gates close behind the Mississippi (towboat). The mooring bitts inside the lock wail like coyotes as the water and the boat go down."[23] In locking through all the Mississippi's locks, I never heard any coyotes. However, as Adam and I descended in this lock, McPhee's words from decades ago rang true as we heard those same coyotes wail.

Shortly after paddling onto the Atchafalaya and into Cajun country, we met our first real, live Cajuns. They had been fishing and offered us a share of their catch of fresh fish. Shortly after, we discovered this would not be a rare occurrence. In my research, I recalled *The Rivergator* reporting that this sharing was a good way to cozy up to the Cajuns. "You might be offered a cup of coffee or tea. By all means, accept this offering. Sharing a cup of coffee is a Cajun tradition as old as the arrival of the Acadians. . . . Be sure to sample at least one chicory blend. Chicory is as SoLa as it gets! Coffee, and the serving and sharing of it, is a fine tradition honed to perfection in Southern Louisiana. Ce Bon!"[24]

Coffee. In several sections of Ruskey's *Rivergator*, he lavishly touted the bayou's chicory blend and how one must try it for the true Cajun

---

22. John McPhee, *The Control of Nature* (New York: Farrar, Straus and Giroux, 1989).

23. John McPhee, *The Control of Nature* (New York: Farrar, Straus and Giroux, 1989), 17.

24. John Ruskey, "Cajun Culture and the Atchafalaya Wilderness," *The Rivergator*, https://www.rivergator.org/river-log/atchafalaya-river/atchafalaya_upper/pg/14/.

experience. It sounded enticing, but over several trips I had become spoiled with Adam's morning cup of eye-opening, French-pressed Mississippi Joe.

As we paddled down this much more peaceful river, Adam pointed to the shore and indicated an alligator sunning himself. As a guide, Adam had been an expert at pointing out to this city boy all types of river fauna. We had talked of alligators on previous trips. I had read the tales of river travelers' encounters with these reptiles of lore, and Adam had seen his share on the river. On my river trips, I had seen a variety of river life including black bear, deer, otters, armadillos, and coyotes, but not one gator. I was excited. Then, in a moment, I realized that this was Johnny Reb's joke on the visiting Yankee. It was no alligator, just a reptilian-looking log on a sandy shore.

This "log appearing as a gator" became the running joke as we paddled the hours away. As the miles and days passed, there were quite a few gator-looking logs that each of us tried to pass off as the real thing.

We had allowed ourselves five days to reach the Gulf just beyond Morgan City. The weather and the paddling conditions were fine, and we did not miss the constant commercial traffic of the Mississippi. There were some towboats with barges, but the two-by-threes seemed much more friendly than the six-by-seven barge trains of the larger river.

We did encounter two distinct challenges, one in the morning and one in the evening. The weather conditions were such that most mornings we awoke to a thick, eerie fog. We experimented one morning by trying to paddle in the fog but quickly abandoned the attempt when we could not see each other after a few seconds on the river. On the foggy days, it would be mid-morning before the sun lifted the gray veil to reveal the blue-on-blue canvas awaiting our paddling strokes.

Tow pushing through another foggy Atchafalaya River morning

The evening challenge was the onslaught of mosquitoes. This was the same scourge that Lewis and Clark's Corps of Discovery encountered two centuries earlier. Luckily, since then, technology's advances have provided today's discoverers with the bug suit. I felt like a beekeeper wearing the mosquito suit, which I hadn't donned since Camp Ripley, near Brainerd, Minnesota.

As we made our way, we were met by several Cajuns skippering their johnboats. The Cajuns are passionate about their hunting and fishing. Over the next few days on the river, the locals offered us fresh-caught fish, "fresh-kilt" squirrels, cold beer, and tequila. Hunting, fishing, and drinking—an outdoorsman's trifecta. On day four, as we stopped for lunch, one of the johnboats ferried across the river to join us. As we talked, two more boats pulled ashore to join the fun. All three knew each other and had stopped just to be social and to see who these kayakers were. They proudly referred to themselves as Coonasses. Each of their boats was high powered: seventy horses strapped to the transom and several high-powered rifles and shotguns secured in the boat's flat hull.

Lunchtime with genuine Coonass with high-powered johnboat and high-powered artillery

One man was scouting out a special hunting place so he could take his grandson deer hunting the following week. He talked of a little trouble he had been having with an interloper.

"I have been hunting here since I was a kid. A while back this guy starts questioning me about what right do I have coming here? We did not hit it off from the beginning."

He mentioned there had been several other occasions where the two crossed paths. He went on to describe how he settled things.

"Now I'm the type of guy who'll fight at the drop of a hat. And sometimes I'm the one dropping the hat! I knew what tree his deer stand was on, and so one day I waited for him on the path to his stand. When he came by, I said, 'Where are you going?'

'I'm going hunting,' he answered.

'No, you're not,' I said.

'Why not?' he asked.

'Cause I cut the tree down with your deer stand in it!'"

End of story.

The words fall short in describing the moment. His expressions, eyes, gestures, and Cajun tongue all made for a wonderful peek into the bayou life of a Coonass. I realized there was an entire country that separated my snow-covered woodland of Paul Bunyan and this Cajun's moss-draped cypress bayou of Loup Garou.

Moments later, one of the other men, right out of Coonass central casting with the weathered face, long beard, and long hair, asked what I did for a living. I replied, somewhat sheepishly, "I'm a human resources consultant." He followed up with, "Is that like OD?" His response surprised me. He went on to tell me that he had left his career of directing the organizational development (OD) department for one of the large oil corporations in Morgan City. "I retired three years ago, and I haven't had a shave or haircut since. I haven't been back, and nobody would recognize me if I had."

Our lunch was more entertaining than any movie I had ever seen! Our up-close-and-personal moments with this slice of Cajun diaspora was exactly what I signed up for. What a country!

During our afternoon paddling, Adam pointed out another alligator log, but as we approached, we realized this log was the real deal. We quietly paddled closer to get a picture of the full-grown gator soaking up sun on the sandy shore. We were just thirty yards away when the alligator stirred, took a few steps, and slipped into the river. It was a memorable moment. I had spotted my first live gator on the shore, and now it was swimming just feet below me. I tried to imagine how many of its relatives were also schooling about as I paddled through their playground. See ya later.

Because of the fog-delayed starts on several mornings, we fell behind our original five-day schedule. At the end of day four, we realized that we would be able to make it to Morgan City but would not be able to paddle to the Gulf itself. It took a while for me to make peace with the realization that to return to Morgan City to finish the "to sea" portion of the "source to sea" plan would require another two-thousand-mile round trip to paddle those twenty miles to the Gulf.

I struggled with balancing this disappointment against the days of experiencing the Atchafalaya River, its topography, and especially its people, from towboat skippers to the ubiquitous Coonasses. As I spent another night tucked in on another riverbank, I weighed the options. There was no immediate salve to counter the sting of coming up short of our target. I tried not to let the "no sea" reality weigh too heavily. We were still in the middle of a wonderful Atchafalaya exploration, so I chose to accept the reality and get back to the adventure at hand.

We awoke the final morning and were greeted by the Lewis and Clark scourge—legions of mosquitoes. Enjoying breakfast, breaking camp, and filling my thermos with a final jolt of Adam's French-pressed finest while encumbered by the bug suit was a true river man's morning. We would arrive in Morgan City mid-day, meet up with Brooks, and head home. I put aside my earlier concerns and accepted our revised game plan. I was good to go.

The morning proved to be an ideal day for paddling our final stretch. We encountered little commercial traffic and had a nice marine radio chat with a couple of towboat skippers. One jokingly questioned if we had run into any "banjo players" on our way down the river. The *Deliverance* reference brought a few guffaws.

As we approached Morgan City, we paddled by a couple in a johnboat who were out enjoying their morning fishing. We exchanged morning greetings and accents. The woman asked if we would like to share a cup of coffee. What appeared as a quite simple question was a bucket list check off for this Yankee city slicker. This was the chicory coffee moment John Ruskey had emphasized in his *Rivergator* scouting report!

I accepted her offer and reveled in the celebratory ritual of transferring the prized chicory blend from her thermos to mine. I had been anticipating this moment ever since I first poured over John's suggestion in my trip-planning stages back in St. Paul.

It was one of the most memorable cups of coffee I have ever enjoyed. Yesterday an alligator, today an Acadian chicory communion.

The harbor in Morgan City offered its own trademark. This was a bicameral city, with two distinct industries sharing the same real estate. Shrimpers and oil riggers had tied up all the premium parking along Morgan City's watery esplanade. My years on the river had presented a pageant of floating vessels, including rafts, pleasure boats, johnboats, oil tankers, and towboats. But as we entered this harbor town, I was introduced to a new type of watercraft. As we paddled past countless shrimp boats, moored in the harbor with their thick hawsers and what appeared to be MacGyver-designed outriggers, trawl nets, and winches, I realized this was as close to the Gulf as I had ever kayaked.

As we paddled past the commercial harbor, we found our exit. Tucked behind a wharf was a bougainvillea-choked boat ramp occupied by Brooks with the truck and two serious fishermen. One had arrived on his umbrella-topped riding lawnmower. I approached the other for a quick chat. We discussed fishing and that his name, Lamond, meant "the world." As we prepared to head for home, Lamond flashed a gold-toothed smile as he steered us to Rita Mae's for the best Cajun food in town.

Once we loaded the boats and gear in the truck, the three of us headed to Rita Mae's. I noticed several Stars and Bars in various sizes displayed on houses and businesses as we made our way across the Gulf town of ten thousand. The Confederate flag, or saltire, reminded this Yankee that he was a long way from home.

Morgan City was the site of the first *Tarzan* movie—the bayous made great jungles—and had lost a third of its population over the past couple decades due to cutbacks in the oil industry. We learned this firsthand from Rita Mae's grandson, who waited our table. He was back at the restaurant after being laid off from one of the oil companies.

He described the house specialties as I took in the small but vibrant five-table restaurant. Being in the Atchafalaya River Basin, the largest river swamp in the country, I decided to go Cajun. Chicken and sausage gumbo with fried fish, potato salad, and sweet tea were perfect for the moment. If extra seasoning had been required, the most famous pepper sauce in the world was being produced minutes away. The McIlhenny Company, the one that has been pouring Tabasco Sauce into worldwide food markets for over 150 years, was just down the road in Avery Island.

The three travelers were stuffed but decided to force down a little dessert while at Rita Mae's. If onion, celery, and bell peppers make up the holy trinity of Cajun fare, then peach cobbler, bread pudding, and pecan pie hit the trifecta of Cajun desserts. Lamond, with his big, gold-toothed smile back on the fishing pier, could not have steered us any better.

On the way home, sixty miles up the road, we drove through Baton Rouge, Louisiana. This city represented the beginning of Cancer Alley for those paddlers choosing to stay on the Mississippi River on their way to the sea. We had a chance to scout out the river and its traffic, and the Huey P. Long Bridge that spans the Mississippi at the very top of Cancer Alley.

Back in Natchez, we went through the loading and unloading ritual once again, said our "bye, y'alls," and I headed home. On my way out of Natchez, I did stop at Gail Guido's Silver Street Gallery & Gifts Under the Hill to report to Gail that we had just kayaked the Atchafalaya. Gail fixed me up with some early Christmas shopping for my granddaughters. I left the store carrying a trio of four-foot-long plush alligators for Clara, Natalie, and June.

Somewhere between Natchez and Vicksburg, I discovered something had gone awry in the loading of my vehicle. I was now miles from Natchez when I realized that a container belonging to Adam had mistakenly been put in with my things. Imagine the dismay when I opened it to discover the quite healthy-sized portion of Adam's bread pudding, fresh from Rita Mae's. C'est bon!

As I headed north toward Memphis, I thought of the last week and my stop at Dale Sanders' house. "Source to sea via Atchafalaya. . . ." Well, I hadn't quite made it to the sea. I also recalled different paddlers' discussions about the Atchafalaya route. It was something like, "Yes, the Atchafalaya will get you to the sea, so you can call it *source to sea*, but it is not the same as paddling the entire Mississippi from its headwaters to its mouth below Venice, Louisiana."

My view of the Mississippi River from the bridge in Baton Rouge had been reassuring. The river and the traffic didn't look that scary!

The 1,100-mile drive gave me a lot of time for thinking. Somewhere between Memphis and St. Paul, I knew I was going to have to do the real Mississippi River, head to toe, or head to mouth. Big Easy, here I come!

Someday.

To summarize my SoLa sojourn I've pirated a sentiment from one of our true American heroes, and our country's first woman in space. In 1983, astronaut Sally Ride, following her first ride into space, proclaimed, "Ever been to Disneyland? That was definitely an E ticket!"

I went to Disneyland as a child. In the early days of the destination theme park, the rides were classified from A tickets to E tickets, with E tickets being the best, most exciting, and most expensive (50 cents). The

Jungle Cruise, Mark Twain Steamboat, and the Matterhorn Bobsleds were all E tickets. The Matterhorn Bobsleds were a rollercoaster ride through the alps. Your bobsled flew by torn-up tracks only to come face to face with the menacing Yeti. This creature guarded his collection of torn-up bobsleds and other mountain climber loot. The twists and turns, the furry beast, the loud, scary sounds, and the splash-down ending made for a thrilling ride. In all, I believe the ride lasted four minutes. Today, the average wait-in-line time is ninety minutes.

Looking at the Atchafalaya River as if it were a Disneyland ride:

First you will experience the massive ORCS as you enter this country's largest bayou. You self-propel yourself by paddling 150 miles on a very scenic and diverse river and bayou system with all types of flora and fauna. You might come face to face with an alligator or two. After the morning fog burns off, you will meet and greet with real live Cajuns who will offer you a variety of food, fresh caught, fresh killed, or fully prepared. With your new Cajun buddies, you will share a cup of Louisiana's freshest home-grown chicory-blend coffee. To top off your Cajun experience, you will be dining on authentic, prepared-with-love Coonass cuisine, with the best bread pudding offered in the oil-rigged, shrimp-boating town of Morgan City. The ride lasts five days. Currently there are no lines.

That was definitely an E ticket!

18

FROM PEANUTS TO POPEYE

Spring 2017

March. I heeded the month's imperative message: time to get moving. It had been almost six months since I stepped out of my kayak at the harbor in Morgan City, Louisiana, and the long Minnesota winter had provided much-needed opportunity to plan. March is my golf addiction's shoulder season, so this was my window for river time.

"When the student is ready the teacher will appear." Laozi, a Chinese sage and contemporary of Confucius, is credited as the author of the statement as found in *Tau Te Ching*, the world's second most published book, right behind the Bible.

This Taoist heeding, from its lofty Eastern origins eight centuries ago, had applied itself to this snowbound student of the river in the form of a mid-winter email, with the subject line: Rivergator Celebratory Expedition Itinerary, March 20 to May 10, 2017—St. Louis to Gulf of Mexico.

In a simple description, the teacher, John Ruskey—who else could it be—was offering a hands-on seminar and syllabus to this oh-so-ready student. "Put me in, coach. I'm ready to play!"

Not so fast, grasshopper. There was fine print. The expedition was going to be conducted in the friendly confines of two huge voyager canoes—not kayaks. My sentiments were reminiscent of Joe Pesci lamenting to Marisa Tomei at the end of *My Cousin Vinny* that he wanted to win the case all by himself.

The announcement promoted a seven-week journey. My business, and my golf, could not survive an absentee landlord for that stretch of time.

The ports of call were scheduled from St. Louis to the Gulf. Having already covered major portions of the river, I still had a lot of new river to paddle. I did not want to paddle through old territory when I had so much new water lying in wait, and this trip would be retracing a lot of my previous trips.

John and I talked and emailed and talked again. We decided I would join the expedition party mid-route in Chester, Illinois, where I would attach myself to them, like a remora to a shark, until we arrived in Memphis, Tennessee, where I would depart. I would paddle my kayak and bring my tent and supplies, but I would camp and eat with eight other explorers. My itinerary established, now I just had to count the days.

On March 24, the ice was finally off the river in St. Paul, Minnesota, and I was on the road to Chester, Illinois, by way of Memphis, Tennessee, for the next paddling trial. This would be the longest chunk I had taken on: 330 river miles, thirteen days on the water, and four days on the road.

Four hours into my road trip, I needed a break and pulled into Urbana, Iowa. The name Urbana belies the character of this rural stop-off settled between the Cedars—as in Falls and Rapids. There was nothing urban about it. It had a population of one thousand, with one Main Street and one bar. The hole-in-the-wall bar was the O-Zone, and I was happy to see it was open at 9 a.m. In fact, it was the only place that was open at that time. Upon entering, I was treated to a living tribute to Wrigley Field, Ernie Banks ("Mr. Cub"), and everything Chicago Cubs. Decked out in Cubs blue, white, and red, the O-Zone's decor featured Wrigley's famed scoreboard covering one wall, Cubs memorabilia, and a most-welcoming proprietor sporting a Cubs cap and a blue "Straight Outta Wrigley" jersey. At that hour, it was just the two of us, so we chatted about the Cubs, the bar, and kayaking. Then I was on my way. It was a wonderful bar and a wonderful break. A customer's review rang true: "Best lil bar in Iowa." What a country!

I took advantage of Mike Clark's hospitality once again as he invited me to stay at Kanu House on my way through St. Louis. We talked of canoes, kayaks, rivers, and paddlers. He mentioned a friend of his with whom he had been paddling, Janet Moreland. She was a world-class kayaker who had gained paddling notoriety by being the first woman to solo kayak both the Missouri and Mississippi rivers from source to sea. Big Muddy, Dolly the Mastiff, and Kanu House were becoming recurring players in my cross-country journeys.

Heading for Memphis, Tennessee, my Missouri waypoints included Ste. Genevieve, Cape Girardeau, and New Madrid. Although all three towns share the same Mississippi river town lineage, each of these gems offer their own distinct sparkle. I had previously paddled past Ste. Genevieve on an earlier trip, with my only memory being to be on the lookout for the French Connection, formally known as the Ste. Genevieve–Modoc ferry. Seventy miles south of St. Louis, I pulled off Highway 61 to take a quick tour. Founded in 1735 by French Canadian colonists, the town has not lost its French accent or beauty. I drove north along the levy to see the ferry boat moored on the river side of the town's massive floodgates. For lunch I discovered the Anvil Saloon and Restaurant. I learned that a restaurant had occupied the building since 1855. The historic bar came from an 1850s steamboat that traveled the Mississippi River. Ste. Genevieve was a historic, clean, friendly, and beautiful French-accented town that was well worth the stop.

Chester, Illinois, where I would be meeting up with John Ruskey's paddling troupe the following morning, was just twenty miles from Ste. Genevieve, but on the other side of the river. For logistical reasons I was first driving to Memphis so my vehicle would be waiting when I finally stepped out of the river.

After leaving Ste. Genevieve, I made a brief stop in Cape Girardeau. In geological terms, a cape is a high point of land that extends into a river, lake, or ocean. Cape Girardeau drew its name from a large promontory rock overlooking the Mississippi River. I learned not to bother looking for it because this natural feature was demolished during earlier railroad construction.

The Anvil Bar—Serving Rivermen for Over 150 years, Ste. Genevieve, Missouri

The town may not have had its namesake cape anymore, but it did flaunt a Mississippi River Tales Mural—an impressive panoramic river history that extends for several city blocks—as well as the Trail of Tears State Park and the sleek and shiny Bill Emerson Memorial Bridge, which connects Cape Girardeau to East Cape Girardeau.

One geographical phenomenon I had noticed in my travels along the Mississippi is that whenever a bridge spans two river cities, the city on the west side of the river generally is more developed and has the larger population, as seen with Cape Girardeau, Missouri (pop. 40,000), and East Cape Girardeau, Illinois (pop. 400). Other examples include Minneapolis, Minnesota (pop. 425,000), and St. Paul, Minnesota (pop. 304,000); Dubuque, Iowa (pop. 58,000), and East Dubuque, Illinois (pop. 1,600); and St. Louis, Missouri (pop. 302,000), and East St. Louis, Illinois (pop. 26,000).

One social studies theorem of this occurrence is that historically, as the new nation's population expanded westward, the Mississippi River, stretching the entire length of the country, loomed as a major hurdle to be crossed. St. Louis, Missouri, may be the best example, with its Gateway Arch symbolizing the "New Frontier." Once the westward expansion had crossed the river, there was a brand-new country waiting to be settled. The west side of the river was now the easternmost border of this new frontier. Colloquially, there was no looking back. One exception to the rule is the eastern city of New Orleans, Louisiana (pop. 390,000), and its western counterpart, Algiers, Louisiana (pop. 26,000). Lake Pontchartrain may be the contributing attraction for settlers staying on the east side of the river.

Just below Cape Girardeau are two Illinois river cities bearing Egyptian cities' names, Thebes and Cairo. Several other nearby Egyptian-named cities on the Illinois side of the river, Carmi, Karnak, Goshen, and Dongola, have earned the southern tip of Illinois the title of "Little Egypt." There are several versions of the origins of this Egyptian connection. A commonly cited tie to Egypt refers to the fertile soil of the River Nile's floodplain and the floodplain found in the wedge-shaped land between the Mississippi and Ohio rivers.

Leaving the Little Egypt area and heading toward Memphis, another Egyptian-named city, I stopped in New Madrid, with its Spanish-themed name. I learned the town was not named for any influx of Spanish immigrants but instead for an American Revolutionary War hero, George Morgan. In a self-serving manner, he named the town New Madrid to curry favor with the king of Spain and hopefully be rewarded with a land grant. What puts New Madrid, with the accent on "Mad," on the map is its earthquakes. Three large earthquakes, with magnitude measurements ranging between 7.2 and 8.2, occurred between 1811 and 1812. This was a quick stop on my drive south, but more time would be spent in New Madrid on the upcoming paddling section of this trip.

In true "the river connects us all" style, John had connected me with Billy Wilkerson in Memphis. Billy would put me up at his home; drive me and my kayak back to Chester, Illinois, to link up with the Rivergator Celebratory Expedition; and then deposit my vehicle on the Mud Island boat ramp in Memphis for when I exited the Mississippi. Billy also gave me a valuable tip. He said I could not go wrong stopping at Central BBQ for their slow-smoked, Memphis-style ribs.

I arrived in Memphis in the early evening and found the recommended ribs joint. It was easy to spot with the Saturday night crowd lined up around the building waiting to get in for their weekend feast. Billy's recommendation was well worth the wait, and after dining on ribs and mac and cheese, I headed to Billy's house.

We were two river men, meeting in the shadows of Graceland. We introduced ourselves and talked of our exploits on the Mississippi. After the day's travels, I quickly fell asleep in the comfort of Billy's spare room. It would be the last time sleeping indoors for the next two weeks.

The next morning, Billy and I retraced my route back to Popeye's hometown of Chester, Illinois. One cannot drive into Chester without learning that this is the birthplace of Elzie Crisler Segar, the cartoonist who created "Popeye the Sailor Man" and his cast of characters. In fact, the town has an annual Popeye festival. Being from St. Paul and therefore serving as the unofficial ambassador of my hometown's very own Charles M. Schulz, creator of Charlie Brown and all the Peanuts characters, I thought it was fitting that the river had linked these two iconic cartoon superstars.

Billy and I drove the 210 miles in just over three hours. My return kayak trip to Memphis would take thirteen days. As we crossed the Chester Highway Bridge from Missouri into Illinois, signs and statues of Popeye confirmed we were in Chester. We came to a fork in the road, and just to the north, on the banks of the Mississippi, sat the Menard Corrections Center, an Illinois State maximum security prison. The eerie juxtaposition of the free-flowing river and the caged mass of humanity was not missed.

We headed south to the Chester boat ramps. Once there, we noticed two voyager canoes coming under the bridge we had just crossed. The logistics had worked! The Rivergator Celebratory Expedition had arrived right on schedule. Mark Rivers guided *Grasshopper* and John Ruskey was helming *June Bug* to the shore. The teacher had arrived!

But would the student in his kayak be able to keep up with these huge voyager canoes? That fear had been in the back of my mind since I signed up for this adventure. The student was about to be tested.

The paddlers hit the shore; Billy and John caught up with each other as Big Muddy and I were reunited once again. The boat landing appeared more like a crowded bus stop. Some people were leaving the expedition at this point, and I was joining. It was a mix of boats, gear, people, and hugs. There were lots of introductions, with names that I would have to relearn in the days to come. John was leaving the expedition due to a family commitment but would be rejoining us in a few days downriver. Big Muddy would be pinch hitting for him.

On the boat landing, I struck up a conversation with one of the voyageurs and we started exchanging our paddling exploits. Days earlier, she had started the Rivergator Expedition with the others in St. Louis but was going to be jumping off now in Chester. She was a great conversationalist,

Hors d'oeuvres courtesy of Rivergator Celebratory Cruise, URM 0.0

and I discovered she was an even greater paddling adventurer. She talked of not just the Mississippi but also the Missouri rivers. She had kayaked both, from source to sea—alone! It was then I realized I had been talking with Big Muddy's friend Janet Moreland, a hall of famer in the kayaking world. It seemed like it was time to add a fifth president, this one a woman, to the Mount Rushmore of paddlers.

So much for the social amenities. The river was waiting! I recalled Laozi, the Chinese sage, from eight centuries earlier. This student was ready!

The moment called for handing the baton forward to a more current Chinese muse, Bruce Lee, as Longstreet's Li Tsung. "Be water, my friend."

From Peanuts to Popeye, my journey was exceeding expectations, and I had not yet touched the water. As I anticipated the freedom of the river, I thought of the 3,400 inmates confined to their seven-by-twelve-foot cells just a few blocks upriver. I stepped into the confines of my two-by-seventeen-foot plastic cell and escaped.

A Richie Havens soundtrack would have fit the occasion.

19

CELEBRATING *THE RIVERGATOR*

Spring 2017

What exactly is *The Rivergator*? The website offers this description:

> *The Rivergator* is a mile-by-mile paddler's guide written for canoeists, kayakers, stand-up-paddleboarders, and anyone else plying the waters of the Lower Mississippi River in human-powered craft . . . 1,155 miles from St. Louis to the Gulf of Mexico. The name Rivergator is adopted from the best-seller, *The Navigator*, first published in 1801 by Zadok Cramer, with the hope that Americans would rediscover their "wilderness within," the paddler's paradise created by the Middle Lower Mississippi River.[25]

To say *The Rivergator* is a paddler's guide is analogous to saying the Mississippi River is a body of water running through my hometown of St. Paul, Minnesota. Both statements are accurate but fall a little short in their description. Yes, the Mississippi River does run through St. Paul, but it is also the Father of Waters. It is an integral part of our country's history including first discovery days, expansion, and the Civil War. It is a life-sustaining artery for commerce, travel, and recreation. It has been the inspiration for books, songs, and poems. For centuries, couples have stopped to enjoy the moments and create memories along the banks of this majestic river. Old Man River, he just keeps rollin' along.

The Rivergator is not just a paddler's guide, it is the Gutenberg Bible of paddler's guides. History tells us it took Johannes Gutenberg twenty years to develop his new printing press. It took John Ruskey thirty years to create the most complete and detailed historically, geographically, and romantically written guide for all Mississippi mariners.

---

25. John Ruskey, *The Rivergator*, accessed September 4, 2022, https://www.rivergator.org.

The Ojibwe, launching their birchbark jiimaanan onto their "Great River" or misi-zibi, established the first paddling routes on this watery network and served as the earliest European explorers' premier paddling guides. From these early scouting reports evolved a vast assortment of path-finder aids for marine navigators including word-of-mouth advice, hand-drawn sketches, maps, "not-to-be-used-for-navigation" plastic place mats, sextants, local and state maps, and the super official, spiral-bound *USACE Mississippi River Navigation Charts* (weighing in at about five pounds each). And now John Ruskey's three decades of nose to the grindstone had presented us with *The Rivergator*.

Adhering to Heraclitus's adage from two and a half millennia earlier, "No man ever steps in the same river twice," this guide outlines the Mississippi during the four seasons and at high, low, and medium water levels. *The Rivergator*, with its gestation period of thirty years, leverages the expertise of scores of contributors including river guides, towboat pilots, river agency experts, biologists, ornithologists, historians, paddlers, and John Ruskey himself. This jewel is safely lodged in cyberspace, accessible with a few keystrokes, and available free of charge to all eager big river explorers. It is one thousand pages and about one million words, or a word for every paddle stroke.

Although mariners have many navigation options available, it was, in retrospect, an embarrassingly naive process for me to ramp up my own navigational learning curve. In my first experience kayaking, my son, Joe, and grandson, Earl, served as my guides. No navigation aids were needed as my two guides had completed the route just days earlier. The following day, I soloed the next stretch, six miles from Hidden Falls to Harriet Island near downtown St. Paul. No charts, guides, or maps were needed, as I had grown up here and knew where I would be putting in and taking out.

I had caught the fever to continue my kayaking and exploration of this big river, but I had no idea of the river's route below St. Paul. I decided to take my car and drive downriver looking for places to exit from my next journey. I drove past Newport, St. Paul Park, and Cottage Grove, all the way to Hastings. There is not one road that follows the river, so I had no idea how many river miles were in each segment between these small river towns. I also had no idea how fast I would be kayaking through this new territory. My first two days on the river had been eight and six miles, so I was planning a day trip of about the same length. Hastings at thirty miles was too far. After two advance exploratory car trips of two hours each, I discovered there was a place seven miles downriver where a person could exit the river under the I-494 bridge near South St. Paul. I had found a spot, but it had been a very time-consuming process.

Shortly after my "road trip" exercise in scouting out entry and exit points on the river, a friend of mine, who worked with the USACE, mentioned the agency publishes a mariner's navigation book that provides detailed navigation charts of the Upper Mississippi from the Twin Cities to Cairo, Illinois. It also publishes one for the Lower Mississippi. I learned bound copies were for sale to the public, and there was also public access to the charts online at no cost. The USACE charts begin with the Twin Cities but do not cover any of the five hundred river miles north of the Twin Cities. I discovered that the Minnesota Department of Natural Resources published nine separate pamphlets covering the first 525 miles of the river, from Lake Itasca to Hastings, Minnesota. These proved to be most valuable as they included charts of the river, portages, campsites, and a wealth of historical and geographical information for each section covered.

I discovered that navigation charts and paddling guides, like the river itself, were appreciated more fully once I jumped in and started using them. From my experience, *The Rivergator* had proven itself to be one of the brightest jewels in the crown of paddling guides. It deserves to be celebrated, and as such, I was humbled to be part of the Rivergator Celebratory Expedition.

We pushed off from the Chester boat landing in two vessels: one thirty-foot, hand-built, cypress-strip voyageur canoe, *June Bug*, powered by eight voyageurs and loaded above the gunnels with hundreds of pounds of gear and supplies; and one orange kayak powered by a single paddler who was spotting the other crew members somewhere between twenty-five to fifty years in age. The original expedition party might have been thinking, "Will the graybeard be able to keep up?" They *might* have been thinking that, but I *knew* I was thinking that. My anxiety was not rooted in how I would do over the scheduled fortnight, it was about how the next fifteen minutes were going to play out. The answer would be revealed in the time-proven, left-right-left-right formula.

Form follows function. I focused on my paddler's form and rhythm. I was not supposed to be focusing on the basics. At this stage of my game, a natural fluid motion was required, along with positive self-talk. Don't forget to breathe. Settle down. They are still in sight.

I had previously paddled with Big Muddy, who was now skippering *June Bug*, when we had run the gauntlet through the deadly St. Louis harbor last year. That had been a successful passage, except for the white-knuckle aspect. With a few more river miles under my skirt, my fears were tailing off in my wake. Maybe this was going to work out.

Our first leg from Chester to Rockwood Island was a short one at eight miles. I had kept up with the group and we had some time to set up our tents and get acquainted over a great shore supper. To date, my on-the-river meals typically involved pouring boiling water into a pouch of freeze-dried pasta or some other bland concoction. I could get used to the alternate reality of a full meal, freshly prepared over the cutting board and campfire. As the sun went down, I spent some time sitting by the glowing embers with Big Muddy and Andy McLean, who had ventured all the way from New Zealand. Andy had been on a river paddle before and was drawn to the expedition to experience a bigger river challenge. He also wanted to peel some layers back on the big what-do-I-want-to-do-with-my-life onion. Having had a full day, my tent and sleeping bag were welcome on this peaceful first night.

"Time to pack up. We have some weather coming in," senior guide Mark "River" Peoples said, rousing the troops with an early awakening. Weather coming in? We had some weather at that moment. I broke down my tent and repacked my gear into my kayak in the early morning rain. Once my tent was stowed, a couple invited me to squeeze in with them under a small, makeshift shelter created by the massive root structure of a fallen tree.

I soon learned this was not just any port in a storm. I had hit a home-run with this refuge. John and LaNae Abnet were a couple from Indiana who had shared many world-class adventures together including the Appalachian Mountains, the Arctic, and the Canadian wilderness. They were experienced paddlers too. They had previously paddled 1,600 miles from the source of the Wabash River, down the Ohio River, and down the Mississippi River to the Gulf of Mexico. LaNae published a book, *Paddling Edna*, about their experience. As we swapped stories, John seemed curious about my career choice of leaving the stability of corporate life twenty-five years ago to take a stab at an entrepreneurial approach to earning a living. Riding out the early morning thunderstorm, I wasn't expecting to be drawn back to the world of human resources, business, sales, and marketing, but we had an interesting chat. I mentioned that I didn't realize how much I did not like having a boss until I didn't have one. John admitted to having a keen interest in making the same leap toward independence. A few months after our trip concluded, John informed me that he had finally jumped into the risky world of entrepreneurial consultancy—and he was liking it!

We pushed off and headed toward Grand Tower. I had some personal history on this leg. Two years earlier, I had soloed the thirty river miles from Chester to today's destination, just across from Tower Rock. As mentioned in a previous chapter, this stretch of the river has been well chronicled, the first reference being the earliest European inhabitants who, as river pirates, used Tower Rock as an ambush site for their unsuspecting prey. Also Meriwether Lewis—on his Corps of Discovery Expedition— mentions this spot in his journals, stating that rivermen who passed the rock would celebrate in a way similar to sailors crossing the equator, by raising a drink of spirits.

Pirates. Lewis and Clark. Was that the hand of history helping guide my kayak through these timeless waters? Nope. It was just me pushing my paddle, stroke by stroke, doing my best to keep up with the voyageurs. On the Missouri side of the river, we finally spotted the six-story tall monolith, Tower Rock, launching itself from the rushing waters. We pulled ashore across the river on a nice sandy beachhead just below Devil's Backbone campground, near Grand Tower.

We had the campground all to ourselves. Having arrived early in the day gave us the opportunity to settle in and spend the afternoon under the shelter of a spacious concrete pavilion. Out of the rain, we dried out our tents and clothes and were able to recharge our batteries, both literally and metaphorically. The time on dry land also offered the opportunity to learn more about my fellow expeditioners.

The crew members were drawn from points scattered around the globe. Our senior guide, Mark "River" Peoples, was based out of Clarksdale, Mississippi. A former pro football player with the New York Giants, he was our expedition's strongman. If there was a boat to be pulled ashore or a tree trunk moved, he was our guy. Also stationed with the Quapaw Canoe Company in Clarksdale was guide Lena von Machui, a German ex-pat. She greeted me with, "You're from Minnesota. I bet you know how to play cribbage." She had a board and had been looking for someone to play. I hadn't realized that cribbage was a regional thing. We were able to enjoy "pegging away" the time at our various campsites.

The other guides were paddlers I knew: Big Muddy and John Ruskey himself. John would be rendezvousing with us downriver. John, or "Driftwood," grew up in the shadows of the Colorado Rockies and then was introduced to music and the river. He originally came to Mississippi for the Delta Blues scene, but he stayed for the Mississippi mud.

Our Kiwi adventurer, Andy McLean, was exploring life choices and career options. I suggested that if he chose to work in the United States, his charming accent should boost his salary by an extra $15K. My estimate was not based on any human resource algorithm but merely a number I tossed out. He mentioned the concept to the group, and there was general agreement that his accent would buy him more toys on this side of the ocean.

My tree-trunk shelter partners, John and LaNae Abnet, were true kayakers and delightful traveling mates. We talked about boats, adventures, and careers. Their caring and sharing attitudes were infectious.

The early invitations for the Rivergator Celebratory Expedition included a call for paddlers who could adequately chronicle the significance of this adventure, specifically writers and videographers. The two youngest members of our expedition met the requirements. Boyce Upholt, originally from Connecticut with a stop-off in South Dakota, and based out of New Orleans, was an explorer and an award-winning writer. His published stories, often with a focus on Southern life, have appeared in a variety of upscale publications including *TIME*, *The Atlantic*, and the Sierra Club's magazine, *Sierra*. He was currently working on a book about the Mississippi River.

Chris "Magique" Battaglia, another New Englander from Portland, Maine, was the expedition's videographer. As our group was drying out and recharging batteries, I got to meet Magique as he checked various components of his impressive inventory of cameras, computers, and mics. His trove of technology was surpassed only by his personality. Completely outfitted by Patagonia, a client company of his, he was an outgoing, funny, witty, intelligent, and adventurous team member.

Two years earlier, I had camped for a night at this same location by myself. Now there were nine of us, and we were heading into new territory. As we exchanged stories, I felt welcomed. I did get invitations, should I need a kayak paddling break, to trade places and experience the ride in a voyageur canoe. At first it sounded like a good insurance plan, but as I pondered the invite, something hit me. It surprised me, but I realized it had become important for me to paddle this entire river in my own kayak.

Back on the river, heading toward Cape Girardeau, we encountered some barge traffic. I listened in to discussions on my marine radio between the tow captain and our captain, Big Muddy. A tow was coming downriver and was going to flank around a bend in the river. The skipper was concerned about our presence and our awareness of the space he would be covering in his flanking turn. I learned it is much more challenging for a skipper to guide a tow downriver than upriver. Shortly after the radio conversation and the ensuing maneuvers, we pulled ashore for a quick break. Within minutes, a small river craft coming upriver approached us. The small boat was from the tow and the riverman came ashore and cautioned me about my kayak. He mentioned a craft my size could be impossible to see from the tow captain's pilothouse, and that my boat should be equipped with special reflective tape. He then gave me two sheets of Coast Guard–approved reflective material, one red and one green, to apply to my kayak. He mentioned the towboat's lights would be able to see me much better with these sheets attached. Although the radio conversations had been quite terse on the river, I was impressed with the towboat crew's genuine concern about our safety on the river.

I was curious about the flanking process, which I had encountered numerous times on my journey, so I relied on my cell phone for some quick answers.

> In a turn, the inward hydrodynamic force produced by the drift angle is applied at a point well below the waterline. The outward centrifugal force is applied at the center of gravity, usually located at or above the waterline. This couple acts to heel the ship outward to an angle at which it is balanced by the righting moment resulting from the transverse metacentric stability.[26]

I wondered how Lewis and Clark's Corps of Discovery made it without cell phones. Were they aware of "the transverse metacentric stability?"

A few hours later, we stopped at Island 28 for a shore lunch. The island offered a sprawling sand beach that bordered some woods. Upon arriving at a beach, it was becoming my custom to take a walk to give my legs a chance to recover from the confines of the kayak. On this walk I discovered, partially buried in the sand, a bony skull of a toothy animal. I brought the treasure back to camp and it was confirmed that it was the skull of a goat. Chris Battaglia was enamored with my find and asked if he could have one of its teeth. I countered by giving him the entire skull—teeth and all. He promptly found a stick with which he fashioned a prop for mounting the head on a pike, suitable for photos. The concept of a "goat in a boat" was put into play. Chris would continue the ritual by mounting the skull on a pike in future campsites established downriver. Two guys and a goat's head. Pure fun. The idiom "once a man, twice a boy" rang true.

Mile Zero! That evening we pulled ashore on the right descending bank at mile 0.0 as indicated in the *USACE Upper Mississippi River Navigation Charts*. There was a sense of accomplishment in knowing the Upper Mississippi was above us. USACE Upper Mississippi River charts begin at

---

26. "Naval Architecture—Maneuverability," *Britannica*, accessed September 5, 2022, https://www.britannica.com/technology/naval-architecture/Maneuverability.

mile 865.0 in Minneapolis. Because USACE charts are designated as navigation charts, and there is no commercial navigation above the Twin Cities, the approximately five hundred river miles north of the Twin Cities to the headwaters in Itasca is literally "off the charts."

The Rivergator serves as a paddler's guide from St. Louis to the Gulf, and the *USACE Lower Mississippi River Navigation Charts* provide a nice navigational assist. Where the Army Corps' upper charts end, the lower charts begin, at mile 958.8. Poet Robert Frost's words sum up the situation, "And miles to go. . . ."

Three states (Illinois, Kentucky, and Missouri) border the spot where the mouth of the Ohio River unleashes a thousand miles of river into the Mississippi, doubling the Mississippi's power as it flows toward the Gulf. We had traveled through Illinois's Little Egypt as we passed the village of Thebes, and now were just downriver from Cairo (pronounced KAIR-oh). The Cairo, Illinois, peninsula is tucked between Missouri and Kentucky and was first visited in 1660 by Father Louis Hennepin, the missionary priest, along with early French explorers. As he described the area, "the banks of the river are so muddy and so full of rushes and reeds, that we had much to do to find a place to go ashore."[27]

Sunset near confluence of Mississippi and Ohio rivers

27. "Cairo, Illinois," *Angelfire*, accessed August 25, 2022, https://www.angelfire.com/wi/wisconsin42nd/cairo.html.

Because March was going out like a lion, the expedition, after battling hours of unrelenting strong winds, settled in for two days of turf on our "surf 'n' turf" tour. When on the water, for good or bad, the eight other adventurers, bound by their paddler's position in their voyageur canoe, were never out of earshot of each other. Conversely, I was always on my own, in my seventeen-foot island, paddling to keep up. This two-day respite on shore provided me with some in-person interaction with the others. My human resources background morphed into humor resources. It was a welcome shift.

I was impressed by the trip's two chroniclers, and the dedication to their craft, or better described, their art. These were artists at work. As part of Battaglia's video documentary, he was conducting interviews with select members. No "point and shoot" internet entries, these were high-tech, professional productions. I was honored to be recruited as the boom operator when "Magique" interviewed Big Muddy. I was charged with capturing every word of his watery wisdom.

Paddling the Mississippi can at times feel like a forced march, even if it is self-imposed. It's hard work. Napoleon Bonaparte is credited with the aphorism, "An army marches on its belly." It is fitting. Having traveled solo

March going out like a lion, March 30, 2017, atop levee at UMR 0.0

for much of the river, often sporking some boiled mixture out of a tinfoil food bag or crawling exhausted into my sleeping bag with a candy bar for supper, I knew what Napoleon meant.

To the contrary, on this expedition the meals were a definite high-light. Lena von Machui and Mark "River" Peoples always made sure we were ready for our next march. Their meals, all of them, provided a special time for us, whether it was to stoke us for the upcoming miles or to reward us for the miles behind us. A day on the river cannot end any better than with a full meal, enjoyed with fellow marchers in the flickering light of the "kitchen" campfire.

The time off the river also gave us opportunities to explore the land. I went on several walks, slogging across the muddy batture (that land be-tween the river and the levee) to see the countryside on the other side of the levee. On the Upper Mississippi, a paddler is always in touch with the passing landscape and all the river towns and cities. The Lower Mississippi, however, is hemmed in by a thousand miles of levees, keeping civiliza-tion hidden behind the massive monument to man's attempt at controlling nature. From atop the levee, I was able to take in an expansive view of the countryside, with the farmers' fields showing the earliest evidence of spring's planting efforts. On one of these walks, I came across a snake that had made a bed out of a lone plastic bag caught in some grass. It wasn't a huge snake, but the out-of-context plastic bag as the snake's nest found a spot in my expedition memories.

After two days of shore leave, we were back on the river, which was now emboldened and doubled in size with the Ohio crowding in. There was more paddling, whirlpools, eddies, and boils, the latter of which I had built up a sizeable fear about. Jonathan Raban, in *Old Glory, A Voy-age Down the Mississippi*, is partly responsible for cultivating these riverine anxieties. On boils, he writes:

> There were sharp rips and creases in the current now, as if the Missis-sippi were trying to tear itself apart; but the most scary change was the succession of great waxy boils. I could see them coming from a long way off. Most of the river was lightly puckered by the wind, but there were patches of what looked like dead-calm water: circular in shape, a hundred yards or so across. I took them for quiet millponds, good place to light a pipe or unscrew the cap of a thermos flask. Delighted to find that the Mississippi now afforded such convenient picnic spots, I drove straight for one. As I hit its edge, the boat slewed sideways and I was caught on the rim of a spinning centrifuge. I had mistaken it for calm

Snake resting on a plastic bag near Cairo, Illinois, at UMR 0.0

water because its motion was so violent that no wind could disturb it. I could see the cap of the boil faraway in the middle, a clear eighteen inches higher than the rest of the river. From this raised point, the water was spilling around and down the convex face, disappearing deep into a crack in which my boat (a 16-foot motorboat) was caught. Running the engine at full speed, I yanked myself out easily enough; but I had felt the river trying to suck me under, boat and all, and I was tense with fright. I grounded in a sandbar and scrabbled for tobacco and Valium. . . . I sized up the Mississippi as an enemy. It was dappled with large whorls of treacherously smooth water.[28]

The boils were mostly manageable if you saw them coming. The trick was being alert, always. Paddling is an iterative process, and at times could gnaw away at the required alertness.

---

28. Jonathan Raban, *Old Glory, A Voyage Down the Mississippi* (New York: Simon & Schuster, 1981), 276.

I had invented a game to break up the paddling monotony on an earlier trip. You could only play it when approaching a river bridge with some traffic. As a truck crosses a bridge, find the slice of daylight shining between the cab and the trailer. Now follow that slice of light until another truck approaches from the other direction. The trick is when the two trucks pass each other, catch that instant when the light shines through that narrow space between both trucks. It's all in the anticipation. I attempted to share this game of catching the light with the other members of the expedition but found few takers.

Fifty miles downriver from Cairo, the expedition turned to starboard at LMR 900.0, and we paddled north for the next ten miles. Only at the headwaters at Lake Itasca is there another stretch where the river heads north for an extended length. The first sixty-eight miles of the Mississippi heads north by northeast until veering south at Stump Lake en route to splitting the country from north to south. This northerly route that our group had just encountered was Bessie's Bend. It is also known as Kentucky Bend, New Madrid Bend, or Kentucky's Bubbleland. It's a twenty-mile horse collar that has a land connection at its base of just one mile. It is the longest meander loop on the river.

At the northerly top of this loop is New Madrid. The city's 1812 earthquakes were the most powerful to ever hit this continent east of the Rockies; the force was felt as far away as the White House. The quakes caused the Mississippi to flow backward for a stretch, creating the anomaly of Bessie's Bend.

Two hundred years after all the geological excitement, we pulled our boats ashore in a much calmer time. As we arrived, a lone fisherman, just heading out in his johnboat, pulled over and chatted for a few moments. "There's a grocery store in town where you can get any food or supplies you might need. My truck is parked at the dock about two blocks downriver. The keys are on the floor so help yourself. I'll be gone fishing for a couple hours." He headed his boat upriver and then circled back toward us. As he got closer, he said, "There is a restaurant in town. I've just called them and told them your breakfast tomorrow morning is on me."

We would be camping at New Madrid, so we had an afternoon and evening of shore leave. The New Madrid Historical Museum was nearby and was worth a visit. It promoted two main features of the area: the New Madrid earthquakes of 1812 and the American Civil War in 1862. The museum provided information on the area's "Battle at Island No. 10," and offered, "the Union forces at New Madrid were digging a canal across the neck of land east of the town to bypass Island No. 10."

Seeing the reference to Union soldiers digging a canal, I recalled that on my drive south to Chester, Illinois, to begin this segment, I had listened to an audiobook of James McPherson's Pulitzer Prize–winning *Battle Cry of Freedom*. In one section McPherson describes, "Midwestern farm boys who had joined the army to fight rebels found themselves dredging tons of mud and sawing off trees eight feet under water to clear a channel for gunboats and transports."[29]

It was the "sawing off trees eight feet underwater" that puzzled me. How does one in 1862 go about sawing off a tree eight feet under water? On the road I had pondered the question for quite some time before filing it as another unsolved riddle. Meanwhile, outside the Historical Museum was a modest memorial to the Civil War and, standing right in front of me, was a tall, jerry-rigged, angles askew contraption. It was a wooden combination of tripod and pendulum. Upon closer inspection I had found the answer to my question. It was a Union saw used to cut off trees eight feet under water. Riddle solved!

Union Army saw used to cut underwater trees found in New Madrid Civil War memorial park

---

29. James McPherson, *Battle Cry of Freedom: The Civil War Era* (New York: Oxford University Press, 1988), 1,524.

T. S. Eliot's "April is the cruelest month . . . ," a line from *The Waste-land*, could have described some of the paddling conditions we were experiencing. Due to the windy weather forecast, we passed on the hospitable fisherman's offer of a breakfast in town, and we got an early start on the river. With Missouri on our right descending bank and an exclave of Kentucky trapped in the middle of Bessie's Bend, or Bubbleland, on our left descending bank we headed toward Caruthersville, Missouri, forty miles downriver. Seven miles into our day's paddle, we exited Bessie's Bend and the Kentucky side of the river became Tennessee.

Fighting a windy and rough river we finally landed in Caruthersville. The town is in Missouri's southeastern tip, the Bootheel, in Pemiscot County, mentioned only because Pemiscot is from the Fox Indian dialect word pem-eskaw, meaning liquid mud. It fits.

We found a convenient shelter in a nearby pavilion where we could spread out and dry out. As our batteries were recharging, we were greeted by a local church group who heard of our arrival and brought us a healthy assortment of homemade pastries, cakes, and pies. We were also greeted by several other townspeople who wanted to wish the newly arrived river travelers a warm welcome and a safe journey. By coincidence, one of the men who greeted us was an Abe Lincoln look-a-like, hat and all, and the other could have passed for Willie Nelson. These double doppelgangers had not come together, but both enjoyed their celebrity ambassador status. After some hard paddling it was a fun afternoon.

Later, as scheduled, the expedition's creator, John Ruskey, rejoined our party with another voyageur canoe, *Grasshopper*, and an enthusiastic crew to fill it, including John's sister, Abby Ruskey, all the way from Olympia, Washington. Although the river conditions were harsh, there was still plenty of daylight left so our eager and enhanced expedition pushed off into the nasty chop for our next leg.

The Mississippi, beefed up with the Missouri and Ohio additives, was a tough river. Not since the swollen Missouri joined the Mississippi above St. Louis had I experienced four-foot, bow-drowning waves, now accompanied by a tempestuous, howling wind. The big, thirty-foot voyageur canoes loaded with a ton of crew and supplies seemed to be keeping a steady line through the challenging waters. I, at the mercy of the river, had my hands full keeping the big boats in sight.

I thought I was doing an acceptable job hanging in there, but there was another perspective. Boyce Upholt later would describe this moment in an article he had published in *Sierra* magazine, "Paddling the Lower Mississippi Ain't a Huck Finn Journey Anymore." His description:

We were waiting for Ruskey, who arrived that afternoon with a van full of fresh paddlers. They were all eager, so despite the wind, we launched again—two canoes and Dennis, a kayaker, who soon struggled to follow our path in the choppy water. When he fell out of shouting distance, caught in the channel with the tows, we knew we had to stop.[30]

It was nice to get mentioned in a cool magazine, but I now have a slice of notoriety as the "struggling kayaker" who couldn't keep up. The price of fame.

"Dennis, go to shore!" was the message on my marine radio. It was a welcomed command. It took a while to ferry over toward the Missouri shoreline and reconnect with the rest of the expedition as we searched for a suitable campsite. Eleven miles downriver from Caruthersville, the I-155 bridge spanned the river from Missouri to Tennessee. There was a suitable spot for camping, but it required one to navigate past the onrushing bridge abutments and circle back upstream through a rocky patch in the raging river. Almost home, I got caught sideways in a powerful eddy and was going over.

Over the last couple of winters, I had spent several Sunday mornings in an indoor pool with twenty paddlers from the Inland Sea Kayakers Club. We all worked on paddling techniques, and most of the class also worked on various kayak rolls. Having tried and abandoned my chances to acquire a rolling technique, I spent my time in the pool working on self-rescue, braces, and unassisted reentries should my braces fail.

A self-rescue is self-explanatory; a brace is a paddling maneuver in which one—on the way to capsizing—saves oneself by instinctively and aggressively "spanking" the water with the paddle held broadside. The trick is to hold the paddle broadside because if you don't, you run the risk of the paddle just slicing into the water and, in effect, accelerating your fate. In a pool, that misstep leads to changing from practicing braces to practicing self-rescues. These practice sessions, paddling an empty kayak with plenty of help nearby, is one thing. Being in a swollen river, with a fully loaded kayak, is a different picture.

"Oh, shit!" I gasped. My fears said, "I'm in the river!"

But then the hours spent on those wintery Sunday mornings kicked in. At the last instant, the brace was textbook. I righted the ship and headed for home. No self-rescue required. I had never been happier to step onto dry land at the campsite.

---

30. Boyce Upholt, "Paddling the Lower Mississippi Ain't a Huck Finn Journey Anymore," *Sierra*, June 28, 2018, https://www.sierraclub.org/sierra/2018-4-july-august/feature/paddling -lower-mississippi-aint-huck-finn-journey-anymore.

We were able to settle in at this new campsite for a couple days. It gave us time to meet the new crew, explore the land, and pursue our varied personal interests. "Magique" Battaglia planted his prized goat-skull-on-a-stick in a place of prominence. Maybe to ward off evil spirits? He then occupied himself with an impressive assortment of audio and video technology. Boyce, absolutely dedicated to his authorly craft, displayed his nonstop commitment as the expedition's chronicler. Ruskey, amid his leadership duties, painted his stylized interpretations of the ever-changing land and waterscapes—a turtle yesterday, today the I-155 bridge. I felt his paintings never diminished his position as our chief scout and leader but actually enhanced his role. Abby Ruskey, an environment and climate educator and consultant, showed the Ruskey artistic bent by creating a "sticks and stones" landscape to grace her personal campsite. It was beauty in and from the wilderness. As we welcomed a different pace of time off the river, an intermittent musical score was provided by Ruskey and Battaglia trading licks on John's guitar.

Chris "Magique" Battaglia posing with goat skull totem at UMR 0.0

John Ruskey watercolor painting of I-155 bridge at LMR 838.0

John Ruskey with guitar just downriver from Caruthersville, Missouri

The group also practiced a few almost daily rituals, one of which included having one member read aloud to the group a passage from our adopted bible, Mark Twain's *Life on the Mississippi*. As my turn came, I grabbed a few lines from chapter 1 describing what happened after Hernando De Soto's 1542 discovery of the river.

> De Soto merely glimpsed the river, then died and was buried in it by his priests and soldiers.
>   The Mississippi was left unvisited by whites during a term of years which seems incredible in our energetic days. One may "sense" the interval to his mind after a fashion, by dividing it up in this way: after De Soto glimpsed the river, a fraction short of a quarter century elapsed, and then Shakespeare was born; lived a trifle more than half a century, then died; and when he had been in his grave considerably more than half a century, the second white man saw the Mississippi. In our day we don't allow a hundred thirty years to elapse between glimpses of a marvel.[31]

During our second night at this campsite, I was awakened early by nonstop howling. This time it was not the ubiquitous coyotes serenading through the night. It was the wind. It seemed that my now-awakened body was the only thing keeping my tent in place. As I lay there in the dark, wondering if the wind would ever release us, I got surprised. Mark "Rivers," the stocky former New York Giants football player, was walking from tent to tent announcing we had to pack up early because of the weather. I guess it was possible to venture out on this dark, gusty morning.

We broke camp in the dark and were on the river at first light. As the two voyageur canoes and I, in my kayak, pulled away from the shore, we rafted together for a new ritual. To start the day's journey, Abby led us in a smudging ceremony. At the time, I didn't know what smudging was and thought maybe the new paddlers were into smoking weed. I quickly learned that smudging, originating in native cultures, refers to the practice of burning herbal material for spiritual, ceremonial, or practical purposes. This rookie found it to be a new and interesting process.

We were off. With "Magique's" apotropaic goat skull totem, and Abby's evil-averting fumes, we were a prepared and protected group of explorers. And it was good that we were, because our day on the river would be a long one. It would be the longest of all my days on the river. We paddled from first light to dusk. Magique's bony goat head and Abby's smoking herbs delivered us safely to Sunrise Towhead, exactly sixty-two

---

31. Mark Twain, *Life on the Mississippi* (New York: Barnes & Noble, Inc., 2010), 4–5.

Sunrise at Sunrise Towhead, LMR 732.0

river miles from our starting point. A sixty-two-mile day! I think it's even more impressive to record it as one hundred kilometers.

The following day, we covered twenty-two choppy, windy river miles and camped at LMR 754.0, just above the Shelby Forest, and just twenty miles upriver from my soon-to-be exit point, Memphis, Tennessee. This would be the last time I would share a campsite with the expedition.

I pulled my kayak up on the shore and, for safe measure, attached a rope from my boat to a nearby tree. I left my PFD and neoprene paddling pants in the boat to dry off. Looking back, this may have been the cause of what soon became a problem. I believe the scent of my body, lingering in the pants and PFD, had put out a signal to all the ants nearby: permission to come aboard! The problem was small, but there were many of these small problems. As can be imagined in a Disney cartoon, complete with marching music, this parade of ants was using the rope as a boarding ramp to my boat. Thousands, yes, thousands of ants had infested my kayak, my PFD, and my paddling pants. I don't know if they were fire ants, but they looked mean, and they were everywhere. It was fortunate that I spotted them when I did because the ant-removal process took a good part of an afternoon dousing, muttering, and rinsing the pests from my boat and gear. I was imagining the scene the following morning had I not discovered the

Tow heading into choppy river at LMR 754.0

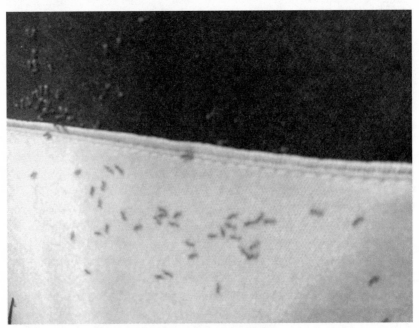

Ants swarming on personal flotation device at LMR 754.0

ants when I did. Their numbers would have multiplied, and I would have been stuck with a very antsy problem as twelve ready-to-shove-off paddlers waited for the one guy in a kayak. Crisis averted.

The extreme winds we had been facing in the previous days had abated and we enjoyed paddling on a friendly river down the home stretch. Chris Battaglia was filming, and I was a featured subject for a few paddle strokes. I was careful to heed our videographer's directive, "Don't break the fourth wall."

I would be the only one leaving our group when we arrived in Memphis, but the expedition would be adding more paddlers and more voyager canoes when we reached that point. They would have 730 miles left before reaching their final destination at Head of Passes at mile "0."

As we approached Memphis, we could see the glassy Bass Pro Shops Pyramid, formerly known as the Great American Pyramid. At 321 feet tall, some refer to this as the tenth tallest pyramid in the world. Paddling around the final bend, we spotted the iconic M-shaped Hernando De Soto Bridge. As we approached Mud Island, I was entering familiar territory. Mud Island is where Adam Elliott and I launched our 150-mile river trip from Memphis to Rosedale, Mississippi, the previous fall.

As we approached the large concrete boat ramp, the newcomers assisted in pulling us ashore. Billy Wilkerson, my Memphis host and shuttle driver, had deposited my vehicle on the ramp, ready to go. Because it was early afternoon, I had asked our expedition's excellent chef, Mark "Rivers," about lunch recommendations in Memphis. He steered me to Gus's Chicken.

The boat ramp was a beehive with introductions, boats being loaded, my kayak getting strapped to my vehicle, and orientation for the new arrivals. There were goodbyes and hugs from my paddling mates. John Ruskey fashioned a brief goodbye ceremony for me that included the presentation of a Rivergator applique for my kayak and a book, *I Am Coyote: Readings for the Wild*, by Jay Schoenberger. To my pleasure, John had inscribed the first page:

Gator Dennis,

To a fine paddler and river rat. Thanks for helping us break in the Rivergator!

Many Blessings, John

John Ruskey and I said our goodbyes. Laozi, the Chinese sage with his ancient wisdom, had captured both ends of our trip with his words, "When the student is ready the teacher will appear. When the student is truly ready the teacher will disappear."

As the expanded group of Rivergators prepared for the river, I headed into town. Within fifteen minutes, I was seated at a table with a crowd of other patrons at Gus's World Famous Fried Chicken in the heart of Memphis.

The fried chicken came close to the self-proclamations, but the news blaring from Gus's wall-mounted TVs was a rude awakening. I was surprised by the shock of my reentry into civilization. I did not realize how much I didn't miss hearing about the president, Congress, the Dow Jones, wheat futures, blah, blah, blah. Welcome back.

I made it about 150 miles into my eight-hundred-mile road trip before the day's activities finally caught up with me. I found a nondescript motel and called it a day. Settling in, I opened the book John had given me, *I Am Coyote*. It was an anthology of thirty-some wilderness writings from a worldwide, blue-ribbon panel: Albert Camus, Henry David Longfellow, Herman Melville, Mark Twain, Jack Kerouac, Meriweather Lewis and William Clark, Theodore Roosevelt, and John Ruskey himself. Before I got to Ruskey's entry, I noticed on the second page that the other expedition members had also signed the book. My cribbage-playing mate's comments provided the perfect recap of our wilderness adventure: "Still can't believe you're unbeatable. Fifteen for two, and knobs is three. You're awesome!!" Lena.

In *I Am Coyote*, John Ruskey's chapter, "The Wilderness," begins:

> The wilderness is the window of our souls, and water our smoothest passage through. Rivers were our first highways, our first newspapers. They were our original world wide web because they connected people far and near.[32]

On the road back to St. Paul, I mulled over John's words. I thought of the past two weeks and what the three hundred river miles and the dots on the globe represented in the huddles by those riverside campfires. We were from Germany, New Zealand, Maine, Connecticut, Colorado, Washington, Indiana, Missouri, Mississippi, and the Mississippi's headwaters state, Minnesota. Far and near, we were all connected. We were explorers, exploring the wilderness of the river and the meanderings of our human condition. I am a river man . . . oops, I Am Coyote!

---

32. Jay Schoenberger, *I Am Coyote—Readings for the Wild* (San Francisco: Kimbrough Knight Publishing, 2014), 142.

20

TAKE THE LAST TRAIN TO . . .

Fall 2017

It had been six months since I stepped out of my kayak and off the Mississippi River at Mud Island in Memphis, Tennessee. I had not dipped my paddle in the Mississippi in that time. My summer paddling had been limited to a few local lakes for a couple of hours at a time. Although my golf addiction had resumed its role as front runner during this season, it had not limited my ability to make paddling plans. The section-by-section approach I had been taking to explore each mile of the Mississippi River provided me with ample time between trips for researching, planning, and anticipating the remaining sections. My route down the river was not always a north-to-south journey but more of a hopscotch approach dependent upon a few variables including weather, river levels, guide availability, logistical support, and personal whims.

My southern guide, Adam Elliott, and I had already covered the stretch from Vicksburg, past Natchez, to the ORCS near Angola Prison. My Rivergator Celebratory Expedition experience in the spring had focused my interest in following this magical, watery ribbon all the way to the southern edge of our continent. I had three big bites left: Burlington, Iowa, to Clarksville, Missouri (135 river miles); Rosedale, Mississippi, to Vicksburg, Mississippi (155 river miles); and finally from the ORCS in Louisiana to Mile Zero (305 river miles), one hundred miles below New Orleans, Louisana. With just under six hundred river miles left, I could still cross the finish line this year.

I would solo paddle the first leg from Burlington, Iowa, to Clarksville, Missouri. It wasn't a hard sell to enlist Adam for the final two legs. My calendar, the weather, river levels, and logistical support were all falling nicely into place. The anticipation was palpable.

It was the middle of October, and with a connection from Big Muddy, I was shuttled to Burlington, Iowa, while my vehicle would be delivered 135 river miles downriver to my planned exit point in Clarksville, Missouri. I was dropped off with my kayak, gear, and four days' supplies at the boat ramp in the old railroad town of Burlington. It was late afternoon and my plan was to load my kayak, push off, and paddle through the remaining hours of daylight before finding a campsite miles downriver.

The "remaining hours of daylight" quickly became an issue. Rough, dark weather was approaching that eliminated any hours of daylight at all, which scrapped my plans for getting on the river. The rest of the day and evening turned into a violent thunder and lightning storm. The nonstop torrents of rain ruled out setting up camp at the boat ramp. I was under a nearby bridge, soaked to my skin, and homeless. A couple drove by and kindly inquired about my safety. Later on, another car stopped and offered a ride to the nearest motel several miles away. I quickly grabbed a small bag with my phone, marine radio, and wallet, leaving my kayak and everything else at the mercy of the storm at the boat ramp.

The boat ramp I was leaving was the same one that I had used on an earlier trip to Burlington. I recalled from my previous trip that some towns-people had warned me a paddler making his way down the river had his canoe stolen from this very ramp. Now on this trip, on this very afternoon, another local had mentioned that just a few days ago, another paddler had his boat stolen from this ramp. Over the dozen years of my trips down the entire Mississippi River, I had heard of only two boat thefts, and they both occurred at the ramp where I was now leaving my kayak, with all my gear, unguarded for the night. My anticipation for a great river trip was shifting toward anxiety. Would I ever get dried out? Would I ever see my kayak again?

I was deposited at a half-star motel in the still-pouring rain. The check-in process was quick. I slipped fifty dollars cash under what appeared to be a bulletproof, bank-style glass window. This was not a "we'll leave the light on for you" experience. Once in the room, I was met with rather questionable décor. Crudely scribbled on a mirror by previous guests were two shuddery, gargoyle-esque faces. For an extra nice touch, next to the graffiti art was a broken headboard with a trashy trifecta scrawled in bubble-gum pink nail polish: "pussy-$-weed."

I was out of the monsoon and I was out of my soaked clothes. I experimented with trying to dry them in the microwave. Not recommended. Morning arrived, and I climbed into my still damp duds and hailed a cab to the boat ramp. Much to my delight, and amazement, my kayak and gear were waiting for me. As I was loading my boat, preparing for the morning launch, a car approached. It was the same couple, Tom and Jean Crotts, who had stopped during the storm. They were glad I made it through the night. Before driving off, they handed me an envelope they had prepared with a brief note:

Dennis,

We were very worried about you last night in the storm. When we came back from having supper we could not find you anywhere. Hope you will be OK on the river. It is going to be windy and cold—39 tonight. Be careful. Be safe. We were going to ask you to go home with us last night. If you need us, call. God bless you.

It's funny how two people, and a few words on a note, can change one's perspective on an entire town. What a great place, Burlington, Iowa!

Having been off the river for six months, I was now back on the Mississippi, paddling beneath the bluffs overlooking this historic river town. These were the same bluffs where two centuries earlier, Zebulon Pike, of Pike's Peak fame, had raised the first American flag on what would become the state of Iowa.

In my thirties and forties, prior to ever holding a kayak paddle, I was a runner. Not fast, but enduring, and I had a few marathons under my belt. The endurance gene seems to have sprouted in the family tree. My son, with a spur-of-the-moment decision, knocked off his first marathon, having never run more than a few miles at a time before that. He did pay for it in the days to follow. My daughter has done a few marathons and has also completed two full-length iron man triathlons. The reason for this reference to running has to do with beginnings.

One thing I experienced in my running days was that no matter how many years I had been running, the first few minutes of any run seemed to be laced with a touch of negative energy. Representative thoughts included, "This is going to be a rough run. Will I ever get the kinks out? Can I find the right pace?"

Now running roads had been exchanged for paddling rivers, but the same sentiments accompanied the beginnings of these forays. The good news is that oftentimes, early on in these running or paddling bouts, the negativity dissipates almost unknowingly, and I am back to the welcomed, one-with-nature, easy-breathing Zen-type experience.

Not having studied any Eastern philosophies, I'm really not sure what Zen had in mind, but I have found that certain desired state of consciousness, and the Mississippi has been part of this transcendental process. Serenity and solitude.

The solitude was welcome. It had been over a year since I had paddled the Mississippi by myself. The previous fall I had been with my guide, Adam Elliott; this spring I shared the river with the Rivergator Celebratory Expedition. Alone, one can think, talk, swear, and sing loudly. There were at least a hundred moments on the river that were subject to a very off-key version of my favorite, a Tin Pan Alley classic from a hundred years ago, "Take Me Out to the Ball Game." It wasn't pretty, but it was loud.

Paddling alone also requires a constant level of alertness, which I found impossible to consistently sustain. Questions continuously vie for attention: How far have I gone? What time is it? What's my pace? There's a scary eddy approaching; can I cross to the other side before it catches me? How far is that tow approaching me from upriver? How far can I paddle with my eyes closed? Where can I stop for lunch? How did that battered nun buoy get up on that shore?

To determine my speed, I had resorted to recording various USACE river mile markings and times on the hull of my kayak with a grease pencil. That also gets confusing when you're trying to make calculations while paddling and looking at a score of markings smeared across the deck.

Battered nun can on Iowa shore

So then you make deals with yourself: I'm not going to look at my watch for at least another hour, or until I get to that bend in the distance. You also dwell on the reality of your situation: I've got to get out of this boat fast, nature is calling! Or the sun is dropping and I haven't seen a place to camp for the past hour.

I've treasured the times when it was just me, my thoughts, and the river.

The clouds were low, but the day was dry. It was duck hunting season and I paddled through acres of decoys and house-sized duck blinds. By late afternoon, the day had turned sunny and I had found a suitable campsite in Fort Madison, Iowa, in the shadows of a giant steel and stone structure. The sign read "Iowa State Penitentiary—1839." It was another riverside prison, with its own unique history. The prison was built seven years before Iowa achieved statehood. Of questionable fame for the prison was the execution of Victor Feguer. After final appeals were denied by President John F. Kennedy, Feguer was hanged on the Ides of March, 1963. Shortly after this execution, Iowa abolished the death penalty. Feguer's execution was the last in the federal prison system until Timothy McVeigh's execution nearly forty years later in 2001.

Iowa State Penitentiary, 1839

While I was sizing up this latest in a string of riverside "Big Houses" from my campsite, I met one of the locals who was on a walk. We chatted for a while and he mentioned the prison had been decommisioned a few years back, but while it was still active, there had been a breakout and one of the fugitives on the lam had stolen his bicycle. He eventually got it back, only to have it stolen again when he parked it outside of a bar one evening. I did some fact checking later and found that two convicts escaped in 2005.

In my last two river towns the scoreboard read: two escaped convicts, a bike stolen twice in Fort Madison, and a canoe and a kayak stolen just twenty miles upriver in Burlington. The next morning, I was glad to find my boat and gear all intact. I broke camp and made my downriver getaway from the crime scenes.

It was a bluebird day without a cloud in the sky, and the river was calm. As noon approached, I crossed to the Illinois side and found a peaceful looking exit point. I was not the first to seek peace at this remote shore.

As I walked up the landing, seeking respite from my north-to-south journey across the country, I was met by two larger-than-life statues of two earlier travelers who had been on an east-to-west journey—Joseph Smith and Brigham Young. Smith founded Mormonism, and the two were both presidents of the Latter Day Saints movement. They led their followers west to escape persecution first in New York, and then Ohio. In 1839, Joseph Smith settled in this serene on-the-river countryside. He named it Nauvoo, from the Hebrew word meaning "a beautiful place." Over the next five years, the riverside Mormon enclave grew to over ten thousand members.

And then things changed. Joseph Smith was shot in a jail cell by an angry mob just twenty miles from Nauvoo. Following Smith's death, Brigham Young, the second Mormon president, commenced the Mormon Pioneer Trail, moving the believers westward to Salt Lake City, Utah. At the Nauvoo landing, there is a memorial park that includes a full-size replica of the large wooden raft used to ferry the Mormon pioneers across the Mississippi to Iowa and points west. Standing on the raft, I tried to imagine those travelers and their trials before I climbed back in my kayak. I took in the significance of the crossroads as I pushed off with my paddle.

The afternoon paddling was peaceful. I locked through Lock and Dam 19 without incident, then pulled off the river to camp just below Keokuk, Iowa, at the confluence with the Des Moines River and just across from Mud Island at LMR 361.0 (not to be confused with Mud Island in Memphis, Tennessee, or Mud Hole in Louisiana). I had paddled twenty-three miles from where I left the penitentiary in Fort Madison that morning. It

Joseph Smith and Brigham Young statues in Nauvoo, Illinois

wasn't a lot of miles, but the day had included a touristy stop at Nauvoo and navigating through another lock. I was on schedule.

The next morning, the marine radio's NOAA local weather forecast called for the day to be dry and sunny with favorable wind conditions. My day's goal was to navigate Lock and Dam 20, paddle into Missouri, and camp somewhere near La Grange, which was about twenty-five miles downriver. It was a modest goal, and with favorable paddling conditions, I was set up for a nice day on the river. That is until I encountered hours of tension-filled, expletives-not-deleted, minefields of flying Asian silver carp.

I was initially introduced to these kayak terrorists on an earlier trip below the Mel Price Lock and Dam, just above St. Louis. A few of them had startled me with their aerial antics, with a couple of close calls. The experience had lasted for just a few miles, and then conditions returned to normal.

When I was a kid, my friends and I would go carp fishing. We headed to the bank of the Mississippi in St. Paul, just below the Indian mounds, with our fishing gear and a can of corn. We would stack our hooks with kernels of corn, load up the line with some heavy weights, and cast out into the river. We could spend a day reeling in ten to fifteen pounders. I am sorry to report, but when we hauled in a carp, we would ooh and ahh about the size of it, and then we would smash it against the rocks. It's not my proudest memory, but we were kids.

Now, sixty years later, this was different! These missiles, launched from the depths of the Mississippi River, were exploding all around me. There were high-flying schools of them surrounding my kayak. In the afternoon hours, paddling through this gauntlet, I saw hundreds if not thousands of these unwelcome intruders. There were twenty to thirty of them airborne at any one time. One monster slammed into my shoulder with the force of a knockout punch. "Ow! Fuck!" Their violent thrashing and up-close proximity ruined what would have been a nice day on the river.

Was it retributive justice for boyhood deeds done six decades ago?

As John Ruskey says, "The Mississippi River connects us all."

How did these invading warriors arrive here? In John McPhee's *The Control of Nature*, McPhee refers to "any struggle against natural forces—heroic or venal, rash or well advised—when human beings conscript to fight against the earth, to take what is not given, to rout the destroying enemy, to surround the base of Mt. Olympus demanding and expecting the surrender of the gods."[33]

I saw firsthand what McPhee had described about man's attempt to control nature at the Atchafalaya River. Man erected the ORCS in his attempt to guide the massive Mississippi River down man's desired path to New Orleans.

In the same way, the flying carp were born out of our attempts to control nature. According to a government publication, in the 1960s and 1970s, man imported these fish from Asia to the Southern United States to control weed and parasite growth in retention ponds and sewage lagoons. By the 1980s, through flooding, these fish escaped their ponds and spread into local water bodies. They now occupy the entire Mississippi River all the way to Minnesota, the headwaters state. Oops.

We can also include the Asian lady beetle as another example of man messing with fauna. And if we want to examine man controlling flora, it's hard to overlook the ubiquitous kudzu. This Asian import, the "mile-a-minute" plant, or "the vine that ate the South," as reported by the Nature Conservancy, was first introduced at the Philadelphia Centennial Expo-

33. John McPhee, *The Control of Nature* (New York: Farrar, Straus, and Giroux, 1989), inside cover.

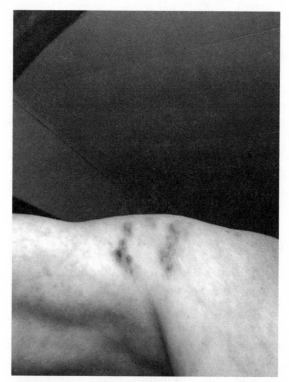

Battle scar on shoulder from tangling with Asian flying carp

sition in 1876. It was touted "as a great ornamental plant for its sweet-smelling blooms and sturdy vines."

Yes, tangents like these help one endure the seemingly endless hours of paddling.

Locking through Lock and Dam 20 went well, and I found myself pulling ashore at La Grange, Missouri, in the late afternoon. I had time to set my campsite near a local riverside park with hours of daylight to spare. I walked into town past the Mark Twain Casino and stopped at a Casey's General Store for a juicy California hamburger, fries, and a Coke. There's something about paddling all day in the great outdoors that makes eating special. Looking back, I don't really think it was the best burger I've ever tasted, but at that moment it was.

A peaceful night on shore was followed by another sunny morning. Quincy, Illinois, the town that hosted the sixth of seven Abraham Lincoln versus Stephen Douglas debates, lay just ten miles downriver.

As I approached the "Gem City," there seemed to be some unusual activities occurring on the river ahead. As I got closer, I noticed sheriff's department boats were dredging the river. There were lots of serious faces amid a macabre setting. My thoughts turned somber as I could only imagine what might have initiated this gruesome scene by which I had to paddle. Two days later, I found out from a local newspaper that a nineteen-year-old man, Ean Michael Reinhold, had been out with two of his buddies setting up duck blinds when a wave capsized their sixteen-foot johnboat. The other two had been rescued but Ean remained missing. Ean's body wouldn't be found for ten months. He came to rest near Hull, Illinois, twenty miles downriver.

T.S. Eliot's words fit the moment. "I do not know much about gods; but I think that the river is a strong brown god—sullen, untamed and intractable . . ."[34]

Later in the afternoon, with a few wispy clouds hanging high in autumn's crisp blue sky, a train screamed directly overhead just as I paddled under the lift bridge approaching Hannibal, Missouri. Fittingly, there were two paddlewheelers moored at the docks of Riverboat Pilot Sam Clemens's hometown. The first of these two stately vessels was the *America*, the newest paddlewheeler on the Mississippi. Christened just one year earlier, this bunting-festooned, six-decked, football-field-size beauty was heading downriver to New Orleans, Louisiana. Passengers making the entire three-week journey from St. Paul to New Orleans would fork over somewhere between $20,000 and $40,000 cash on the barrelhead. The $20,000 difference depended upon how much luxury one could stand.

Tucked behind the *America*, almost out of sight, was the local, scaled-down version of Mississippi paddlewheelers. It was Hannibal's own, the *Mark Twain*. What else *could* they name it? Coming in at one-third the length of the *America*, the tariffs were also scaled back, ranging from $20 to $40, depending on if you wanted a meal with your out-and-back, three-hour cruise. Surprisingly, the triple-decker *Mark Twain* could pack in 350 passengers when fully loaded, while the *America* was limited to just 185 passengers, allowing ample room for baubles, gowns, and sea chests.

A few miles downriver, I locked through Lock and Dam 22 and continued paddling this history-rich river until finding a place to camp somewhere between Hannibal and Louisiana, Missouri. I had paddled forty-three miles. A few days back, this trip started in thunder and lightning before I had even touched the water. Now on my last evening, the

---

34. Eliot, T. S. "The Dry Salvages" in *Four Quartets* (London: The New English Weekly, 1941).

The *America* moored in Hannibal with the *Mark Twain* peeking out from behind

National Oceanic and Atmospheric Administration's next-day weather forecast called for another sunny and favorable day. It was good news as I tucked in for my last night on the river. As I thought about the various moments on the trip, I recalled paddling by a small town that was conducting dragon boat races. The decorated boats and people cheering from the river banks were just another one of the sweet yet simple kayaking experiences chronicled in my memory bank.

Getaway day started as another cloudless, perfect fall morning. I packed my kayak and pushed off toward Clarksville, twenty miles downriver. The last day always brought its uniquely mixed emotions. Here I was, having paddled past previous river heists, prison escapes, Mormon trails, dragon boat races, body searches, barge traffic, and paddleboats large and small. Nights had been spent sleeping with the sounds from the river and the land, from the low bass of a towboat's foghorn to the high-pitched wail of wild coyotes.

I had one last stop before my final takeout in Louisiana, Missouri. I opted out of the unpacking ritual required for my last meal on the river and chose the convenience of a one-block walk to "Mom and Pop's Do-nuts & Diner." It had a friendly atmosphere with a river view. I grabbed my last opportunity for genuine, Southern-cooked biscuits smothered in gravy with onion-laced greasy hash browns on the side. While enjoying the brunch, I also took in Mom and Pop's marine decor, a full-sized, fully curved ship's figurehead mermaid, no longer adorning a ship's prow on the high seas but now relegated to standing guard by the diner's checkout counter.

The last ten miles went quicker than I wanted. I pulled off the river at the Clarksville boat ramp, just above Lock and Dam 24. Because Big Muddy had dropped me off just below this lock and dam on an earlier trip, this would be one of a few locks that I would not lock through. I surmised that because this was Clarksville and not Burlington (that kayak-stealing town), there was a good chance my vehicle would still be there. It was, right where my shuttle driver had said it would be. It was always a relief.

I had a seven-hundred-mile drive home and I knocked off the first sixty before stopping at a Budget Inn in Palmyra, Missouri, just off the Great River Road on Highway 61. It was a step up from the "any-port-in-a-storm" motel that I had endured in Burlington. This place did not have the two shuddery, gargoyle-esque faces smeared on the room's mirror, but the new room's mirror did also show a rather scary image. It was an ugly mass of greens, blacks, blues, purples, and yellows. The unsightly reflection was my now fully ripened shoulder bruise earned from my encounter with the flying Asian carp three days earlier.

As I was falling sleep, I realized it wasn't the miles paddled, or the tows dodged, that earned me the honor of saying, "I am a river man."

It was the battle scar imprinted on my shoulder from my tangle with a fish.

21

CROSSROADS

Fall 2017

This would be my fastest turnaround yet. I had just returned from my paddle to Clarksville, Missouri, on Saturday, and by early Wednesday morning, just four days later, I was once again leaving my driveway in the dark, heading for Natchez, Mississippi. There was a reason for the home-and-gone-again itinerary. There were only two segments left to complete the entire river: Rosedale, Mississippi, to Vicksburg, Mississippi (155 river miles), and ORCS, Louisiana, to Mile Zero, just past Pilot Town, Louisiana (305 river miles). Adam Elliott signed on with me for this final, big push.

I stashed my golf clubs in the basement for the season, made some last-minute accommodations to ensure my business would still be in existence upon my return, and cleared my calendar for the next three weeks. My on-river calculations indicated I had only 460 river miles left to Mile Zero. If I allowed three days each way for the 1,200-mile drive into the Deep South and back, that would leave fourteen days for paddling. The numbers indicated that if we paddled an average of thirty-one miles a day, we would reach our long-standing goal—the Gulf of Mexico—completing the S2S river odyssey. As I considered the huge, mile-wide Lower Mississippi, I assumed the current would provide a nice paddling boost.

Two hours after I left home, the sun peeked over the horizon, casting a long shadow riding tandem in the fields to my right. I had observed this phenomenon many times and I always welcomed it. It was the early morning shadow of my kayak atop my vehicle, signaling that I was off and running again.

After two days on the road, I arrived in Clarksdale, Mississippi, a small town steeped in the Deep South's artistic history, both literary and musical. America's playwright, Tennessee Williams, spent his boyhood years in

Clarksdale. The town is also renowned as the birthplace of the deep Delta blues and proud home to the site of Robert Johnson's crossroads. Almost a century ago, as history tells it, Johnson had made his Faustian pact at the intersection of Highways 61 and 49 in Clarksdale. Later, in 1967, Bobbie Gentry made her mark on the Delta blues scene lamenting Billie Joe MacAllister's demise on the Tallahatchie Bridge. Her song was number one on *Billboard*, and the famed bridge and river were less than an hour's drive from Clarksdale. The Tallahatchie River becomes part of the Yazoo River, the same river I kayaked at the finish line of the aptly named Bluz Cruz one year earlier.

I would have to catch the music later, because I was headed for the home of the Quapaw Canoe Company. At Quapaw, I received a warm welcome from my fellow Rivergator Celebratory Expedition crew, Mark "River" Peoples, Lena von Machui, and the founder of Quapaw Canoe Company, John Ruskey. We had not seen each other since I left the expedition six months earlier in Memphis. They gave me the graphic details of the expedition's forced grounding near New Orleans a few weeks after we had parted ways. A powerful storm had blown up, wreaking havoc with the river and their campsite. Several large trees toppled, one landing right on Lena's tent, miraculously on the half of the tent where she was not sleeping. For a while she was trapped between the tent wall and the fallen tree. Another tree completely flattened Chris "Magique" Battaglia's tent. Fortunately, he was not in it at the time. It may have been the spirit of Chris's goat skull totem that spared him for further adventures. The Quapaw crew were now making plans to resume the expedition and complete their celebratory trek to the Gulf.

While at Quapaw, John introduced me to a dozen local teenagers who were proudly showing off their current project—a huge, hand-hewn voyageur canoe. We took a picture of the students with their cypress boat-in-the-making, the Quapaw team wished me bon voyage, and I was back on Highway 61, the "blues highway."

CLARKSDALE, MISSISSIPPI, TO VICKSBURG, MISSISSIPPI

This last leg of the long road trip led me through Alligator, Mississippi, home of the "Alligator Blues," to Cleveland, Mississippi, where I would link up the following morning with Adam. It had been one year since we paddled from Memphis to Rosedale.

It was a nice reunion and Adam introduced me to Joe Harris and Mike Cain, two Natchez natives. Adam covered the on-land logistics just as well as he guided me through the Southland's waterways. He had arranged for Mike to shuttle my vehicle to Natchez and Joe would be traveling with us to Rosedale.

Bluesman Eric Clapton's homage to Robert Johnson and his devil's bargain captured the spirit of our journey in his song "Crossroads," where he is going to bring his barrelhouse blues to the riverside in Rosedale.

We were on that riverside. Just before noon, our kayaks were loaded, and Joe pushed us off into a cold, gray day. He would shuttle Adam's truck back to our endpoint in Vicksburg. From the Rosedale harbor there is a three-mile stretch called Napoleon's Cutoff that leads to the river. We negotiated the busy harbor filled with plenty of barges and plenty of dead fish floating on the surface. Once we exited the wind-protected confines of the harbor, we faced a cold, wind-whipped river. After three days on the road, I was finally back, paddling the Mississippi.

The fetch of the wind was brutal, and every paddle stroke was a fight for any forward motion. I thought, if Adam is doing it, I'd better do it. After about a mile's worth of paddling futility, soaked with the cold river's spray, we pulled off on the Arkansas shore. There we found a campsite just above the conflux with the Arkansas River that offered some protection from the elements. We would mark down four river miles for the first day. I went to bed early, curled up in my sleeping bag wearing a full set of dry clothes, hoping for better conditions to follow.

The next morning dawned bright and blue, and we enjoyed a great day of paddling. We had time to catch up on each other's lives over the past year. Adam talked of joining John Ruskey's Rivergator Celebratory Expedition a few days after I had left it in Memphis. Somewhere along the way, we got around to discussing paddlers' river names. There was John Ruskey's "Driftwood," Mark Peoples's "River," and Mike Clark's "Big Muddy." On a previous trip, I had suggested for Adam's river guide service that he promote himself as "Adam, First Man on the River." Returning the favor, Adam suggested I also needed a river name. He thought the moniker should exude the river's essence and proffered "Dangerous Eddy." Although the link was distant, I could sense the pairing of Dangerous Eddy and Mark Twain, despite the century and a half gap. It was the riverine connection. Fitting appellations, each cribbed from a navigator's chart.

I liked it.

Sunrise shadows on the countryside

Early morning ice on the kayak below Rosedale, Mississippi

No rain and a favorable wind brought us to our next campsite at Island 29, forty-five miles downriver from Rosedale. After another cold night, we arose at sunrise, knocked the morning ice off our kayaks (this was a first), and pushed off into a cloudless day. While paddling, I described my dryland Dixie research for this trip. I had read Greg Iles's novel *Natchez Burning*—all 791 pages of it. Chapter 1 opens with, "Albert Norris sang a few bars of Howlin' Wolf's 'Natchez Burnin.'" It was another instance of connectedness. Natchez native Greg Iles tied his book's title to Howlin' Wolf, legendary bluesman, who frequently partnered up with another legend, Robert Johnson, as they offered their deep Delta blues renditions in Clarksdale.

When I mentioned *Natchez Burning*, Adam recalled the local joke, "Oh, you mean Natchez Churning, the gripping book about the Natchez butter revolution?" Adam said that Natchez's writer-in-residence, Greg Iles, was one of his clients, and he had provided his carpentry artistry for Greg on several occasions.

As the sun completed its arc, we had logged another calm, blue-sky day. For our evening's campsite we discovered a peaceful sand beach, replete with a goose "sand nest" on the shore, laden with three goose eggs. Another forty river miles were behind us.

Daybreak brought a cloudless sunrise. I checked the stick I had stuck in the sand at the water's edge the night before and saw that the river had receded a few inches from the stick's evening position. It was a trick Adam had taught me a few trips ago. We got on the river early, but after only five miles we had to pull ashore to wait out a fierce wind. The long, wind-swept beach offered no shelter, so we set up our tents for a midday nap. With the wind abating only slightly, we resumed our paddling and worked our way down another thirteen miles before calling it quits for the day.

I awoke early and realized it was Halloween, so I texted Adam a picture of a makeshift rendition of me as a river pirate. Buccaneer "Dangerous Eddy" is loose on the riverbanks, matey! We didn't realize it when we beached our kayaks the night before, but checking our navigation charts later, we discovered we had camped less than a mile from the Transylvania Chute—on Halloween.

This would be our last day of paddling for this leg of the trip. Our destination was Vicksburg, with the finish line forty-six miles downriver. It was the same finish line as the Bluz Cruz that we had crossed a year and a half earlier. Another blue sky, with only a slight wind, made for a decent day of paddling and conversation. We reminisced about last year's Bluz Cruz and the trips we had taken over the previous eighteen months including Vicksburg to ORCS, the Atchafalaya River, Memphis to Rosedale (where we met Mickey the perv), and now our final push to the Gulf. We turned to portside and paddled up the last mile on the Yazoo River. Adam's crew member Joe Harris had delivered; Adam's truck was waiting for us on the finish line ramp.

This leg was done. Our wet, cold, and rainy start finished with four dry, cerulean-sky days. Now we would drive seventy miles to Natchez, sleep at Adam's place, and get shuttled to the ORCS. We would then paddle through Baton Rouge to New Orleans, also known as Chemical Alley, and on to the Gulf of Mexico. There was a light at the end of this tunnel.

Heading south, Adam knew a place just outside Vicksburg where we could get supper. The Tomato Place, whose atmosphere is self-described as "a Southern grandma's back porch," was just what a long day of paddling called for. Our server, a Southern hospitality specialist, Desiree, welcomed us with smiles and great food. The tuna melt with tomato, of course, was perfect. Once you got past the bold, garish, sunflower yellow and tomato red decor, you noticed an incredibly wide-ranging inventory of stuff for sale. Pork skins, red popcorn grits, and, no surprise, assorted colors and sizes of John Ruskey's river posters and prints.

Desiree endured our dinner table tales before recommending the bread pudding topped with a huge mound of ice cream. I was glad Adam was driving, as I was done for the day.

The Tomato Place in Vicksburg, Mississippi

22

NATCHEZ AND POINTS SOUTH

Fall 2017

We awoke in Natchez to heavy rains and decided we would spend the day in town and let the storms pass. I joined Adam and a local resident, Steve Huber, for breakfast. Steve and I had previously met on my earlier trips. Steve, "hail fellow well met," can hold his own in any conversation, bolstered by his keen reading appetite. Steve is a purveyor and restorer of high-end furniture, with a specialty in late eighteenth- and early nineteenth-century French pieces. Our reconnection was most welcome as Steve's top-of-the-morning op-ed observations, delivered with a splash of local color, carried over into second and third cups of coffee. After breakfast, Adam tended to some work while I was off to be tourist for a day in Natchez, the "Bluff City."

I learned that Natchez has the greatest collection of antebellum mansions. Unlike the burning of Atlanta, Natchez was spared because the city had voted against cessation prior to the Civil War. With a healthy roster of plantation homes, this Yankee set out to tour some of the Old South's manors and manners. Full disclosure, and I am not proud, but I filched the "manors and manners" from a travel brochure.

I spent a good part of the day visiting Longwood, also known as Nutt's Folly. Haller Nutt, a cotton king, designed his octangular mansion with the onion-shaped dome in 1859, only to have construction halted by the war. Haller died in 1864, with only nine of the thirty-two rooms completed, and that is how the manor remains today—unfinished.

Following the plantation visit, I found a restaurant on the outskirts of town called Roux 61. I passed up the gator bites and shrimp 'n' alligator cheesecake but did try the crawfish étouffée with the catfish platter.

OLD RIVER CONTROL STRUCTURE, LOUISIANA, TO NEW ORLEANS, LOUISIANA

The following morning, Adam's crew member, Joe, shuttled us through miles of kudzu-choked countryside to arrive at the ORCS. Just one year prior we stood at this same launching point, just below Shreves Cutoff.

There is a historical significance to this place on the Mississippi. Back in Christopher Columbus's time, the Mississippi formed a meandering loop, similar to Bessie's Bend up north in Tennessee, in which a twenty-mile loop was formed that required sailors to navigate twenty miles of river bend to gain a one-mile advance on the river. In the early steamboat days, this loop was referred to as Turnbull's Bend, and it added hours to any navigation. In 1831, Henry Shreve, a big name in Mississippi River history and the namesake of Shreveport, Louisiana, dug a canal through the neck of Turnbull's Bend, thereby providing a navigational shortcut for river travelers. As Shreves Cutoff provided a time-saving assist, it also had the effect of speeding up the Mississippi's eventual diversion into the Atchafalaya River, thereby providing a puzzle for navigators, politicians, and engineers of all types. Their solution was the ORCS, which continues to keep the Mississippi River from becoming the Atchafalaya River.

A year ago, we traveled the Atchafalaya, but, as Dale Sanders said, "Some paddlers don't consider that a true source-to-sea route." So we chose to discover this new section of the Mississippi. We would paddle under both Huey P. Long bridges, one in Baton Rouge and one in New Orleans.

The Mississippi River touches ten different states on its way to the Gulf. At its source it flows through Minnesota, then borders eight other states before flowing through Louisiana. There are a few exceptions in which the river, by its meandering ways, briefly jumps its tracks and smudges a mapmaker's state line before returning to its state of origin. With these exceptions noted, there are only two states that the river flows through: its headwaters state, Minnesota, and Louisiana, its endpoint. The rest of our journey would be entirely within the state of Louisiana, the Bayou State.

As we prepared to launch, there was a young man who guided his johnboat ashore at the boat landing. His boat was loaded to the gunnels with hundreds of buffalo fish. He had hauled them in using hoop nets. He proudly hoisted the largest; it was a most impressive fish. With the tail still touching the boat deck, its head reached the man's chest. Life on the Mississippi.

Johnboat filled with buffalo fish at Old River Control Structure, Louisiana

It was mid-afternoon when Joe shoved us off and we enjoyed a good afternoon of paddling. We found our first campsite fifteen miles downriver. On our second day we were trapped in camp until mid-morning because of fog. The same thing happened on our third day. Once the mid-morning fogged burned off, we were back on the river. Adam and I were paddling side by side about five yards apart when just a foot in front of Adam's kayak the water suddenly exploded. A huge Asian carp flew by Adam's face. My guide introduced me to a few new words. Rattled, we decided to take an unscheduled break to recover from the rude intrusion.

With the fog-delayed launch, and the extra-long "get-it-back-together" break, we had worked our way down another twenty-two river miles before we found a suitable campsite. We had to climb atop a sandy shelf to keep our boats, tents, and gear out of the river. It was an interesting evening as we observed the sandy shelf upon which we were perched undergoing its continuous calving process, like the icebergs being pared back in the climate change videos. In addition to the other evening sounds associated with camping on the riverbanks, we listened to the new sound of the bank-carving Mississippi sending more silt to the Gulf.

Except for the foggy mornings, our paddling was what we had experienced on our previous trips on the Lower Mississippi. A typical day was spent paddling all day, looking for the next buoy, keeping an eye out for tows and their huge wakes, drifting in and out of conversations, avoiding wing dams and whirlpools, and looking for spots to rest and camp. We did this over and over again.

Our typical paddling days were about to end, however, as we approached the largest and busiest inland harbor in our hemisphere: Baton Rouge. As a prologue to the next few days of paddling challenges, we successfully maneuvered through a tow captain's nightmare of a hairpin turn just above Baton Rouge, and we found a marginally suitable but historically rich campsite at LMR 235.0, just above the Huey P. Long Bridge, now called the Old Bridge.

Huey P. Long, "The Kingfish," and the bridge's namesake, had been a fiery, flamboyant, and charismatic governor and senator for the state of Louisiana in the first half of the twentieth century. The story goes that this first of the two Huey P. Long bridges was designed to cross the river at a height that would preclude larger vessels, like oil tankers, from advancing any further upriver, thereby monopolizing the ocean-going transportation interests for his beloved state of Louisiana.

Our campsite was on a small and rare patch of sandy beach on Free Negro Point, just on the inside of a bend identified on the USACE navigation maps as Mulatto Bend. The names refer to antebellum times when some New Orleans slaves who had earned or were given their freedom migrated and settled in the same area where we were spending a night in our tents.

Other historical references, all with a French influence, lay just across the river on Scott's Bluff. On this bluff, in 1699, French explorers noted a cypress tree that was stripped of its bark, adorned with animal parts, and stained red from the latest hunt. The tree's significance was that it marked the boundary line between the hunting grounds of two native tribes, the Houma and Bayou Goula. The French explorers called the area "le baton rouge," French for "red stick."

About a hundred years later, the French-born pirate and privateer Captain Jean Lafitte is said to have cached a portion of his pirate's plunder on this very bluff. In one last look back, another traveler and the author of *On the Road*, Jack Kerouac, who was of French Canadian descent, cited this area in his travels.

Our campsite's proximity to antiquity's jewels was obliterated by the sights and sounds of the new day's industry. We were camped just feet from the river, and just feet from a remarkably busy industrial site full of barges and heavy equipment. Another foggy morning greeted us as we were captive to a front-end loader noisily scraping out the last of a barge's cargo just outside our tents.

The morning's cacophony—the high-pitched beep-beep-beep of the loader backing up, the metal-on-metal scraping sounds, and the workmen's barking voices—countered any semblance of two guys getting back to nature by camping out on a riverbank. My musings over whether commerce or creation ruled our campsite's surroundings were quickly answered when I crawled out of my tent and stood to stretch. I saw fresh, deep tracks passing by my tent's courtyard. Deep in the sand with big claw marks newly etched were an alligator's footprints, along with the accompanying grooved gator tail track. These tracks, which were not there when I had climbed into my tent the night before, trailed off into the nearby brush. The spookiness of the moment had this visitor from the Northwoods reflecting on both the mythical Cajun werewolf, Rougarou, and "the Creature from the Black Lagoon." I must have slept well to miss this nocturnal intruder.

When the fog finally lifted, we pushed off into the breach of Chemical Alley. We paddled into the harbor, bobbing and weaving through the churned-up river's real-time version of rush hour traffic. The tows' wakes created a mountain range of waves that continuously swallowed us up to our paddling skirts before releasing us for the next bout. I recall one barge

Fresh gator tracks at threshold of author's tent

crewman as he brought out his camera to catch a picture of us, his face proclaiming, "Do you guys really want to be doing this?" This was the St. Louis harbor all over again.

Seven miles into our route, under the two Baton Rouge bridges, and past the Morgan City Port Allen Canal (another shortcut to the Gulf), we encountered a tow heading toward us. He was crowding to our half of the river (the right descending bank) because there was an oil tanker anchored right in the middle of the river. I wondered what a tanker was doing "parked in the center of the road." It didn't take too long for me to realize this is what oil tankers do: they park wherever that want. Because of the Huey P. Long bridge's low ceiling, and the depth of the river, this was as far up the Mississippi as these monsters could navigate. They're huge.

According to my research, the Knock Nevis Oil Tanker measures 1,500 feet in length (longer than the height of the Empire State Building) and can carry up to two million barrels of oil.[35] By comparison, a kayak is three feet high and can carry one paddler. It was our job to stay out of their way.

---

35. American Petroleum Institute, *Tankers: Fueling American Life* (Washington, DC, 2011), https://www.api.org/~/media/files/oil-and-natural-gas/tankers/tankers-lores.pdf.

We successfully maneuvered through the oil tankers, both moving and anchored, navigated around two more hairpin turns, and found a campsite twenty-six river miles from where we started the day. This was significant, as we had paddled our way through another one of my bigger fears, the Baton Rouge Harbor. There were only a hundred miles left of Chemical Alley to reach New Orleans, and another hundred miles to the Gulf. We were camping just below Plaquemine Bayou, not to be confused with Plaquemine Road, city, parish, or culture. The French Creole named an early military post that was built on the Mississippi River banks "Plaquemine," from a native word "plakemine," meaning persimmon, as the riverbanks were abundant with persimmon trees.

Our riverbank post for that night was not abundant with persimmon trees, but it was abundant with trash. The flotsam-covered sandy shore brought back visions of the 1970s public service announcement, referred to as the "crying Indian ad." It showed a Native American, portrayed by Iron Eyes Cody, paddling his birch bark canoe to a trash-strewn shore, and as more garbage was tossed, the ad ended with one lone tear falling down the paddler's cheek.

Hey, what did we expect? We were in Cancer Alley.

Not the best campsite in "Cancer Alley"

After experiencing another foggy morning, we pushed off. We faced another hairpin turn around the White Castle Revetment. Paddling around a hairpin on the river is nothing like motoring around a hairpin on the "Road to the Sun" in Glacier National Park. The White Castle hairpin is ten miles long and can take up to three hours of paddling to complete it.

In the Mississippi's Chemical Corridor, the traffic includes tows, tankers, and assorted other vessels all jockeying for position. The U-shaped river turn presents the biggest navigational challenge for the commercial traffic, and the biggest need for the recreational traffic to stay out of their way. Amid dodging fleets of barges and a tanker or two, I questioned whether this even qualified as recreation anymore. The ability—or inability—to see what's coming around the bend is the challenge. Am I on the right side of the river? And if I am not, is it possible to cross over to the other side through industry's crowded expressways?

Adam was working the marine radio to monitor the traffic. He knew what he was doing, and it was reassuring that one of us knew where we had to dart (if a paddler can dart) to or fro. Below Baton Rouge, there are three different applicable marine radio channels: one for the fleet boats (channel 13), one for the tows and other commercial traffic (channel 67), and one for the ten-thousand-horsepower tugs (channel 77) that were pushing and pulling the huge ocean-going vessels with their massive wakes rushing toward our log-sized kayaks. We had not yet reached the ocean-going cruise ships and their designated radio frequencies.

Over the next three days, it was more of the same. We were fogged in until mid-morning, and then enjoyed blue sky afternoons where we paddled about twenty miles, commented on the sizes of the tankers, and panicked occasionally about whether a fleet boat entering our paddling lane was going downriver or coming right at us.

On November 8, about ten miles downriver from the day's starting point, we paddled up to the paddlewheeler *America*. She was moored so her passengers could stop for lunch at the Oak Alley Plantation just upriver from Vacherie, Louisiana. This was the same riverboat that, weeks earlier, I had seen moored next to the *Mark Twain* in Hannibal, Missouri. In Hannibal, the *America* had dwarfed the *Mark Twain*. These were different waters. Now the paddlewheeler, coming in at around four hundred feet long, was a runt when side by side with the ocean tanker trade.

We paddled another four miles and stopped for lunch on the right descending bank near Vacherie. Just ten yards into the river there was an upside-down johnboat, mostly submerged, with only a portion of its stern poking out from the waves. Surely there was an untold story.

After lunch, our paddling took us safely past Willow Bend. There was not a real threat at the time, but I did notice after the fact there was a warning on the USACE navigation map: "Dangerous eddies at work below on RDB at River Mile 142.5." My namesake, Dangerous Eddy, was alive and well, deep in the heart of Louisiana.

Paddling the last few days along this stretch of the river, we passed miles and miles of barges moored, end to end, nonstop, along both shorelines. There were hundreds, if not thousands, of barges. It was all heavy industry, nothing recreational or residential. At LMR 138.0 we were able to squeeze ourselves into our most industrial campsite yet. We pulled ashore just yards behind a tanker that was being worked on in dry dock. The sawing, hammering, and welding provided the musical score, all played out under the spotlighted stage of the tanker's transom, and we had front row seats. Not waiting for any intermission, I found my way up and over the levee to a convenience store. I gathered fried chicken, ice cream, and a six-pack of Gatorade for the road. We settled in for the night and fell asleep long before it was "light outs" for the tanker's night shift.

The next morning, we climbed into our kayaks and headed toward The Big Easy, which was now just two days away. It was more of the same: heavy traffic, big industry. About thirty miles upriver from New Orleans, on the left descending bank, we passed the Bonne Carre (Square Hat) Spillway. Shortly after the killer Mississippi River flood of 1927, man was back in the business of controlling nature. A massive, mile-and-a-half long weir was constructed, its floodgates serving as a safety valve to allow man, at times of highwater, to safely divert up to 20 percent of the Mississippi's flow into Lake Pontchartrain, six miles away. The Bonne Carre Spillway is still working successfully today.

It was another day of heavy-traffic paddling. At one time, with the river all jammed up in front of us, we decided to let things sort themselves out, so we slipped into a rare open space near the riverbank, just in front of a parked tug. We were there a few minutes when, to our surprise, this workhorse of a boat, just yards in front of us, decided it was time to go to work. With all ten thousand horses awakened, and the skipper getting ready to head out, we were in a tight spot. To our left was the wall of an industrial dock—no exit there! Behind us was a string of barges all moored to the shore. To our right was the river with all its commerce on the move, and straight ahead was a tug ready to move out, right through the very spot we were occupying. We poked our noses out into the river to take our chances. In that moment of uncertainty and anxiety, I was glad to have Adam as my guide. Not that he knew a sure-fire way to safety, but I felt good that I was not facing these dire straits alone. With Adam in the lead, we managed to wind our way safely through the moving maze of river commerce at work.

Further down the river in calmer waters, one huge oil tanker was anchored off the shores of a smoke-belching refinery. It was memorable for its name and logo. Boldly painted on the ship's massive brown prow was a ten-foot-high, beaming white smiley face. With equally impressive lettering, the name was proudly displayed: *Four Smile*. For all the work put into building this huge tanker, I would have thought someone could get the plural noun correct on the tanker's name.

That evening, we pulled off the river next to a quarter-mile-long wooden barge-loading structure leftover from a different era. Underneath its weathered beams were several half-buried, dented, and out-of-service buoys, both red and green. To find a plot suitable for staking out our tents, it required considerable effort to climb through some hilly, thick brushland. It wasn't just the difficulty of the climb; it was how many times we had to repeat the climb to get our gear and our kayaks clear of the river's reach. We were at LMR 114.0, just above New Orleans. This was our fifteenth day together on our bit-by-bit approach to the Gulf, and due to some foggy

Tanker *Four Smile* just above New Orleans

mornings and a rain-out day, we were behind schedule. It bears repeating: a schedule is one of the most common enemies of safety.

From our separate tents we were discussing our progress when Adam relayed the news that we should be able to make it to Algiers Point—just across the river from New Orleans—by the next day. But because of logistical challenges beyond that point, we should plan to get picked up there for our return trip home. I knew we were running behind, but I had been putting the inevitable out of my mind. The "do the math" realities delivered a harsh, disappointing blow. Coming up just one hundred miles short of our goal (equating to a few days of paddling) would require another 2,500-mile road trip—three days down and three days back. Fuck!

Adam could sense the depth of my disappointment. He tried to soften the blow by saying he knew we wanted to get to the Gulf on this trip, but there would also be next year. And then Adam said something really cool: "I know this trip is important to you. I will make myself available next year and we will do it together. And I won't be doing it as your guide—we will just do it together."

That was a mood-altering moment. Instead of me trying to fall asleep with the reality of a job unfinished, drawing comparisons to Nutt's Folly and Old Haller Nutt and his still-to-this-day-unfinished Longwood Mansion, I dozed off thinking what a classy guide I had picked for my adventures. Once again, I was good to go.

The new day brought no fog. The early morning sun was a nice surprise, and my attitude was right. We took some time and climbed the levy to see the lay of the land. There was a popular bike trail running along the top of the levy and on the other side was the nice, neat town of Kenner. Just below us we spotted two statues: it was two men, squaring off against each other in yesterday's bare-knuckled boxing poses as a tribute to the first World Heavyweight Championship prize fight held in the United States. It happened in 1870 in Kenner. England's Jed Mace defeated Tom Allen of Birmingham, Alabama, in the ten-rounder. Apparently, Kenner was chosen as the location for the fight because the word had gotten out that the boxers would have been arrested had the fight occurred in that other river town just down and around the bend—New Orleans.

A century and a half later, two new fighters were preparing for the final round of this year's bout. Adam and I climbed into our kayaks, bare knuckled and armed with graphite paddles, ready to take our fight to the Big Easy.

Ten miles into the day's trip, a bridge with a fifteen-story-high river clearance came into view. It was over four miles long and had twin railroad tracks and a six-lane highway. Prior to this bridge's construction, trains faced the cumbersome process of ferrying each railroad car across the river. It was the first bridge to cross the Mississippi River in New Orleans, and at that time it was the world's longest railroad bridge. The bridge was opened in December 1935 and was named to honor Louisiana's colorful governor and senator who had been assassinated just three months earlier. The Huey P. Long Bridge, also known as the Old Mississippi River Bridge, is sometimes irreverently referred to as the Puey Long Bridge.

I had encountered many Mississippi River bridges, at least 135 of them up to this point. The significance of paddling under this one bridge was the competition for its navigational space. There were three channels, with the widest being 750 feet, or three-fourths as wide as an oil tanker is long. We were competing with tugs, tows, fleet boats, oil tankers, and an assortment of other commercial traffic. It was not just a matter of staying out of their pathways, it was about contending with all the various wakes that were churned up and spreading across the entire river. The largest wakes presented the opportunity to ride the teeter-totter river, and as the child's game always went, one kid would always hop off at the bottom of the seesaw just to see the other come crashing down from his momentary summit. If you could get past the anxiety, it was a thrilling ride.

Adam led the way, with the assistance of his marine radio. My job was to keep up and keep calm—two tests I was barely passing. But flunking was not an acceptable option.

Once under the bridge, we entered a ten-mile bend with a C-shaped turn in the river that defines the city's shoreline and serves as its namesake, the Crescent City. New Orleans historically has been a welcoming melting pot for different people, music, styles, cultures, and cuisines. But at that moment, a rich Creole blend of watercraft had my full attention.

The stretch of the main harbor of New Orleans is bookended by bridges: the Huey P. Long Bridge at the top (LMR 106.1) and two bridges at the bottom, the Crescent City Connection Upper Bridge (LMR 95.8) and the Crescent City Connection Lower Bridge (LMR 95.7). Within this white-knuckle harbor experience was one of the widest arrays of marine vessels that we would be required to dodge, including oil tankers, tows, tugs, fleet boats, container ships, large and small US Navy vessels, the ocean-going *Norwegian Pearl* cruise ship, the *Steamboat Natchez*, the *Creole Queen* paddlewheeler, and, finally, the Algiers Point *Canal Street Ferry*, which crossed the river every fifteen minutes.

But we made it! The Crescent City! Creole City! Queen City! NOLA! N'Awlins! The Big Easy! The Big Greasy! The Big Sleazy! We

were a $2 ferry ride away from it all because we were on the other side of
the two-hundred-foot-deep river. We paddled to a sandy beach directly
across from the City of Excesses. The quaint little town of Algiers Point is
protected from the river and all the sins of its saintly neighbor by a levy.
On the river side of the Algiers Point levy is a mile-long, well-manicured
grassy parkland, with a ribbon of sandy beach outlining the batture. We
found some protective shrubbery that would serve as our campsite, just feet
from the river, offering a perfect view of N'Awlins by night.

It was suppertime and a ten-minute walk on the levee's paved path
brought us to River Fine Foods Store, just across the street from the Folk
Art Zone & Blues Museum. There were no blues at that time, but the
food store promoted "Home of the Po-Boy Sandwich, the Longest, the
Biggest, the Best Sandwiches in Town." We sat atop the levee, watching
the sunset, enjoying "the best po-boy in town," and relishing the fact that
we had paddled through the best and worst of "Cancer Alley." Just then
we were treated to the cruise ship *Norwegian Pearl* sailing past our campsite,
heading down the Mississippi to the Gulf and points beyond. A quick check
showed the ship had a capacity for 2,400 passengers and a crew of 1,000.
By comparison, the paddlewheeler *America* that we had paddled past a few
days earlier could hold 185 passengers.

It was dark by six o'clock and we settled into our tents for the night.
It was a peaceful, starry evening with the river reflecting the lights from
the Big Easy across the way. To add to the charm, a riverboat, *The City of
New Orleans*, with its big faux paddlewheel, was motoring down the river,
working through its playlist of jazz classics for the entertainment of its paying passengers, and a few nonpaying listeners on the shore. The band was
still playing two hours later as the riverboat passed by our tents, this time
heading back up the river, into the city and its port.

I crawled outside my tent at sunrise and was greeted by the cruise ship
Carnival Triumph sailing into port. Its massiveness blocked out the cityscape
across the river. It was fun to see this monster ply the same waters we
paddled in the kayaks just the day before. I later learned that this luxury
liner, with its eleven decks, pools, spas, mini-golf, and ballrooms, was the
same super cruiser that made world headlines just four years earlier. A fire
on board took out all the power, leaving four thousand people to drift help-
lessly without water, food, lights, and working toilets for four days in the
Gulf before being towed into Mobile, Alabama.

Cruise ship *Carnival Triumph* sailing past our campsite coming into New Orleans, Louisiana

23

FROM THE CITY OF SAINTS
TO THE SAINTLY CITY

New Orleans, Louisiana, to St. Paul, Minnesota
Fall 2017

Our plans called for another of Adam's connections, Ken McLemore, to drive down from Port Gibson, Mississippi, and retrieve us for our return trip to Natchez. Ken and his black-and-white border collie, Piper, arrived mid-morning. Introductions were made, we packed our gear, loaded the kayaks on top of the truck, and set off for Natchez without ever stepping foot into the Big Easy. Ken had spent his engineering career in the world of energy and was an affable sort who proved to be a great storyteller. He also said he knew a spot for lunch.

We arrived at Middendorf's and, while we knew it was Ken's spot, from the parking lot it seemed like it was everybody's spot. "Comfort, Consistency and 75 Years of Mama Josie's Recipes" was the tagline for this destination hotspot in the middle of nowhere. In their seventy-five years of operation, the Middendorfs had figured out how to handle the crowds in a most hospitable, Southernly fashion. Instead of placing my own order, I was ordered to try their famous, thin-cut, fried catfish.

While there, I enjoyed great food and great stories. I noticed an older man seated near us, proudly wearing his veteran's hat. Having been away from civilization and calendars for a couple of weeks, it dawned on me it was November 11, Veterans Day. On our way out, I made a point to stop by and thank the old vet for his service. We chatted briefly. I still recall Middendorf's as a special place, from the great Southern hospitality to the food, friends, and people. What a country!

It was a three-hour drive back to Natchez, following the river past the marshes, bayous, kudzu, and Spanish moss–draped cypress trees. We topped off our successful paddle and good meal with a variety of topics. Ken was a canoe guy. He chided his kayaking passengers about the features of his preferrred craft, "Open boat—open mind." I didn't realize it at the time, but he was one of the race directors for the 2016 Vicksburg Bluz Cruz, which had been my first paddling experience on the Lower Mississippi, and the first time I had linked up with my river guide Adam.

As we approached Natchez, I brought up Natchez's homegrown author, Greg Iles. Author Stephen King's back cover comments about Iles's book *Natchez Burning* prompted me to buy it: "There's a bonus: you'll finish knowing a great deal about the Deep South's painful struggle toward racial equality, and the bloody road between Then and Now. Only a southern man could have written this book, and thank God Greg Iles was there to do the job."

I wanted to ask about that and decided to take the chance with Ken and Adam. As I recall, our conversation went something like, "I'm a little hesitant about bringing this up, and I don't want to offend either of you, but I am curious about your perspectives, as guys who grew up in Natchez, on those times that Greg Iles writes about in his stories. He talks about a lot of racially fueled hatred and violence."

Ken put me at ease about asking the question. He talked of growing up on his family farm in the small town of Roxie, about twenty-five miles from Natchez. He gave a personal account of the times described in *Natchez Burning*. To paraphase Ken:

> We had a young black man, Charles Dee, sixteen years old, who helped us on the farm. I recall the two of us hauling hay one day. The following day he disappeared. Days later they found Charles's body sixty-five miles away, near St. Joseph, Louisiana. He had been thrown into an oxbow lake after being tied to a piece of heavy farm equipment. The young black man's murderer was eventually caught when a police cold case was reopened. His murderer was convicted, sent to prison, and eventually died in prison. I am still troubled, and wonder to this day, how someone could murder this young man just because he was black.

It turned into a good, serious conversation, one that transformed Greg Iles's historical fiction novel into one man's personal history. I am glad I took the chance and asked.

We arrived at Adam's house, unpacked, and reloaded my boat onto my vehicle. We said our "goodbye, y'alls," and I was headed home, 1,100 miles north. Before I left town, however, I made a quick trip "Under the Hill" to stop at Silver Street Gallery & Gifts and have the proprietor (and paddler) Gail Guidry help me pick out a few Christmas presents.

Seventy miles up Highway 61, through Port Gibson, I stopped for a quick bite at the Tomato Place. Desiree, who had been our server as Adam and I passed through two weeks earlier, was working, and I told her about our trip. "Stop in again, Mr. Dennis, next time you're passing through," she drawled. More Southern hospitality.

Returning home is different than starting out on a trip. The beginnings are full of anticipation, curiosity, and energy. Heading home is about putting miles behind you, looking forward to getting home, and replaying the previous days on the river and on the road.

I had been gone for the better part of a month. We had made it to New Orleans, making me one of the estimated fifty people who paddle from Lake Itasca to New Orleans each year. Although I hadn't paddled all that way in one big bite, I was glad to say I was part of the group.

What began as an interest in learning how to paddle a kayak, and look around the next bend in the river, became so much more. As it turned out, the course catalogue was pushing me toward an advanced degree. The curriculum emphasized connectedness, with subjects that included our country, its history, weather, geography, engineering, the Civil War, the river, and all things related to it, such as the food, music, poetry, cultures, and, of course, the people. I was earning good grades in class participation.

We did not make it to the Gulf, but I had no regrets. This was a full trip that exceeded my expectations. And I had recruited Adam to jump back in the river with me next year. A big part of travel is the anticipation.

Over the next two days, the harvested cotton fields turned to harvested fields of corn, marking my return home. Let the anticipation begin.

24

NOLA TO CODA

Fall 2018

It was fall and once again I was heading south to the Lower Mississippi River. In the past four years, because of this river, I had made eight trips to St. Louis, Missouri, and points beyond. These had all been either in the spring or fall, mainly to avoid the flood stages of the river, the hot weather of the Southland, and to feed my golf jones in the summer months. I was driving to meet up with Adam in Natchez, Mississippi, and then proceed on to Venice, Louisiana—the farthest point one can drive along the river.

I had called Big Muddy in advance to inquire about staying at the Kanu House in St. Louis on my way through. As always, he welcomed me but indicated I would be sharing space with some students. I arrived at his place in the early evening and discovered I would be a guest along with seventeen other paddlers—fifteen students and two faculty members from Augsburg University in Minneapolis. The university offered students the chance to earn a semester's worth of credits by getting out of a brick-and-mortar classroom and enrolling in a program called "River Semester." This included one hundred days of traveling the Mississippi River by voyageur canoe and shuttle vans from the headwaters of Lake Itasca to the Gulf of Mexico. The students had started their semester in August at the head-waters and were literally camped out in the backyard of Kanu House for the past several days due to record-setting rainfall and flooding.

Big Muddy invited the school's program director, Joe Underhill, and me to escort him to pick up dinner for everyone from a local hotspot, Playboy El Cappuccino Lounge and Restaurant. It was not a gentrified neighborhood; actually it was in the hood, but Big Muddy assured us we would be fine because he was with us.

It was standing room only, and it was "cash only." We had a long wait for the food, but I could have stood there all night. We were treated to live music including a house-rocking version of Tina Turner's classic "Proud Mary."

Returning to the Kanu House, we were a big hit with the students as we spread out our haul of catfish fillets, steak fries, and hush puppies on the kitchen table. The food and the conversation were both excellent. It was interesting to hear about the twenty somethings' river tales. One student's journal entry read, "I feel incredibly empowered by the program. For the first time in a long time, I am beginning to realize I am capable of so much more than I ever imagined. I actually feel like I can travel almost anywhere, and can do almost anything." Fifty years her senior, I was having the same experience.

There was some envy when I mentioned I was heading to New Orleans in the morning to finsh off the last one hundred miles of a thirteen-year trip. One student, tired of camping in the rain in St. Louis, joked, "Take me with you!" Augsburg University and Joe Underhill had designed a wonderful program that was augmented by Big Muddy in St. Louis, and further down the river, the unofficial dean of river studies, John Ruskey. Their "River Semester" was nothing like the geology course I recalled, sitting in a crowded classroom listening to my professor droning on about a meandering river.

It was dark and raining when I left St. Louis the next morning. My plan was to reconnect with Adam in Natchez. Then we would each drive our vehicles through New Orleans and on to Venice, Louisiana.

Two days later, Adam and I were on the road again. We survived another foggy morning and the New Orleans traffic, and by noon we were in Venice. We parked my vehicle, transferred my kayak and gear to Adam's truck, and backtracked our way to Algiers Point. Across the street from the ferry boat dock that carries people from Algiers Point to New Orleans was the Dry Dock Cafe. It looked like a popular place, so we stopped for a late lunch. It was the Saturday before Halloween, and we were just across the river from let's-celebrate-anything New Orleans, so we joined some early partiers and had a nice lunch. Then it was back to work. Last fall's campsite, on the grassy stretch between the levee and the sandy shoreline, was just blocks away. We would camp the night and then it was just ninety-five miles to Mile Zero, the Gulf of Mexico.

As we were pitching our tents, we noticed two tailgaters nearby celebrating the perfectly sunny, blue-sky fall afternoon. Our kayaks and gear caught their attention, and they invited us over. With that, the size of their party doubled. It sounded a little like the movie *Same Time Next Year*, but we learned Angela and Larry had been connecting and reconnecting for about thirty-five years. The conversation, and the beer, was flowing freely, as attested by the number of dead soldiers stacking up in Larry's truck bed. Larry sported a black "Hotel Alcatraz" T-shirt topped off with a backward red hat, while Angela proudly filled out her "Team Blue" jersey under her crimson coif. As we got friendlier, I referenced Angela's locks with the song from Gershwin's Porgy and Bess, "A Red-Headed Woman." She snapped back, "It's burgundy!" Just as the song goes, this red-headed woman put me in my place.

As we talked, it came out that Angela and Larry celebrated the same birthday. I asked what their birthday was. Maybe it was a combination of a Crescent City voodoo astrologist lining up some Tarot cards, but things turned a little mystical for a moment. We discovered our happy couple really did not share the same birthday. Larry was born on March first and Angela was born on Leap Day, February 29. With a birthday only every four years, she always celebrated birthdays with Larry. I pulled out my driver's license as proof when I revealed I was born on February 28. There we were, February 28, 29, and March first. Adam came in with a March fifth birthday. The four of us were a small school of Pisces, celebrating on the country's greatest waterway. We recruited a woman from a nearby picnic to take a picture of the four of us. Yes, she was also a Pisces, and she was also from Natchez. The New Orleanian pre–Hallows Eve spirits were working.

As an added feature, Adam had contacted Boyce Upholt, the writer I had met on the Rivergator Celebratory Expedition one year earlier. He was living and writing in New Orleans, and he came across the river to join us for part of the afternoon. The Mississippi River connects us all.

After three days on the road, setting up camp, and enjoying a great day with great people, I was ready to get some sleep before engaging the last one hundred river miles over the next three days. The evening was special, looking out on the river traffic with a New Orleans backdrop, and a passing paddleboat's jazz cruise supplying the musical score. I crawled into my tent one more time.

By this point, I had camped on the river at least seventy-five nights, so why did it not surprise me that I did not have my air mattress? This was planned to be our last trip, and I was still learning. There are always a lot of things on the camping checklist and sleeping bag and air mattress are at the very top. It wasn't a deal breaker, but without that cushion under my sleeping bag, I would have to endure a few toss 'n' turn nights.

The following morning, another of Adam's friends, Danny Fraizer, a geologist, met us on the point. He was going to shuttle Adam's truck to his house in New Orleans for safekeeping. Danny was also a paddler, but this morning, instead of a boat, he brought a drone with him. Before we left, he demonstrated some impressive aerial maneuvers. As we departed the New Orleans area, Danny captured the two Gulf-bound kayakers on video from two hundred feet above the river. He later sent us a musically scored video of us heading out of the New Orleans harbor. We looked good from twenty stories high.

The river was still huge, and the traffic included oil tankers, container ships, and trawlers, but it was not as congested as the gamut we had run between Baton Rouge and New Orleans. We had a peaceful day of paddling and found a place near Jesuit's Bend to camp at LMR 68.0. In the field where we settled, there were numerous miniature turret-shaped mud structures, each surrounding an animal's hole in the ground, six inches high. They were constructed by some animal laying rows of tiny mud bricks in a very symmetrical pattern. We never did learn who built them. As I pitched my tent, I tried to find some grassy terrain to cushion the spot where my air mattress should have been.

That evening, we watched another cruise ship, the *Carnival Dream*, sail by on its way to one of its regular ports of call in the Caribbean or Panama.

The fog is lifting with tanker up ahead

With its five thousand–plus passengers and crew, it was like a small city floating by our two tents.

Our second day on the water was a repeat of the previous day and we arrived at a boat launch area near Buras at LMR 25.0. We had paddled forty-three miles and I was tired. Just after sunset, Adam spotted an otter playing at the shoreline and invited me to get out of my tent and check him out. I declined. I guess I couldn't wait to stretch out on the hard ground.

The following morning, our last morning to be spent on the river, Adam talked about the otter sighting the night before. He said there was a whole family of them playing for hours at the shoreline. Just because Adam's a good guide when it comes to nature doesn't mean he always has good students. Adam tried his best with me. The lesson is: listen to your guide, grasshopper.

CREATURES GREAT AND SMALL—
GATORS AND BUCKS AND BEARS, OH MY!

Missing out on the nighttime otter show was regretful, but as my adventure was nearing the finish line, I took an inventory of nature's highlights that I had been able to experience. From top to bottom, the Mississippi River is a fluid, moving museum of natural history. Paddling the river may have started off as a physical exercise, but from the very beginning I found myself immersed in nature's order of things. I became one with the wild. Samuel Taylor Coleridge penned these sentiments in his classic *The Rime of the Ancient Mariner:*

> He prayeth well, who loveth well
> Both man and bird and beast.
> He prayeth best, who loveth best
> All things great and small[36]

Two centuries later, this modern-day mariner can reflect and attest to an old sailor's up close and personal link to nature, to bird and beast, both great and small. The Mississippi River is a real-time, two-thousand-mile-long zoo, without the cages.

Throughout my years journeying down the river, I have experienced a variety of creatures. One evening in Mississippi, Adam had marshaled

---

36. Samuel Taylor Coleridge, "The Rime of the Ancient Mariner, Part VII," first published in *Lyrical Ballads*, 1798.

a short parade of two armadillos right through our campsite. I had never seen a live armadillo and instinctively grabbed my camp chair and assumed a lion tamer's pose to protect myself from the tank-like little beasts. As I took a defensive position, my guide said just one word: "Dennis." It wasn't the word; it was the tone. It signaled disappointment. It showed surprise as to how a grown man could cower in the face of two harmless creatures. In a moment, the two armored critters waddled over to my boots, sniffed around a bit, and ultimately sauntered out of the campsite and into the darkness. How was I to know they were harmless?

Creatures great also presented themselves on a few memorable occasions. In Louisiana, Adam and I sat in our boats, entranced as we watched an alligator slowly slip into the river below us. Also in Louisiana, Adam and I were just feet from a large buck as he charged noisily into the river. Linked with the too-close-for-comfort black bear sighting with Bob Verchota in Minnesota, it became clear that the Mississippi is an equal opportunity attraction. As I look back, these were all thrilling moments, made sweeter because nobody got hurt.

Then there were the creatures small. The wood ticks Bob and I collected on our trip hung on for days to follow, stowed away in our garments, gear, and vehicles. During John Ruskey's Rivergator Expedition, I battled a tide of ants. Thousands of the industrious little tormentors had invaded my kayak, PFD, and clothing at one of our campsites. But perhaps the most egregious pests were mosquitoes. From Minnesota to Louisiana, we suffered countless aerial attacks. The kamikaze-like, blood-sucking dive bombers were also the scourge of the Lewis and Clark Corps of Discovery Expedition two hundred years earlier. Unfortunately, mosquitoes have been a common adversary for explorers throughout history.

Based on a limited sample size of just one—me, paddling down the Mississippi—I have drawn a conclusion. Creatures great, like gators, bucks, and bears, tend to evacuate an area when travelers approach. Creatures small, like wood ticks, ants, and mosquitoes, welcome humans hungrily, swarming us, attacking us, and infesting our bodies and gear. So which creature category would you prefer to encounter?

All this talk of creatures great and small has left out one creature that proved itself to be an unexpected and very aggressive paddler's foe—the flying Asian carp. I am going to need some help if I am to follow the old sailor's advice: "He prayeth best, who loveth best, All things great and small."

THE LAST DAY

My last night of camping on the banks of the Mississippi proved memorable for all the wrong reasons. I missed out on the otter theater, and I once again missed out on an air mattress–cushioned night of rest.

Mark Twain, toward the end of *Life on the Mississippi*, references sunsets and sunrises:

> The Mississippi region has these extraordinary sunsets as a familiar spectacle. It is the true Sunset Land; I am sure no other country can show so good a right to the name. The sunrises are also said to be exceedingly fine. I do not know.[37]

Well, I do know, fellow river man. After thirteen years, this was the last morning we would be waking up on the river, and the sunrise provided a spectacle worthy of the occasion. It was our last day of paddling, and we were on the river early to catch the full effect. It was just fifteen river miles to Venice, and then another ten miles to Mile Zero, and the Gulf of Mexico. We had decided to stop in Venice and unload our gear into my vehicle, parked there a few days earlier, so we would have a lighter load on our run to Zero. It was a two-mile paddle in Tiger Pass from the river to Cypress Cove Marina in Venice. We transferred our gear from our kayaks to my vehicle and stopped for lunch. We then pushed off into Tiger Pass and the Mississippi for our last paddle. Once on the river it was ten miles out and ten miles back. The last ten miles being upstream.

The river had gotten a little choppier and windier in the afternoon. It was fun seeing the mile markers now reporting single digits. Because of the river conditions, our paddling, mine specifically, was slowing down. I was trying to do the math about how we were going to cover the next five miles to Mile Zero, the mouth of the Mississippi, and then paddle upriver ten miles and two more miles up Tiger Pass to the marina in Venice. The math wasn't working.

We were on the right descending bank, and we could see Pilot Town across the river from us at LMR 3.0. Pilot Town is where the pilots make their on-the-river transfers to the incoming ocean vessels. Because of the ever-changing challenges of the Mississippi River, and the Cabotage Provision of the Jones Act, only local bar pilots are allowed to bring the ocean vessels upriver from the mouth of the Mississippi to Venice. From Venice upriver to New Orleans, or Baton Rouge, a river pilot is required. On the

---

37. Mark Twain, *Life on the Mississippi* (New York: Barnes & Noble, Inc., 2010), 313.

Last sunrise on the Mississippi River, LMR 25.0

river, we had witnessed a few of these transfers when a pilot boat would pull alongside a larger, ocean-going vessel and, still under power and on the move, the new bar pilot would climb from the small craft, up a ladder to the larger vessel. It was an impressive maneuver to watch.

Adam had apparently been making the same calculations as I had when he announced the need to turn around because we did not have enough daylight to make it to the Mile Zero marker and return to Venice. It would be too dangerous to be paddling upriver in the dark with the river traffic. It was the last thing I wanted to hear, but I had to agree with him. I had already come to the same conclusion. Adam, in a consoling voice, said that the last three miles were just like what we had been paddling through, but the Mile Zero marker is larger than the other mile markers. It was not that consoling. I spent the next few hours paddling and dealing with this change in plans and change in emotions. I concluded that it would be fine; we could still enjoy our trip.

In 1927, when Lucky Lindy parked his plane in Paris after spending thirty-three hours flying 3,500 miles, CharlesLindbergh.com reports there was a crowd of one hundred thousand people waiting in the dark to celebrate the special occasion. It took me thirteen years, paddling 2,347 miles, and it was early evening when we pulled into the marina in Venice.

It was a sunny evening and there were four men nearby, oblivious to the significance of my moment.

Near a wooden structure, these four men were huddled by their corral of impressive trucks. They were enjoying the evening and appeared to be friendly, confident, in the prime of life, and maybe a little cocky. After years of looking forward to this occasion, I wanted to keep the moment going so we walked over and started visiting with the foursome. We asked about their fishing, and they were curious about our kayaking and from where we had paddled. We gave them both the short story, from New Orleans, and the long story, from the headwaters in Minnesota. They congratulated us and we exchanged high fives.

One of the men was at a cutting bench that held the man's Bud Light and a large, freshly caught yellowfin tuna. He was just starting to carve up the catch of the day. It was fascinating watching this artist at work. He wielded the large knife with the deftness of someone who had been trained by Benihana himself. As I got closer to take in his mastery, he asked if I had ever tasted sashimi. I said I did not know what it was. He expertly cut a few thin slices and spread them out on the wet cutting board and invited me to try some. The taste was special, as if the river itself was serving up one final, unexpected treat to cap off my thirteen-year adventure.

Preparing sashimi in Venice harbor

When I was first pushed into the Mississippi in a rental kayak, it was a memorable moment. Three generations—my son, grandson, and I—were celebrating the day. We were embarking on a cool adventure on our country's greatest river. Carpe diem.

Thirteen years and three kayaks later, I was stepping off this same great river. I believe life's passions are bracketed between anticipation and memories. The middle ground is the moment. For me, this moment was viscerally charged. My body was alive in the elements, paddling all day, and now taking in one last sunset. The sounds and smells of the harbor, the sight of the tuna splayed open on the butcher's table, my first taste of sashimi, guys talking about the river . . . this was, as Mark Twain said it best, "Life on the Mississippi."

As in the beginning, once again it was three generations. I spotted these guys fifty years, and here we were, all enjoying this evening on the river, celebrating a wonderful catch, and a thirteen-year journey. It was a confluence of two recurring themes. The Mississippi connects us all, and river people are happy to give. Tina Turner, you were oh so right!

25

TWELVE HUNDRED MILES UPHILL

Fall 2018

It was November 1, All Saints Day, and New Orleans, home of the Saints, was taking its time coming around after a day and night of Halloween fêtes. My plans for the day included reaching Clarksdale, Mississippi, with a few reconnections along the way. My first stop was Silver Street Gallery & Gifts in Natchez, Mississippi. It had become my traveling tradition to stop and catch up with Gail, report on my most recent trip, and stock up on a few Christmas gifts that could only be found in this nifty, Under-the-Hill gem of a shop.

Having spent the last week with Adam, I decided to give him a break, leaving Natchez and heading north on the Great River Road, Highway 61, to Lorman, Mississippi, and the Old Country Store. It was two and a half years ago, right after the Bluz Cruz, that I had first discovered the home of the "World's Best Fried Chicken." King Arthur Davis's hospitality, accompanied by his acapella singing, made for a most memorable meal. On this day, I made a brief stop, had a piece of peach cobbler, said hi to Mr. D, and was headed just a few miles up the road to Port Gibson. I was hoping to catch a quick moment with Adam's friend Ken McLemore, who had shuttled us from Algiers Point to Natchez one year ago. He was in his shop, and we had an enjoyable visit.

Knowing I still had over a thousand miles to travel, our chat was brief, and I was off to Vicksburg, and the Tomato Place. What started out as a paddle tour had now become a knife, fork, and spoon tour. At the Tomato Place there was no sign of Desiree, the unofficial queen of Southern hospitality, no "Hi, Mister Dennis," and no souvenir Tomato Place coffee mugs for sale. While I enjoyed their signature BLT and avocado sandwich, a staffer made a run somewhere and came back with a half dozen of their

artsy mugs. Now these mugs are part of my morning coffee routine, providing a nice memory of that roadside slice of the Deep South.

My next stop was Clarksdale, Mississippi. Historically, Clarksdale was
a thriving city when cotton was king in the antebellum era. It was known as
"The Golden Buckle of the Cotton Belt." Today Clarksdale is on the map
because of its Deep Delta blues history. With a little research, I learned that
the Mississippi Blues Trail is alive and well in Clarksdale. Blues artists who
were born or lived in Clarksdale included John Lee Hooker, Muddy Waters, Howlin' Wolf, Sam Cooke, and Big Jack Johnson, not to be confused
with Big Joe Williams, from Crawford, Mississippi, or Big Walter Horton,
from Horn Lake, Mississippi. Ike Turner also was born in Clarksdale, but
his better half, Tina, grew up just 150 miles up the Mississippi River in
Nutbush, Tennessee.

My plan was to experience the Delta blues firsthand. On the Rivergator trip one year prior, John Ruskey, a native of Clarksdale, had tipped me
off that actor Morgan Freeman still lived in Clarksdale and owned a juke
joint, the Ground Zero Blues Club. It is a one-hundred-year-old, nongen-
trified, ramshackle building at the end of Blues Alley on Delta Avenue that
has been featured in *National Geographic* and on *60 Minutes*. It is the jewel
of this little burg of fifteen thousand and is "the number one Blues Club in
the nation," according to Bill Luckett, former Clarksdale mayor and Morgan Freeman's best friend. Inside, a tattered sign perched next to a guitar
provided the spirit, "If it ain't been in a pawn shop it can't play the blues."

I arrived there just as the band was heating up. Fitting the vibe of the
evening, the server was the epitome of Southern hospitality. This Delta
queen, with her sweet "y'all," recommended the house special, "fried
green tomato sammich" with a side of sweet potato fries. She later assured
me, with her Southern drawl, that the homemade peach cobbler à la mode
would be a fine choice. On this first travel day out of New Orleans, I had
a tomato sandwich and a peach cobbler two different times, at two separate
places.

As the band took a break, I visited with a couple of travelers from
the state of Washington. While I was working my way down the country
on the river, these guys were serious blues aficionados working their way
across the country doing the Mississippi Blues Trail with planned stop offs
in Memphis and New Orleans. We were travelers crossing paths at Robert
Johnson's crossroads. Cool.

As I settled up with my Southern belle server, I learned that she was
actually from Michigan. Who knew?

After an evening living the bluesy life, the following morning I made one more stop in Clarksdale as part of my northbound farewell tour. John Ruskey had invited me to his place. We visited one last time and he flattered me with several of his river posters. My favorite was his artistic interpretation of the entire river, boldly lettered "Mississippi River Connects Us All." The keynote was John signing it for me right there: "Yo Dennis . . . Good journeys, my friend! May the river be with you always! John Ruskey." It is framed in my living room, and I appreciate it every day.

On this journey's penultimate day, my goal was to reach Hannibal, seven hours north. On the way, I called to see if Hannibal's paddlewheeler, the *Mark Twain*, was sailing that evening. I learned there was a dinner and jazz cruise leaving at 6:30 p.m. The woman at the ticket office allowed me to buy a riverboat ticket in advance. I told her I was going to be cutting it close.

I finally arrived in Hannibal just in time. Just in time, that is, to see the *Mark Twain* departing the dock and heading upriver. I stopped in the gift shop ticket office to say hi to the woman who had been helping me over the phone with cruising information earlier in the day. I introduced myself and she said to wait while she called the captain. The *Mark Twain* was a half mile upriver! It was not my request, but she said they had done it before. The pilot, after receiving her phone call, reversed course, pulled the riverboat back to the dock, and welcomed me to come aboard. Climbing on deck, I stepped into a sea of not-so-friendly faces. I don't think they cared that the skipper had a track record of backtracking.

Once aboard, I did find a group of friendly travelers. We exchanged stories and I enjoyed my last fare of Southern fried chicken with all the classic trimmings. The genuine riverboat jazz band provided a nice musical score for my trip home. I had gone from Delta blues one night to Dixieland jazz the next. It was the ultimate battle of the bands.

It was dark when we arrived back at the dock. I found a motel in Hannibal and climbed into bed for my last night on a road trip that had started thirteen years earlier. I was tired, and the luxury of being indoors in a nice bed was not lost on me. I welcomed it. Yet as I stared at the motel ceiling, I felt a little part of me already missing the feeling of shimmying into my sleeping bag after an exhausting day of paddling, dousing my headlamp, and listening to the owls, coyotes, and sounds of the tows working the river. Those waning moments were always special, even when I didn't have an air mattress.

The final stretch of my adventure was the four hundred miles from Hannibal to St. Paul. As I crossed the Mississippi River driving into St. Paul, I looked east and saw the familiar bluffs of Mounds Park.

In 1882, two decades after his riverboat captain's career ended due to the Civil War, author Mark Twain boarded a northbound packet boat, the *Gold Dust*. He boarded not as a steamboat pilot but as a passenger doing research for what would become America's definitive book on the Mississippi River and the people it touches, *Life on the Mississippi*. In the final pages of Twain's river adventure, we read:

> We reached St. Paul, at the head of the navigation of the Mississippi, and where our voyage of two thousand miles from New Orleans ended. It is about a ten-day trip by steamer. . . . St. Paul is a wonderful town. It is put together in solid blocks of honest brick and stone, and has the air of intending to stay. The town stands on high ground: it is about seven hundred feet above the sea-level. It is so high that a wide view of river and lowlands is offered from its streets. It is a very wonderful town, indeed.[38]

The parallels were not missed. Mark Twain and I were both finishing trips from New Orleans, Louisiana, to St. Paul, Minnesota. I had started my day's journey in Hannibal, Missouri, also the original starting point for Mark Twain, and the characters he created: Tom, Huck, and Becky. And now I was looking at that same "high ground" referenced by Twain; the very same bluffs and Indian mounds that served as my boyhood world.

Three miles later, I was pulling into my driveway. I made a point to stop before driving into the garage, thereby avoiding ripping the kayak off the top of my vehicle. I was grateful I remembered.

Home. I hauled my kayak down and stowed it. As I unloaded my gear, I made one last check of my boat. I stuck my head into the kayak cockpit and peered forward to make sure I hadn't missed anything. I had. There, stuffed neatly into my kayak's pointy bow, was my achingly missing-in-action air mattress.

---

38. Mark Twain, *Life on the Mississippi* (New York: Barnes & Noble, Inc., 2010), 325.

26

BOARD 'N' BOTTLE

On a shelf in my office there is a wooden board measuring seventeen inches long, five inches high, and a half inch thick. On a table in my living room, there is a clear glass bottle that holds twelve ounces of water. These two displays—wood and water—are two of nature's gifts that I garnered as souvenirs from my years of being one with the river.

The board, its man-made function washed away years ago, has transformed into driftwood. Its smooth but scarred, silvery-gray surface has been beaten up and worn down. It has endured the currents and waves of time. Its size belies its light weight; it was carried some unknown distance only to be deposited on a muddy shore at Upper River Mile Zero—the confluence of the Mississippi and Ohio rivers.

Board 'n' bottle

As I sit at my office desk, that piece of driftwood brings back the moment of a time passed. My mind recalls the people, the food, the campsite, a goat's skull, the weather, and the power of the newly merged river flowing past Cairo, Mississippi.

Mile Zero. So much was behind us, but so much still lay ahead.

The glass bottle appears to contain clear water, but upon further inspection you can notice a silty layer of sediment covering the bottom of the vessel. Somewhere early on in my river trips, I remember dipping a container into the Upper Mississippi River and scooping out a bottle's worth of Old Blue. Unlike finding the driftwood, I cannot recall the exact location, but I did collect a sample from a place where the river appeared fairly clean. Looking back, I am surprised that I collected the river's water only once considering the thousands of miles I spent floating in it.

The river starts with the clear waters of Itasca in northern Minnesota, which derives its name from a Dakota Sioux word "mni sota" meaning "clear blue water." (Full disclosure: Some say the word Minnesota may be derived from a similar, but contradictory, Dakota Sioux word "mnisota," which means "cloudy water.")

Below the clear blue waters of Minnesota, the Mississippi River receives the contributions of the Wisconsin, Illinois, Missouri (The Big Muddy), Arkansas, Tennessee, and Ohio rivers, along with more than a thousand other tributaries, until its muddy brown waters roll to the Delta, one hundred miles below New Orleans.

I will occasionally take this bottle of clear water and give it a shake, causing the silty bottom to disintegrate and, in snow globe fashion, the turbidity of the Mississippi River comes to life in my pint-sized bottle.

The wood, snatched from a riverbank after being shaped by countless years of the Mississippi's forces, and a few ounces of water, interrupted on its way to the Gulf by a kayaker breaking up the monotony of the day's paddle, now serve as treasured links to time well spent.

27

REFLECTIONS

Don't quit your day dream.

—Anonymous

Journeys can be described as opportunities to find oneself, and through my thirteen years on the river, I did find myself. I found myself getting smarter about rivers, paddling, and people. I learned that man's connection to the river covers a wide swath.

Through this experience I've become a richer man. Over the miles logged, the creatures, cultures, people, food, and music created thousands of miles of open-air theater. The performances changed daily, from comedy to tragedy, melodrama to musical. Old Man River always played the lead.

As I continued south, I noted that while the river was ever changing, so was I. One notable way was my age: I found myself getting older. I was a different man in my early sixties compared to my mid-seventies. I was aging, and at times it seemed I was doing so at an accelerating pace. I could feel it.

Over the years with Adam Elliott as my guide, I noticed that it became increasingly more common with each trip that Adam would slow down and wait for his client-in-tow. Don't get me wrong, each of those respites was most welcomed! But as an active guy, it wasn't something I was used to.

I think my age was most noticed on the turf side of my surf-and-turf scamper down the middle of the country. My ability to crawl in and out of the tent with ease had become a little less easy. On top of the camping moments were the portages and lugging my kayak and gear at the put-in and takeout spots. It was getting tougher. And as my trips took me farther from home, the road trips were longer, but due to my age, my driving stretches became shorter.

Yes, what started out as a reenactment of Mark Twain's Huck Finn and his riverine adventures was heading toward Papa Hemingway's *The Old Man and the Sea*.

My sentiments are not to be construed as complaints but as honest observations of what happens to us all over time, but perhaps more notably when we're pushing our bodies further than our birth certificates would attest.

Travel in general can be an opportunity to find oneself, and I did, but I also moved beyond this concept to embrace a more action-oriented approach. I ramped up my efforts to align with author George Bernard Shaw's proclamation, "Life isn't about finding yourself. Life is about creating yourself."

Indeed, over thirteen years, I created a new me—I became a river man. Through intensive reading; year-round paddling practice in rivers and pools; wisdom gleaned from river people, guides, and philosophers; and thousands of miles spent on—in!—the river, I was changing. I could tell a nun from a can, pass on the one whistle or two, and recount the difference between a brace and a batture. I was scaling riprap and skirting wing dams. I was a new man. I was a river rat!

I had paddled two and a half thousand river miles, from the source of the Mississippi River to its mouth at Mile Zero. Well, almost. We had to turn around at Lower River Mile 3. So maybe it was only 2,497 river miles. Do those last three missing miles bother me?

I searched for solace in T. S. Eliot, America's poet from St. Louis, a river town if there ever was one, and his fitting words, "The journey, not the destination matters."

Another Elliott, my guide Adam, also offered some salve: "Mile marker zero is just like all the other mile markers, except it is a little bigger."

And of course, I could not forget the words of Henry Crepeau, my mountain-climbing, world-class fellow adventurer who had himself come up short of the finish on a Mont Blanc climbing expedition. Due to bad weather, his group had failed to summit. They had to turn back at the last moment, after being ever so close to the peak. Henry's statement was a tonic, wise at any altitude: "Nothing's up there but ego."

Actually, maybe there was something else up there because the next summer, Henry returned to the French-Italian Alps to personally inspect the top of Mont Blanc.

It takes a certain kind of person to be able to persevere like that. Through my Mississippi River travels I have met paddlers who have been the first (Natalie Warren), fastest (K. J. Milhone), farthest (Janet Moreland), and even the oldest (both Stan Stark and Dale Sanders). These men and women earned world records. Their trips and their writings are amazing.

My paddling claims are not even in the same ballpark as these phenoms, and that's okay. What the river offers is the chance for each of us to experience whatever the river brings. As I carved a slice down our continent's greatest river, I can lay claim to my personal *firsts*, my *fastests* and *farthests*. I'm pretty sure there's an *oldest* in there somewhere too. But I'm not finished yet. Sorry, Adam, but I'm not buying it that mile marker zero is just like the others. It is different, and there is something more than ego out there.

So the original band is getting back together. What started as a Saturday afternoon outing in 2005 with my son and two-year-old grandson will come full circle. Our plans include my son, Joe; my guide, Adam; and my grandson, Earl, who is now a nineteen-year-old man, joining me in southern Louisiana to chase down that last mile marker—the big zero.

The words of Jack Kerouac, author of *On the Road*, are fitting not only for this final leg in my journey, but for the sum of it:

> Because in the end, you won't remember the time you spent working in the office or mowing your lawn. Climb that goddamn mountain.[39]

---

39. "The Most Inspirational Jack Kerouac Quotes," *Gentleman's Journal*, accessed September 27, 2022, https://www.thegentlemansjournal.com/the-most-inspirational-jack-kerouac-quotes/.

ACKNOWLEDGMENTS

One hand can't tie a bundle.

—A Cameroonian proverb[40]

Summoning a few sports analogies with reference to one's life span, in my ball game I was somewhere near the bottom of the seventh inning. It had been a phone call that started a run of events that fell onto the field of good fortune, blessing, serendipity, or just dumb luck.

My son was the caller, and he was fired up about floating down a river in a plastic boat. "You should come with us. We're going again tomorrow." He invited me to join him in a three-hour cruise on Mark Twain's Mississippi River, in a kayak.

Mark Twain's Mississippi River. In those four words lie clues to two life-affirming adventures. The first was kayaking a couple thousand miles on America's River, and the second was writing about my years on Mark Twain's Mississippi. At the stage in the game where the coach might be looking for some relief from the bullpen, I was still in the game, and anxious to see how the next innings played out.

In both paddling and writing you are in it by yourself. You make every one of those never-ending paddle strokes, and you are the one to make every one of those numberless keystrokes. Having now said, "look what I did," I want to acknowledge a few of the people who transformed both the paddling and the writing adventures from what could have been lonely, tedious, isolated hours wedged in a boat or staring at a screen into genuine, roller-coaster, what's-coming-next, E-ticket rides.

---

40. This proverb was first told to me by two friends from Cameroon, James and Rose Kukwa.

217

These people who pushed me forward fall into two camps: one relates to the river currents (paddle strokes), and the other to words on a page (keystrokes).

RIVER CURRENTS

I thank my son, Joe Van Norman, and grandson, Earl Van Norman, for giving me that first push off the concrete boat launch and into the river, accompanied by words of encouragement, "You'll figure it out."

There are scores of individuals who helped me maneuver through the river's meanderings, and I have mentioned many of them in the preceding pages, but I want to acknowledge a special few at this point.

The Inland Sea Kayakers (ISK) kayak club deserves recognition for coaching me up the beginning paddler's learning curve. Herb Bourque, Jeff Forseth, Fred Linehan, and Peggy O'Neal were all kind and effective coaches. Their self-rescue, navigation, eddy orientation, and bracing techniques were most relevant and helpful.

Although I was just learning about the river and paddling, I was able to entice an intrepid few to travel with me early on. Terry Cooper and his wife Pam Davis; Henry Crepeau, who reintroduced me to camping after a forty-year hiatus; and Bob Verchota, an outdoorsman of the first rung. Each made those earliest sections most memorable with their great company and conversations.

Another river-time mention goes to Gail Guidry, a paddler and proprietor of Silver Street Gallery & Gifts. Gail was always ready to supply me with a special, one-of-a-kind collection of gifts for my family every time I left Natchez heading for home.

I must also mention my daughter, Kelly Stauff, for consistently offering her daughterly advice and caution. "Dad don't go. You will die." Those words never sounded clearer than that one moment in a crowded St. Louis harbor with a formidable towboat bearing down on one terrified miniscule kayaker.

WORDS ON A PAGE

In recalling my river stories, I have received guidance and inspiration from many. The generosity and talents offered by them have added an enjoyable and recreational aspect to the process of writing this book. A few of those whose encouragement and advice on how to link this adventure into words on a page are mentioned here.

They have spent hours selflessly reviewing various stages of drafts and providing their invaluable feedback. Their diverse talents and backgrounds draw from authors, journalists, bloggers, newspaper executives, playwrights, artists, book lovers, a magician, a screenwriting professor, a librarian, and one river city mayor. Roll the credits: Daniel (Predictably Lost) Alvarez, Lisa Brienzo, Roger Buoen, Steve Carlson, Bill Casey, Bill Decker, Mayor Jimmy Francis, John (The Amazing Hondo) Hughes, Steve Larson, Michael B. Miller, Patti and Richard Palahniuk, Jeff Redmon, Steve Stauff, Stan Trollip (one half of the Michael Stanley writing team), Boyce Upholt, and Jeff Wright.

A special thanks to Don Shelby, who wrote the foreword for this book. What better meld of talents and interests could one select to begin this story? Don's résumé includes an award-winning journalist, a top-tier media personality, decades of public performances as a Mark Twain impersonator, an around-the-globe adventurer and explorer, a paddler, a bibliophile with a sweet spot for river books, and a bona fide river rat.

This book would not be without the talent, skill, and creative touches of Dita Squires. At a chance first meeting I asked Dita what she does. "I'm a copywriter." I followed with, "Would you read two chapters of a book I'm writing?" She thought we might have something, and with that we became a river-connected writing team. She has provided insight, suggestions, new ways to present an idea, and cheerleading throughout this writing adventure. She's fantastic!

My family was instrumental in helping me tell this story. My sister, Barb Frame, with her artistic and creative talents, has provided two personalized maps, one of the Upper Mississippi and one of the Lower Mississippi, to help visualize the ups and downs of this slice through the country.

On a weekend trip to my daughter's family cabin I had, not accidently, left a couple early chapters of my manuscript lying on a table, hoping for some family feedback. My daughter, Kelly, took the bait. "I read your chapters. You should finish it and make some money." Although remuneration wasn't the motivation, a daughter's (almost) unsolicited encouragement was plenty. It was a go.

My wife, Jean Van Norman, generously accepted the challenge to jump into this story-telling process. She knows me and my language and communication quirks and customs. Along with this personal knowledge, she brings a background in proofreading and book layout. With her keen eye and wordsmithing talents, she offered many key suggestions and advice

("I think you mean descendants, not ancestors"). Her encouragement, along with her critical analysis, was always offered in her caring manner.

As the paddling journey began with one phone call, so did the publishing adventure. Three minutes into Brittany Stoner's phone call she asked, "Can you send a manuscript?" Like my river guides, Brittany, Chris Fischer, and the others at Globe Pequot and Lyons Press have guided this rookie through the new and mysterious world of publishing in a most professional, competent, we-are-in-this-together style.

The Cameroonians are right. I could not have embarked on this adventure or bundled up this story by myself. My thanks to all the caring and giving people who helped me along the way.

ABOUT THE AUTHOR

Dennis Van Norman was born and raised in a river town, St. Paul, Minnesota. His childhood included playing in Indian Mounds Park, climbing on the limestone bluffs and cliffs overlooking the Mississippi River, and exploring the caves scattered along the river's banks.

He earned his undergraduate and graduate degrees from the University of Minnesota and the University of St. Thomas. His professional writing has been in the corporate world and includes a business journal publication, writing strategic plans, mission statements, and executive speeches.

His writing for fun has included a regular column for a small town Wisconsin newspaper. The column, *Random Shots from a Grassy Knoll*, featured different golf courses and the characters that crowded them. He has published a book of poetry, *Courtside Chatter*, that covered his daughter Kelly's four years of varsity basketball at Gustavus Adolfus College, earning him a Varsity Athletic Award and Letter as Honorary Poet Laureate.

This book, *Threading a Kayak down the Mississippi*—part history, nature, travel, adventure, and memoir—is Dennis's first published book. When he is not traveling, Dennis still enjoys his regular morning walks along the timeless Mississippi River, at the foot of those same bluffs he scrambled about as a boy.